CCNA™ Exam Notes™: Cisco® Certified Network Associate

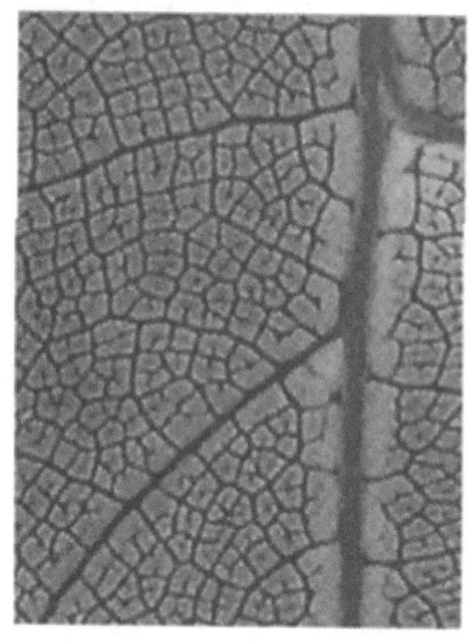

Todd Lammle

San Francisco • Paris • Düsseldorf • Soest • London

Associate Publisher: Guy Hart-Davis
Contracts and Licensing Manager: Kristine O'Callaghan
Acquisitions & Developmental Editor: Neil Edde
Editor: Vivian Jaquette
Project Editor: Elizabeth Hurley-Clevenger
Technical Editor: Devin Akin
Book Designer: Bill Gibson
Graphic Illustrator: Tony Jonick
Electronic Publishing Specialist: Adrian Woolhouse
Production Coordinator: Catherine Morris
Indexer: Ted Laux
Cover Designer: Archer Design
Cover Photographer: The Image Bank

Library of Congress Card Number: 99-61311

ISBN: 0-7821-2535-2

Manufactured in the United States of America

10 9 8 7 6 5 4 3 2 1

Acknowledgments

Many thanks go to those who helped me complete yet another Sybex book.

I would like to acknowledge Devin "Devinator" Akin for doing such a fantastic job of making sure I stayed technically in tune. I would also like to take this time to personally thank Brian Horakh for introducing Devin to Sybex. Brian has a great Web site that can help you pass all your Cisco Certification exams: `http://www.networkstudyguides.com`.

For the Sybex crew, Elizabeth Hurley-Clevenger and Vivian Jaquette did a terrific job of keeping this book flowing and readable. Kudos to them both for keeping up with my hectic schedule and keeping me busy with lots of queries!

Production Coordinator Catherine Morris and Electronic Publishing Specialist Adrian Woolhouse did a great job of marrying the manuscript with the art. It's hard work, but people like them make it look so easy!

Neil Edde, Acquisitions Editor, and the person I've once referred to as Gandhi, thanks again (and again...) for always keeping your calm and patient demeanor in the craziest of times.

Table of Contents

Introduction

This book is intended to start you out on an exciting new path toward obtaining your CCNA certification. It reaches beyond popular certifications like the MCSE and CNE to provide you with an indispensable factor in understanding today's network—insight into the Cisco world of internetworking.

If you've purchased this book, you are probably chasing one of the Cisco professional certifications: CCNA/CCNP, CCDA/CCDP, or CCIE. All of these are great goals, and they are also great career builders. Glance through any newspaper and you'll find employment opportunities for people with these certifications—these ads are there because finding qualified network administrators is a challenge in today's market. The certification means you know something about the product, but more importantly, it means you have the ability, determination, and focus to learn—the greatest skills any employee can have!

You've probably also heard all the rumors about how hard the Cisco tests are—believe us, the rumors are true! Cisco has designed a series of exams that truly challenge your knowledge of their products. Each test not only covers the materials presented in a particular class, it also covers the prerequisite knowledge for that course.

Is This Book for You?

This book covers everything you need to know to become a Cisco certified CCNA. It will teach you how to perform basic configurations on Cisco routers using multiple protocols. Each chapter begins with a list of the CCNA test objectives covered in it; make sure to read over them before working through the chapter.

You'll also learn how to start up and configure a Cisco router, as well as attain a clear and detailed understanding of the OSI reference model and how to configure the relevant protocols used in the OSI model. This book covers how to configure TCP/IP, how to subnet an IP scheme into multiple subnets, and how to apply those abilities in a lab. You'll also learn how to route IPX and create access lists to provide traffic management for your multiprotocol network.

The Sybex Exam Notes books were designed to be succinct, portable exam review guides. They can be used either in conjunction with a more complete study program—supplemented by books, CBT courseware, or practice in a classroom/lab environment—or as an exam review for those who don't feel the need for more extensive test preparation. It isn't our goal to "give the answers away," but rather to identify those topics on which you can expect to be tested and to provide sufficient coverage of these topics.

Perhaps you've been working with Cisco internetworking technologies for years now. The thought of paying lots of money for a specialized Cisco exam preparation course probably doesn't sound too appealing. What can they teach you that you don't already know, right? Be careful, though. Many experienced network administrators, even CCIEs, have walked confidently into test centers only to walk sheepishly out of them after failing a Cisco exam. As they discovered, there's the Cisco of the real world and the Cisco of the Cisco certification exams. It's our goal with these Exam Notes books to show you where the two converge and where they diverge. After you've finished reading through this book, you should have a clear idea of how your understanding of the technologies involved matches up with the expectations of the Cisco test makers.

Or perhaps you're relatively new to the world of Cisco internetworking, drawn to it by the promise of challenging work and higher salaries. You've just waded through an 800-page Cisco CCNA study guide or taken a class at a local training center. Lots of information to keep track of, isn't it? Well, by organizing the Exam Notes books according to the Cisco exam objectives, and by breaking up the information into concise, manageable pieces, we've created what we think is the handiest exam review guide available. Throw it in your briefcase and carry it to work with you. As you read through the book, you'll be able to quickly identify those areas you know best and those that require more in-depth review.

NOTE The goal of the Exam Notes series is to help Cisco certification candidates familiarize themselves with the subjects on which they can expect to be tested in the certification exams. For complete, in-depth coverage of the technologies and topics involved in Cisco networking, we recommend the Cisco Certification Study Guide series from Sybex.

How is This Book Organized?

As mentioned above, this book is organized according to the official exam objectives list prepared by Cisco for the CCNA exam. Within each chapter, the individual exam objectives are addressed in turn. Each objective section is further divided according to the type of information presented.

Critical Information

This section presents the greatest level of detail on information that is relevant to the objective. This is the place to start if you're unfamiliar with or uncertain about the technical issues related to the objective.

Necessary Procedures

Here you'll find instructions for procedures that require a lab computer to be completed. From logging into a router to configuring RIP and IGRP routing, the information in these sections addresses the hands-on requirements for the CCNA exams.

NOTE Not every objective has a hands-on procedure associated with it. For such objectives, the Necessary Procedures section has been left out.

Exam Essentials

In this section, we've put together a concise list of the most crucial topics of subject areas that you'll need to comprehend fully prior to taking the Cisco exam. This section can help you identify those topics that might require more study on your part.

Key Terms and Concepts

Here we've compiled a mini-glossary of the most important terms and concepts related to the specific objective. You'll understand what all those technical words mean within the context of the related subject matter.

Sample Questions

For each exam objective, we've included a selection of questions similar to those you'll encounter on the actual Cisco exam. Answers and explanations are provided so you can gain some insight into the test-taking process.

How Do You Become a CCNA?

The CCNA certification is the first certification in the new line of Cisco certifications and a precursor to all current Cisco certifications. With the new certification programs, Cisco has created a stepping-stone approach to CCIE (Cisco Certified Internetwork Associate) certification. You can become a Cisco Certified Network Associate for the meager cost of this book plus $100 for the test. And you don't have to stop there—you can choose to continue with your studies and achieve a higher certification called the Cisco Certified Network Professional (CCNP). Once you are a CCNP, you have completed all the coursework and acquired all the knowledge you need to attempt the CCIE lab.

Why Become a CCNA?

Cisco has created a certification process, not unlike Microsoft or Novell's, to give administrators a set of skills and prospective employers an authenticated way to measure those skills. Becoming a CCNA can be the initial step of a successful journey toward a new or refreshed, highly rewarding and sustainable career.

As you study for the CCNA exam, we can't stress this enough: It's critical that you have some hands-on experience with Cisco routers. If you can get your hands on some 2500 routers, you're set! But if you can't, we've worked hard to provide dozens of configuration examples throughout this book to help network administrators (or people who want to become network administrators) learn what they need to know to pass the CCNA exam.

SEE ALSO One way to get the hands-on router experience you'll need in the real world is to attend one of the seminars offered by Globalnet System Solutions, Inc. (`http://www.lammle.com`), produced by the author of this book.

SEE ALSO Keystone Learning Systems is producing high-quality training through videos featuring Todd Lammle. Go to `http://www.klscorp.com` for more information about all Cisco certification videos.

It can also be helpful to take an Introduction to Cisco Router Configuration (ICRC) course at an Authorized Cisco Education Center, but be aware that this class doesn't cover all of the test objectives. If you decide to take the class, reading this book in conjunction with the hands-on course will give you the knowledge you need for certification. There are hundreds of Cisco Authorized Training Centers around the world—see the Cisco Web page (`http://www.cisco.com`) for the location nearest you.

Where Do You Take the Exams?

You may take the exams at any one of the more than 800 Sylvan Prometric Authorized Testing Centers around the world. For the location of a testing center near you, call 800-204-3926. Outside the United States and Canada, contact your local Sylvan Prometric Registration Center.

To register for a Cisco Certified Network Associate exam:

1. Determine the number of the exam you want to take. (The CCNA exam number is 640-407.)

2. Register with the Sylvan Prometric Registration Center nearest you. You will need to pay in advance for the exam. At this writing, registration costs $100 per exam, and the test must be taken within one year of payment. You can sign up for an exam up to six weeks in advance or as late as one working day prior to the day you wish to take it. If something comes up and you need to cancel or reschedule your exam appointment, contact Sylvan Prometric at least 24 hours in advance. Same-day registration isn't available for the Cisco tests.
3. When you schedule the exam, you'll be provided with instructions regarding all appointment and cancellation procedures, the ID requirements, and information about the testing center location.

What the Cisco CCNA Exam Measures

The CCNA program was not only created to provide a solid introduction to the Cisco internetworking operating system (IOS) and to Cisco hardware, but to internetworking in general, making it helpful to you in areas not exclusively Cisco's. It's hard to say at this point in the certification process, but it's not unrealistic to imagine that future network managers—even those without Cisco equipment—could easily require Cisco certifications of their job applicants.

So if you make it through the CCNA and are still interested in Cisco and internetworking, you're headed down a certain path to success.

To meet the CCNA certification skill level, you must be able to understand or do the following:

- Install, configure, and operate simple-routed LAN, routed WAN, and switched LAN networks.
- Understand and be able to configure IP, IGRP, IPX, serial, AppleTalk, Frame Relay, IP RIP, VLANs, IPX RIP, Ethernet, and access lists.
- Install and/or configure a network.
- Optimize WAN through Internet access solutions that reduce unnecessary broadcasts and reduce WAN costs using features such as filtering with access lists.

- Provide remote access by integrating dial-up connectivity with traditional, remote LAN-to-LAN access, as well as supporting the higher levels of performance required for new applications such as Internet commerce, multimedia, and so on.

Tips for Taking Your Cisco CCNA Exam

The CCNA test contains 70 questions, which are to be answered in 90 minutes. You must schedule the test at least 24 hours in advance (unlike the Novell or Microsoft exams), and you aren't allowed to take more than one Cisco exam per day.

Many questions on the exam will have answer choices that at first glance look identical—especially the syntax questions! Remember to read through the choices carefully, because a "close" answer won't cut it. If you choose an answer in which the commands are in the wrong order or there is even one measly character missing, you'll get the question wrong. So to practice, take the sample quizzes at the end of each objective section over and over again until they feel natural to you. All of the exam questions are multiple-choice, just like the examples in the text. Unlike Microsoft or Novell tests, the exam has answer choices that are really similar in syntax—some syntax will be dead wrong, but more than likely, it will just be very *subtly* wrong. Some other syntax choices may be almost right, except that the variables are shown in the wrong order.

Also, never forget that the right answer is the Cisco answer. In many cases, they'll present more than one correct answer, but the *correct* answer is the one Cisco recommends.

Here are some general tips for exam success:

- Arrive early at the exam center so you can relax and review your study materials—particularly IP tables and lists of exam-related information.
- Read the questions *carefully*. Don't jump to conclusions. Make sure you're clear on *exactly* what the question is asking.

- Don't leave any unanswered questions. These will be counted against you.
- When answering multiple-choice questions you're not sure about, use a process of elimination to get rid of the obviously incorrect answers first. Doing this will greatly improve your odds should you need to make an "educated guess."
- Because the hard questions will eat up the most time, save them for last. You can move forward and backward through the exam.
- If you are unsure of the answer to a question, choose one of the answers anyway. Mark the question so that if you have time, you can go back to it and double-check your answer. Remember, an unanswered question is as bad as a wrong one, so answer questions even if you're not certain of the correct choice; if you don't and you run out of time or forget to go back to the question, you'll get it wrong for sure.
- Since you're *not* allowed to use the Windows calculator during the test, memorize the table of subnet addresses that appears in Chapter 4 and write it down on the scratch paper supplied by the testing center after you enter the testing room, but before you start the test. Remember that you must understand IP subnetting to pass this test! Chapter 4 will arm you with all the knowledge you need to understand IP subnetting.

Once you have completed an exam, you'll be given immediate online notification of your pass or fail status, plus a printed Examination Score Report indicating whether you passed or failed, along with your exam results by section. (The test administrator will give you the printed score report.) Test scores are automatically forwarded to Cisco within five working days after you take the test, so you don't need to send your score to them. If you pass the exam, you'll receive confirmation from Cisco, typically within two to four weeks.

There's one more thing you can do to prepare. Visit Brian Horakh's Web site—`http://www.networkstudyguides.com`–and go through the exercises and practice test questions he provides. This will really help you keep abreast of any changes made to the test.

How to Contact the Author

Todd Lammle can be reached at his integration and consulting company located in Colorado at `info@lammle.com`.

How to Contact the Publisher

Sybex welcomes reader feedback on all of their titles. Visit the Sybex Web site at `http://www.sybex.com` for book updates and additional certification information. You'll also find online forms to submit comments or suggestions regarding this or any other Sybex book.

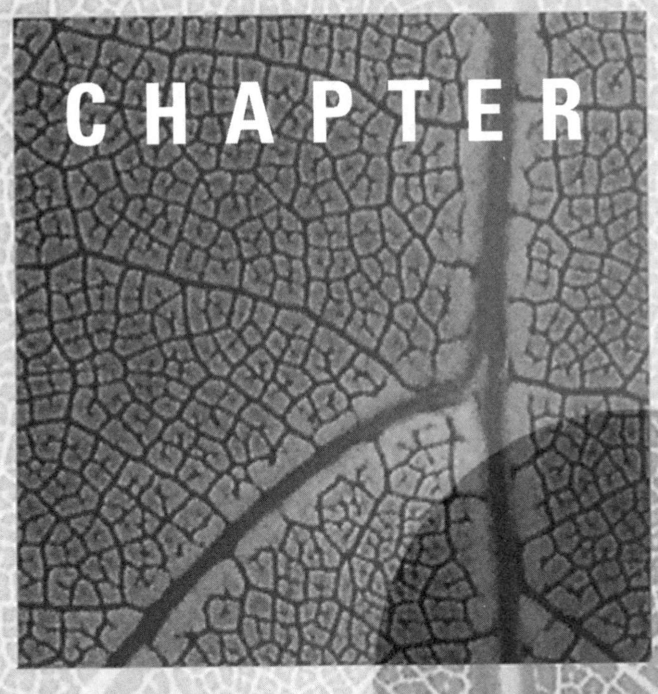

1

OSI Reference

Cisco CCNA exam objectives covered in this chapter:

- **Identify and describe the functions of each of the seven layers of the OSI reference model.** *(pages 3 – 13)*
- **Describe connection-oriented network service and connectionless network service, and identify the key differences between them.** *(pages 13 – 16)*
- **Describe data link addresses and network addresses, and identify the key differences between them.** *(pages 17 – 21)*
- **Identify at least 3 reasons why the industry uses a layered model.** *(pages 21 – 23)*
- **Define and explain the 5 conversion steps of data encapsulation.** *(pages 24 – 27)*
- **Define flow control and describe the three basic methods used in networking.** *(pages 27 – 31)*
- **List the key internetworking functions of the OSI Network layer and how they are performed in a router.** *(pages 31 – 36)*

In this chapter, we are going to discuss the Cisco way of looking at the OSI reference model. When you take the CCNA exam, it is important that you can describe the aspects and specifications of each layer of the OSI reference model.

When looking at the different specifications related to each layer, we will concentrate on a few specific details, such as the differences between connection-oriented and connectionless network services and between Data Link and Network layer addresses.

We will continue to concentrate on the OSI reference model as we present reasons that the networking industry uses a layered model when creating a variety of networked applications, not just when using the OSI reference model. We will also review the process of data encapsulation as user data is sent from one host to another.

The last two topics covered in this chapter are flow control at the Transport layer and internetworking functions at the Network layer. Although flow control is specified at more than one layer of the OSI model, we will focus only on the flow control generated at the Transport layer.

Identify and describe the functions of each of the seven layers of the OSI reference model

The OSI model is the primary architectural model for networks. It describes how user data and network information are communicated from applications on one computer to an application on another computer through the network media. The OSI reference model breaks this approach into layers.

The OSI reference model is important in that it helps facilitate troubleshooting. There are many reasons why you must understand the OSI model (see the section "Identify at least three reasons why the networking industry uses a layered model" later in this chapter), and Cisco thinks this knowledge is especially important for troubleshooting and understanding data conversion in internetworks.

The OSI reference model has seven layers:

- Application
- Presentation
- Session
- Transport
- Network
- Data Link
- Physical

These layers are sometimes grouped together. For example, the Session, Presentation, and Application layers are referred to as the "upper" layers. This is because application developers can make one protocol that spans the specifications of all three layers.

Critical Information

To fully understand how protocols work in a network, you must have a fundamental understanding of each layer and its function. Figure 1.1 shows how the OSI layers stack up.

FIGURE 1.1: The OSI reference model

Application	File, print, message, database, and application services
Presentation	Data encryption, compression, and translation services
Session	Dialog control
Transport	End-to-end connection
Network	Routing
Data Link	Framing
Physical	Physical topology

Application Layer

The Application layer of the OSI model supports the communication components of an application and provides network services to application processes that span beyond the OSI reference model specifications.

The Application layer is also responsible for the following:

- Understanding the resources needed to communicate between two devices and establishing their availability
- Synchronizing applications on the server and client

- Agreeing on error control and data integrity of communicating applications
- Providing system-independent processes or program services to end users

These are some of the most popular network services specified at the Application layer:

- The World Wide Web (WWW)
- E-mail gateways
- Electronic Data Interchange (EDI)
- Special interest bulletin boards
- Internet navigation utilities
- Financial transaction services

Presentation Layer

The Presentation layer is so named because it presents data to the Application layer. It's essentially a translator, making sure that the data sent from one system is readable by the Application layer of the receiving station. The Presentation layer is responsible for code formatting, conversion, and negotiating the data transfer syntax for the Application layer.

A successful data transfer technique is to convert the data into a standard format before transmission. Computers are configured to receive this generically formatted data and then convert the data back into its native format for actual reading (for example, EBCDIC to ASCII). It is important to remember that the Presentation layer is the only layer that can actually change data.

The OSI has protocol standards that define how standard data should be formatted. Tasks such as data compression, decompression, encryption, and decryption are associated with this layer.

Some Presentation layer standards are involved in multimedia operations. The following file format standards serve to direct graphic and visual image presentation:

- PICT
- TIFF
- JPEG

Others standardize video and audio formatting:

- MIDI
- MPEG
- QuickTime

Session Layer

The Session layer's job can be likened to that of a mediator or referee. Its central concern is dialog control between devices, or *nodes*. For example, a database running within an internetwork could use Session layer protocols to keep track of the transactions occurring on each system. The Session layer establishes, manages, and terminates sessions between applications. It also provides data transfer control and management between cooperating application processes over a session connection.

Responsible for coordinating data communication between two Presentation layer systems, the Session layer organizes their communication by offering three different modes—simplex, half-duplex, and full-duplex. It also splits a communication session into three different phases: connection establishment, data transfer, and connection release. This allows the Session layer to coordinate requests and responses that occur when applications communicate between different hosts.

These are some examples of Session layer protocols and interfaces:

- Network File System (NFS)
- SQL

- RPC
- X Window

Transport Layer

Services located in the Transport layer both segment and reassemble data from upper-layer applications and unite the information onto the same data stream. They also provide end-to-end data transport and establish a logical connection between the sending host and the destination host on an internetwork. This layer is responsible for reliable network communication between end nodes. (Note that *reliable* does not mean *guaranteed.*)

The Transport layer is responsible for providing mechanisms for multiplexing upper-layer applications, sequencing, and session establishment, as well as maintenance and termination (tear-down) of virtual circuits. It also hides details of any network-dependent information from the higher layers by providing transparent data transfer and fault recovery.

This layer ensures data integrity by maintaining flow control and by allowing users the option of requesting reliable data transport between systems. Flow control prevents the problem of a sending host on one side of the connection overflowing the buffers in the receiving host—an event that can result in lost data. Reliable data transport employs a connection-oriented communications session between systems, and the protocols involved ensure that the following objectives will be achieved:

- Upon receiving the segments, the recipient sends an acknowledgment to the sender.
- Any segments not acknowledged are retransmitted.
- Segments are sequenced back into their proper order upon arrival at their destination.
- A manageable data flow is maintained in order to avoid congestion, overloading, and the loss of any data.

Network Layer

The Network layer is responsible for routing within an internetwork. Cisco and all other types of routers are defined at this layer.

An internetwork must continually designate all paths of its media connections. In Figure 1.2, each line connecting routers is numbered, and those numbers are used by routers as network addresses. These addresses possess and convey important information about the path of media connections. They're used by routing protocols to pass packets from a source onward to its destination.

FIGURE 1.2: Internetwork addressing

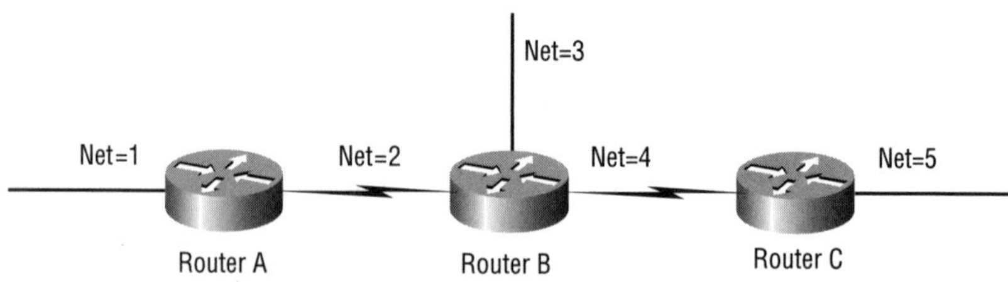

The Network layer creates a composite "network map"—a communication strategy system—by combining information about the sets of links into an internetwork with path determination, path switching, and route processing functions. It can also use these addresses to provide relay capability and to interconnect independent networks.

Consistent across the entire internetwork, Network layer addresses also streamline the network's performance by not forwarding unnecessary broadcasts, such as NT server advertisements. Unnecessary broadcasts increase the network's overhead and waste capacity on any links and machines that don't need to receive them. Using consistent end-to-end addressing that accurately describes the path of media connections enables the Network layer to determine the best path to a destination without encumbering the device or links on the internetwork with unnecessary broadcasts.

Data Link

The Data Link layer ensures that messages are delivered to the proper device and translates messages from above layers into bits for the Physical layer to transmit. It formats the message into data frames, which add a customized header containing the hardware destination and source address.

The IEEE divides the Data Link layer into two sublayers, MAC and LLC, described below.

MAC

The MAC (Media Access Control) sublayer of the Data Link layer is responsible for the following:

Framing: This layer is responsible for taking the packets from the upper layer and framing the packet with both a header and trailer, hence the name framing. The frame contains the hardware addresses (MAC address) of both the source and the destination host.

Media Access: This is the way that hosts or network devices communicate with the physical medium.

Logical Topology: This defines the digital signal path through the physical topology. For example, in a Token Ring network, the physical topology is typically a star topology. However, the logical topology in a Token Ring network is a ring.

LLC

The LLC (Logical Link Control) sublayer can provide optional services to an application developer. One option is to provide flow control to the Network layer by using stop/start codes. The LLC can also provide error *correction,* while the MAC sublayer only provides error *detection.*

The LLC enables the upper-layer protocols to remain independent over different LANs by providing a Destination Service Access Point (DSAP) and a Source Service Access Point (SSAP). The DSAP and SSAP provide a method of communication between the Network layer and Data Link/Physical layers by identifying the Network layer protocol regardless of the type of physical and logical medium being used.

Physical Layer

The Physical layer is responsible for the electrical, mechanical, and procedural specification for physical links between hosts on an internetwork. This layer sends and receives bits. The Physical layer communicates directly with the various types of actual communication media.

At the Physical layer, the interface between the Data Terminal Equipment, or DTE, and the Data Circuit-Terminating Equipment, or DCE, is identified. The DCE is usually located at the service provider, while the DTE is an attached device, such as a router. The services available to the DTE are most often accessed via a modem (asynchronous) or channel service unit/data service unit (synchronous).

Necessary Procedures

NOTE There are no hands-on procedures directly related to this objective. Throughout the rest of this book, you will see this subsection only for objectives that involve procedures.

Exam Essentials

You will not be able to pass the CCNA exam without a complete understanding of the OSI model and how the protocols function within this model. Keep the following points in mind when going through the various objectives covering the OSI model and the IP (Internet Protocol).

Understand the different layers and their functions. Just knowing the order of the layers won't suffice. You must have a good understanding of what function each layer provides, including its protocols and specifications.

Understand the different protocols in the IP protocol suite. You need to understand how ARP (Address Resolution Protocol), RARP (Reverse Address Resolution Protocol), UDP (User Datagram Protocol), IP (Internet Protocol), TCP (Transmission Control Protocol), and ICMP (Internet Control Message Protocol) function in an internetwork environment. You should also know how each protocol relates to the OSI reference model. (See Chapter 4 for more information on network protocols.)

Key Terms and Concepts

Logical Topology: The signal path through the physical topology. There are typically only two logical topologies: bus and ring.

OSI: An acronym for Open System Interconnection, this network architectural model was developed by the International Organization for Standardization (ISO) and ITU-T in 1977. Their basic purpose was to develop a data communication standard for multivendor interoperability. The OSI model consists of seven layers (described previously), each with different specifications.

Physical Topology: The actual layout of the network medium. There are five different physical topologies: bus, ring, star, mesh, and cellular.

Sample Questions

1. Which layer is responsible for providing mechanisms for the building and tearing down of virtual circuits?

   A. Application

   B. Presentation

   C. Session

   D. Transport

E. Network

F. Data Link

G. Physical

Answer: D. The Transport layer is responsible for virtual circuit connection and termination between hosts.

2. Which layer is responsible for negotiating data transfer syntax?

   A. Application

   B. Presentation

   C. Session

   D. Transport

   E. Network

   F. Data Link

   G. Physical

   Answer: B. The Presentation layer is responsible for data conversion. This is the only layer that can actually change the data.

3. Which layer is responsible for understanding the resources needed to communicate between two devices and establishing their availability?

   A. Application

   B. Presentation

   C. Session

   D. Transport

   E. Network

   F. Data Link

   G. Physical

   Answer: A. The Application layer is responsible for understanding the resources needed to communicate between two devices and establishing their availability.

4. Which of the following are Presentation layer standards? (Choose all that apply.)

   A. PICT

   B. TIFF

   C. JPEG

   D. NFS

   E. SQL

   F. MIDI

   G. MPEG

   Answer: A, B, C, F, G. The Presentation layer standards include PICT, TIFF, and JPEG for graphic and visual images, and MIDI, MPEG, and QuickTime for movies and sound. NFS and SQL are Session layer standards.

Describe connection-oriented network service and connectionless network service, and identify the key differences between them

Connectionless and connection-oriented services can be used at almost all layers of the OSI model, and the decision to use them at any given layer is completely up to the application developer. Understanding the differences will help you troubleshoot an internetwork, configure Cisco routers correctly, and find the correct answers on the CCNA exam.

Critical Information

When talking about the difference between connection-oriented and connectionless network service, people usually refer to an actual protocol as an example. For instance, IP is connectionless and TCP is connection-oriented. This is true; however, these are just protocols that use the specifications of the Network and Transport layers to set up and deliver data to network devices. They do not actually define the network service.

Perhaps the best and most often used analogy is the difference between sending a postcard and a registered letter. We'll use that analogy in the following sections.

Connectionless

Connectionless network service is similar to sending a postcard or letter. You put the correct source and destination host addresses on the postcard and then drop it in the mailbox. Does it get to its destination? You hope so. Since the message on the postcard is probably not a matter of life or death, you don't need an acknowledgment of its receipt. Using this type of delivery saves time and overhead, but at the cost of reliability.

As mentioned previously, the decision about whether to use connectionless service is totally up to the application developer and not up to the end user. An application developer chooses this type of service when he or she needs a quick transfer at a specific layer and is not overly concerned with reliability.

Connection-Oriented

To return to our postal analogy, connection-oriented service is like using registered mail instead of dropping a letter in the mailbox. This is the type of service you'd want when sending your winning lottery ticket to the Lottery Commission. Although it's still not guaranteed, the service will be more reliable. A connection-oriented session is likewise not guaranteed, but it's created using a basic transfer mechanism and provides flow control, windowing, reliability, and error checking.

In a connection-oriented session, acknowledgments are used. If the destination host does not send an acknowledgment within a specified time, the sending host will retransmit the data.

Application developers use this type of service when they need a more reliable connection. In some instances, developers use connectionless service on some layers and connection-oriented service at other layers to add reliability. An example of this would be TCP/IP. IP is a connectionless service for quick routing of datagrams between internetworks, but it uses the TCP protocol for reliability and flow control at the Transport layer to put everything back together before the upper layers receive the data.

Exam Essentials

You may not get any specific questions about connectionless and connection-oriented sessions on the CCNA exam; however, to pass the test, you must comprehend the differences between the two.

Understand what makes a reliable session. It is important to understand both the protocols that make a reliable session and how a reliable connection is created. (See the previous section of this chapter and the section on TCP/IP Transport layer protocols in Chapter 4.)

Be familiar with the protocols used in a connectionless service. You need to understand how IP and UDP work in an internetworking environment. (These points are covered in Chapter 4.)

Key Terms and Concepts

Connection-Oriented: Data transfer that requires the establishment of a virtual circuit. Typically called a *reliable* connection.

Connectionless: Data transfer that does not use a virtual circuit. Typically described as *best-effort* delivery of datagrams.

Sample Questions

1. Which of the following describes a connection-oriented session?

    A. UDP (User Datagram Protocol)

    B. Analogous to sending a postcard

    C. Data transfer that does not use a virtual circuit

    D. Data transfer that requires the establishment of a virtual circuit

    Answer: D. A session is set up before any data is transmitted in a connection-oriented session.

2. Which of the following describes a connectionless network service?

    A. TCP (Transmission Control Protocol)

    B. Analogous to sending a registered letter

    C. Data transfer that does not use a virtual circuit

    D. Data transfer that requires the establishment of a virtual circuit

    Answer: C. A session is not set up before data is sent.

3. Of the protocols TCP and IP, which is connectionless and which is connection-oriented? (Choose both correct statements.)

    A. TCP is connectionless.

    B. IP is connectionless.

    C. IP is connection-oriented.

    D. TCP is connection-oriented.

    Answer: B, D. IP is connectionless and TCP is connection-oriented. (These protocols are covered in more depth in Chapter 4.)

Describe data link addresses and network addresses, and identify the key differences between them

To understand the difference between Data Link and Network addresses, you must have a fundamental knowledge of the OSI reference model. You need to know how these addresses are used in an internetwork in order to create a reliable network and to troubleshoot it. When you are working with Cisco switches and routers, the Network and Data Link layers are the most important layers to understand.

You should know by now that Data Link addresses are really hardware addresses. They are sometimes called MAC addresses because of where they are specified in the OSI reference model. Network addresses, or logical addresses, are specified at the Network layer.

Critical Information

Data Link layer, or physical (hardware), addressing is a unique address that is burned into each network interface card (NIC) by the manufacturer. Think of the hardware address like the address to your house. It's got to be different from the other addresses or your mail just isn't going to get to you. The hardware address is a 48-bit address expressed as six bytes, as shown in Figure 1.3. The first three bytes, known as the vendor code, are given to the manufacturer by the IEEE. The IEEE administers this Organizational Unique Identifier (OUI) so that there aren't any duplicate hardware addresses floating around. The second three bytes are made up by the manufacturer and are generally part of the serial number of the card.

MAC, hardware, and Data Link addresses are all different terms for the same thing. It is important to understand that hardware addresses

FIGURE 1.3: The MAC address format

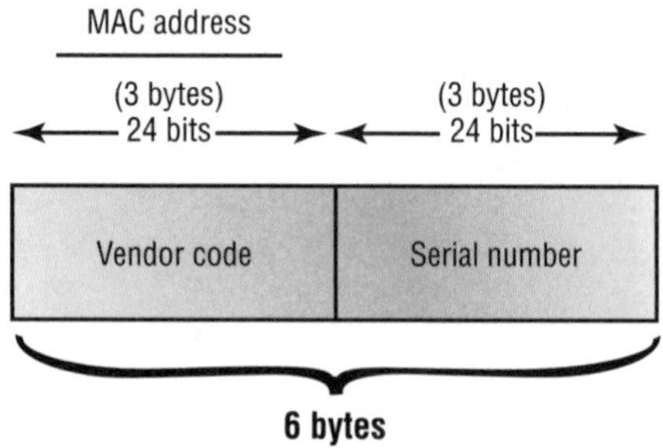

are only used when sending information or data on the local LAN. These addresses are never forwarded on to remote networks through routers.

Logical addressing, sometimes referred to as *virtual* addressing, is used at the Network layer and is hierarchical in scheme, unlike physical addresses, which use a flat addressing scheme. The logical address defines more than the house number, to return to our street address analogy. The logical address can define the city, street, and house address. Examples of protocols that use logical addresses are IP and IPX (Internetwork Packet Exchange). Figure 1.4 shows how a logical address can be used to specify the city, street, and house of an internetwork device.

Exam Essentials

As with the previous objective, the CCNA exam does not directly ask about hardware and logical addresses. However, if you don't have a fundamental understanding of the differences between address types and how they are used, picking the right answer for some questions will be difficult.

Understand when a hardware address is used. In terms of basic IP routing, logical addresses are used to get packets from one network to another. Hardware addresses are used to find a host on a network or LAN.

FIGURE 1.4: Logical addresses

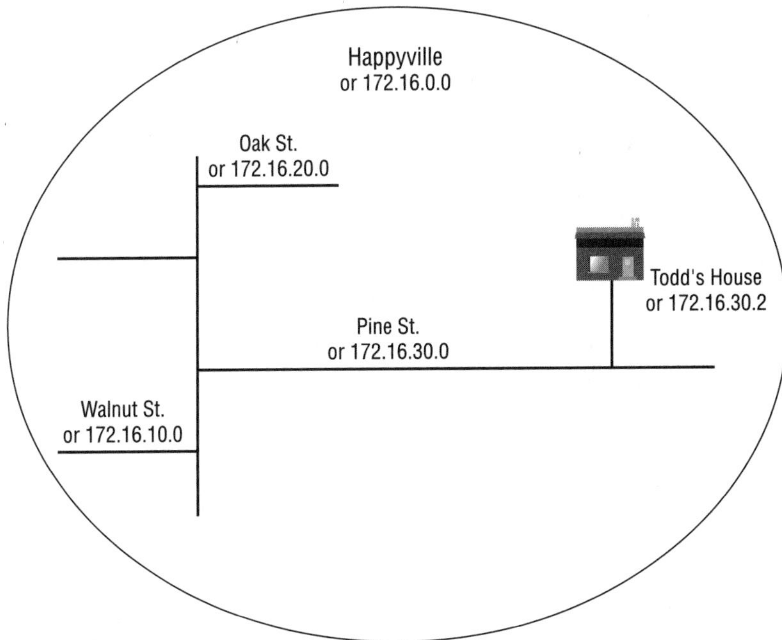

Have a good grasp of the difference between a hardware address and a logical address, including IP and IPX. Again, logical addresses are defined at the Network layer and used to name networks or streets. Hardware addresses are defined at the Data Link layer and are used to identify a host on a LAN. (IP and IPX addressing are explained in more detail in Chapter 4.)

Key Terms and Concepts

Hardware Address: Also known as the MAC or physical address, a hardware address is a Data Link layer address that is required for every host or device that connects to a LAN. These addresses are used by routers and other network devices to find a specific host on a LAN. Hardware addresses are six bytes long.

Logical Address: Sometimes called a protocol or network address, a logical address is a Network layer address referring to a logical, rather than a physical, network device.

Sample Questions

1. Which of the following are true? (Choose all that apply.)

   A. Hardware addresses are used to find WAN devices.

   B. Hardware addresses are 12 bytes long.

   C. Hardware addresses are used to find devices connected to a LAN.

   D. Hardware addresses are also known as physical or MAC addresses.

   Answer: C, D. Hardware addresses, also known as MAC or physical addresses, are used to find a local device on a LAN.

2. What type of addressing is used to create internetworks?

   A. Hardware

   B. MAC

   C. IP

   D. Logical

   Answer: D. Connecting networks together with a router creates internetworks. The administrator assigns a logical address to each network that is connected to the router. An example of this is an IP address or IPX address; these are both logical addresses.

3. When a router receives a packet, how does the router forward the packet to the destination host or next hop?

   A. By using IP or IPX.

   B. By using an ARP broadcast to locate the IP address of the next hop or final destination host.

C. By placing the packet in a frame with the destination hardware address of a host on a locally attached LAN or the router interface of the next hop.

D. By placing the packet in a segment with the destination logical address of a host on a locally attached LAN or the router interface of the next hop.

Answer: C. When a router receives a packet, it first checks the destination's logical address (its IP address, for example). If the router is not the final destination, then it checks the routing table to find the network of the final destination. Once that is found, it puts the packet in a frame and puts the destination hardware address of the next hop or destination host on a locally attached LAN.

Identify at least 3 reasons why the industry uses a layered model

One of the first things to understand is that Cisco presents many different reasons why the industry uses a layered model, not just three. In the following sections, we will define many of the reasons that we think are the most important for you to remember for the exam.

You should have a fundamental understanding of the OSI model, including knowing why the industry uses a model and what the benefits are. Knowing this can help you fulfill business requirements in the real world as well as prepare for the CCNA exam.

Critical Information

There are many advantages to using a layered model. Because developers know that another layer will handle functions they're not currently working on, they can confidently focus on just one layer's functions. This promotes specialization. Another benefit is that if changes to protocols are made to one layer, it doesn't necessarily change protocols within the other layers. A third big advantage of using layered models is compatibility. If software developers adhere to the specifications outlined in the reference model, all the protocols written to conform to that model will work together. This is very good. Compatibility creates the foundation for a large number of protocols to be written and used.

Cisco's official reasons for why the industry uses a layered model include the following:

- It clarifies the general functions, rather than the specifics, on how to do it.
- It divides the complexity of networking into more manageable sublayers.
- It uses standard interfaces to enable ease of interoperability.
- Developers can change the features of one layer without changing all the code.
- It allows specialization, which helps the industry progress.
- It eases troubleshooting.

Exam Essentials

Use this information, along with the first objective (on the seven OSI layers), to see the "big picture" of how Cisco looks at the OSI model.

Remember why developers use layered models. Ease of troubleshooting, a standard interface, and industry specialization are three good reasons Cisco gives for using a layered model in the networking industry.

Key Terms and Concepts

Compatibility: This is a key reason for reference models. Application developers can ensure compatibility between disparate systems if they use the specifications of a layered model, such as the OSI reference model.

Sample Questions

1. Which of the following are reasons the networking industry uses a layered model? (Choose all that apply.)

   A. Allows gigabit speed between LANs

   B. Allows administrators to make changes in one layer without changing all the layers

   C. Speeds up network industry progress by allowing specialization

   D. Facilitates systematic troubleshooting

   Answer: B, C, D. Troubleshooting, specialization, and the ability to change protocols in one layer without changing all the layers are key reasons why the industry uses a layered model.

2. Which of the following are benefits of having layers in a reference model? (Choose all that apply.)

   A. Allows gigabit speeds between LANs

   B. Allows specialization of applications while still maintaining interoperability

   C. Allows databases to update and back up at any time

   D. Allows ease of troubleshooting between internetworks

   Answer: B, D. Specialization and troubleshooting are two reasons why the industry uses a layered model.

Define and explain the 5 conversion steps of data encapsulation

Data encapsulation is the process in which the information in a protocol is wrapped, or contained, in the data section of another protocol. In the OSI reference model, each layer encapsulates the layer immediately above it as the data flows down the protocol stack.

It is imperative to understand the encapsulation method when troubleshooting an internetwork. For example, when running a network analyzer or running troubleshooting commands, you will not be able to find the problem if you do not understand the encapsulation method. Practice running through the conversion steps in your head before taking the CCNA exam.

Critical Information

The logical communication that happens at each layer of the OSI reference model doesn't involve many physical connections because the information each protocol needs to send is encapsulated in the layer of protocol information beneath it. This encapsulation produces a set of data called a *packet*.

Looking at Figure 1.5, you can follow the data down through the model as it's encapsulated at each layer of the OSI reference model. Starting at the Application layer, data is encapsulated in Presentation layer information. When the Presentation layer receives this information, it looks like generic data being presented. The Presentation layer hands the data to the Session layer, which is responsible for synchronizing the session with the destination host. The Session layer then passes this data to the Transport layer, which transports the data from the source host to the destination host. But before this happens, the Network layer adds routing information to the packet. It then passes the packet on to the Data Link layer for framing and for connection

FIGURE 1.5: Data encapsulation at each layer of the OSI reference model

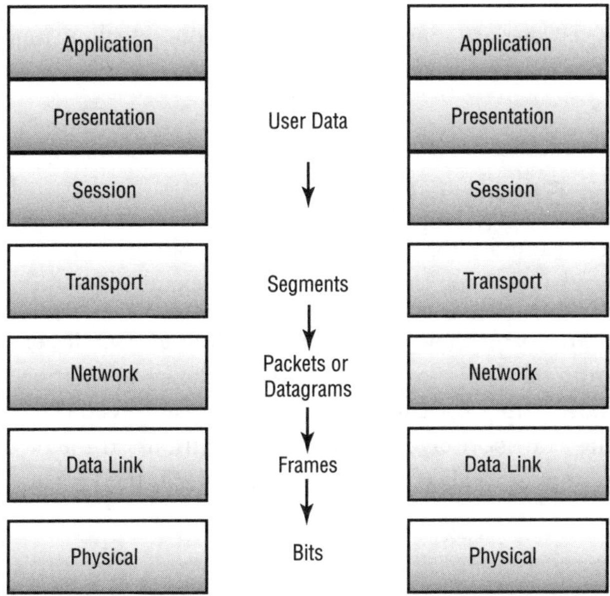

to the Physical layer. The Physical layer sends the data in binary format to the destination host across fiber or copper wiring. Finally, when the destination host receives the 1s and 0s, the data passes back up through the model one layer at a time. The data is de-encapsulated at each of the OSI model's peer layers.

At a transmitting device, the data encapsulation method is as follows:

1. User information is converted to data for transmission on the network.
2. Data is converted to segments and packaged with control information for a reliable connection.
3. Segments are encapsulated with a Network header and converted to packets, or datagrams, which specify the source and destination logical addresses.

4. Packets, or datagrams, are converted to frames to allow a connection over an interface to the network.
5. Frames are converted to bits with some clocking functions to allow transmission on a network medium.

Exam Essentials

The exam is direct: You must understand the exact functions of each layer if you want to pass the CCNA exam.

Memorize the encapsulation method of each layer. Remember, from the upper layers down, this is the encapsulation method: user data at the Application, Presentation, and Session layers; segments at the Transport layer; packets, or datagrams, at the Network layer; frames at the Data Link layer; and bits at the Physical layer.

Key Terms and Concepts

Bits: The Physical layer takes the binary data handed down from the Data Link layer and converts the 1s and 0s to a digital signal to be sent out over the physical topology.

Frames: These house the packets, or datagrams, handed down from the Network layer to be delivered to a device on a LAN.

Packets: Sometimes called *datagrams,* these house the segments handed down from the Transport layer to be routed through an internetwork.

Segments: Defined at the Transport layer, these are parts of a data stream that are handed down from the upper layers to be transmitted to a destination device.

Sample Questions

1. At the Transport layer, user data is converted to:

   A. Packets

B. Frames

C. Segments

D. Bits

Answer: C. The Transport layer breaks data streams into segments and then numbers these segments to be put back together at the destination host. This is called *segmentation*.

2. At the Data Link layer, packets are converted to:

   A. Packets

   B. Frames

   C. Segments

   D. Bits

   Answer: B. Frames are used to house a packet or datagram to be delivered on a local LAN.

3. At the Network layer, segments are converted to:

   A. Packets

   B. Frames

   C. Segments

   D. Bits

   Answer: A. Packets, or datagrams, are defined at the Network layer.

Define flow control and describe the three basic methods used in networking

Flow control is a function that prevents network congestion by ensuring that transmitting devices do not overwhelm receiving devices with data. There are a number of possible causes of network congestion. For example, a high-speed computer might generate traffic faster than the network can transfer it or faster than the destination device can receive and process it.

Typically, application developers need to understand flow control when creating an application. They decide where and when to use this function. Understanding flow control and what protocols work with it can help you troubleshoot Cisco internetworks and help you find the right answers on the CCNA exam.

Critical Information

Flow control is used to help solve network congestion problems. Cisco uses three types of flow control: buffering, source-quench messages, and windowing.

Buffering

Buffers are a section of memory allocated for storing incoming requests. This is not unlike waiting in line at Disneyland. If the line gets too long, employees just add more rope sections to make the waiting area larger; eventually, the area overflows and people start leaving. Routers do the same thing; they keep allocating memory until they have no more room, and then they start discarding segments—ouch! Buffering works fine until requests come in faster then the router can handle them.

Source-Quench Messages

Source-quench messages are used by receiving devices to help prevent their buffers from overflowing. When a receiving device's buffers start filling up, it sends a source-quench message asking the transmitting device to *slow down!* This is what happens:

1. A network device receives too many segments and starts discarding them.
2. Each time the receiving device drops a segment, it sends a source-quench message to the transmitting device.

3. The transmitting device receives a source-quench message for each segment that was discarded. It does not stop transmitting, however; it just slows down the process until source-quench messages are no longer being sent from the receiving device.
4. Once the transmitting device stops receiving source-quench messages, it slowly increments the number of segments being sent until it starts receiving the source-quench messages again.

Windowing

In windowing, the transmitting device transmits segments and the receiving device acknowledges them, but an acknowledgment is not expected for each transmission. If the devices agree on a window size of three, for example, the transmitting device will send three segments before expecting an acknowledgment. Here is how it works:

1. The transmitting device sends three segments to the destination device.
2. After receiving the three segments, the destination device sends an acknowledgment to the transmitting device.
3. Once the transmitting device receives the acknowledgment, it then sends three more segments.
4. If the transmitting station does not receive an acknowledgment from the receiving station, it will resend the segments after a timeout period. Since the receiving device may have overflowed its buffers, the transmitting device resends the segments at a slower rate.

Exam Essentials

You must both have an understanding of the different types of flow control and be able to "read between the lines" when looking for the right answer in a flow control exam question. The only way to do that is to make sure you understand exactly what happens in any flow control situation. (Review the previous section on data encapsulation methods.)

Remember what happens if a device receives more segments than it can handle. A device will drop segments if it receives more segments than it can digest. Source-quench messages are used to tell the transmitting device that the receiving device is dropping segments.

Understand windowing and acknowledgments. When devices set up a session, they agree on a window size. The transmitting device expects an acknowledgment from the receiving device after it sends the agreed-upon number of segments.

Key Terms and Concepts

Acknowledgment: Notification sent from one network device to another to acknowledge that segments have been correctly received.

Buffer: An area of memory used as temporary storage for data being sent or received. This can refer to any area of memory in a computer.

Source-Quench Messages: Used by receiving devices to help prevent their buffers from overflowing, these messages tell the transmitting device that the receiving device is dropping segments.

Window: The number of segments allowed to be transmitted from a transmitting device to a receiving device before an acknowledgment is received.

Sample Questions

1. What happens if a receiving device receives too many segments to process?

   A. It receives a source-quench packet.

   B. It adds more acknowledgments.

   C. It opens the window to a larger size.

   D. It starts to discard segments.

   Answer: D. If a device's buffer is full, it will discard any new segments received.

2. After a device discards segments, what does it do?

   A. It adds more buffers.

   B. It sends a source-quench message for every segment dropped.

   C. It opens the window to a larger size.

   D. Nothing.

   Answer: B. When source-quench is used, the receiver will send a message to the transmitting device after each segment is dropped.

3. When windowing is used as a flow control method, which of the following is true?

   A. The transmitter and receiver agree on the window size before transmitting any segments.

   B. The transmitter and receiver agree on the window size after transmitting all segments.

   C. The transmitter and receiver agree on the window size after transmitting segments, and a source-quench segment is received at the transmitter.

   D. The transmitter tells the receiver the window size it must accept before transmitting any segments.

   Answer: A. Window size is decided upon when a connection-oriented session is set up.

List the key internetworking functions of the OSI Network layer and how they are performed in a router

Of course, you'll need to understand the routing process to pass the CCNA exam. After all, this is a Cisco certification test!

Remember that internetworks are created using routers, not switches or bridges. Only routers can administratively assign a network address to a LAN or WAN link, which is then referred to as an internetwork.

Routers are used to connect LANs to LANs, LANs to WANs, and so on. The function of a router is to send data from a device on a local network to a device on a remote network, hence the term *routing*.

To be a successful network administrator, it is crucial that you understand how frames and packets work together to send user data to remote networks. This section explains that process.

Critical Information

An internetwork must continually designate all paths of its media connections. As shown in Figure 1.6, each line that connects routers is numbered, and those numbers are used by routers as network addresses. These addresses possess and convey important information about the path of media connections. They're used by routing protocols to pass packets from a source onward to its destination.

The Network layer creates a composite "network map"—a communication strategy system—by combining information about the sets of links into an internetwork with path determination, path switching, and route processing functions. It can also use these addresses to provide relay capability and to interconnect independent networks. (Refer to the Network layer section of the first objective covered in this chapter for more information.)

When an application on a host wants to send a packet to a destination device located on a different network, a Data Link frame is received on one of the router's network interfaces. The router then de-encapsulates and examines the frame to establish what kind of Network layer data is in tow. After this is determined, the data is sent on to the appropriate Network layer process. (Because the frame's mission has been fulfilled, it's simply discarded.)

FIGURE 1.6: Communicating through an internetwork

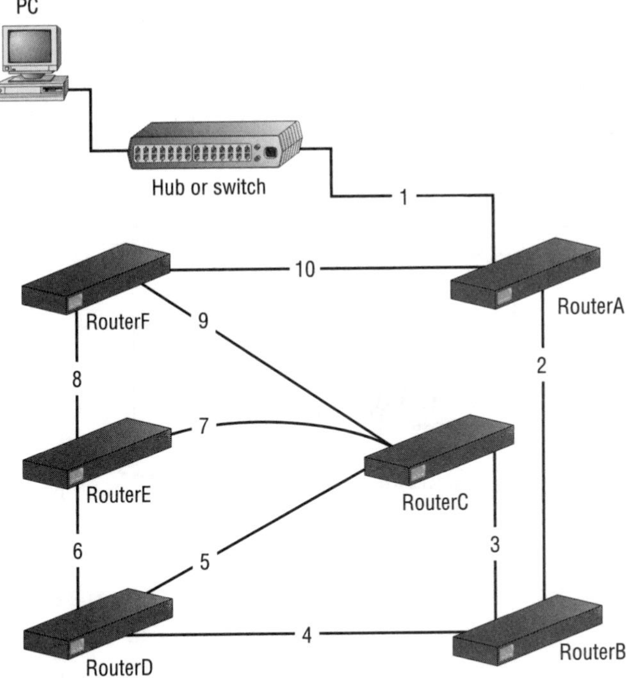

Figure 1.7 illustrates how the Network layer process works. (This process is described in more detail below.) After examining the packet's header to discover which network it's destined for, the Network layer refers to the routing table to find the connections the current network has to foreign network interfaces. After one is selected, the packet is re-encapsulated in its Data Link frame with the selected interface's information and queued for delivery to the next hop in the path toward its destination. This process is repeated every time the packet is routed to another router. When it finally reaches the router connected to the network on which the destination host is located, the packet is encapsulated in the destination LAN's Data Link frame type. It's now properly packaged and ready for delivery to the protocol stack on the destination host.

FIGURE 1.7: The Network layer process

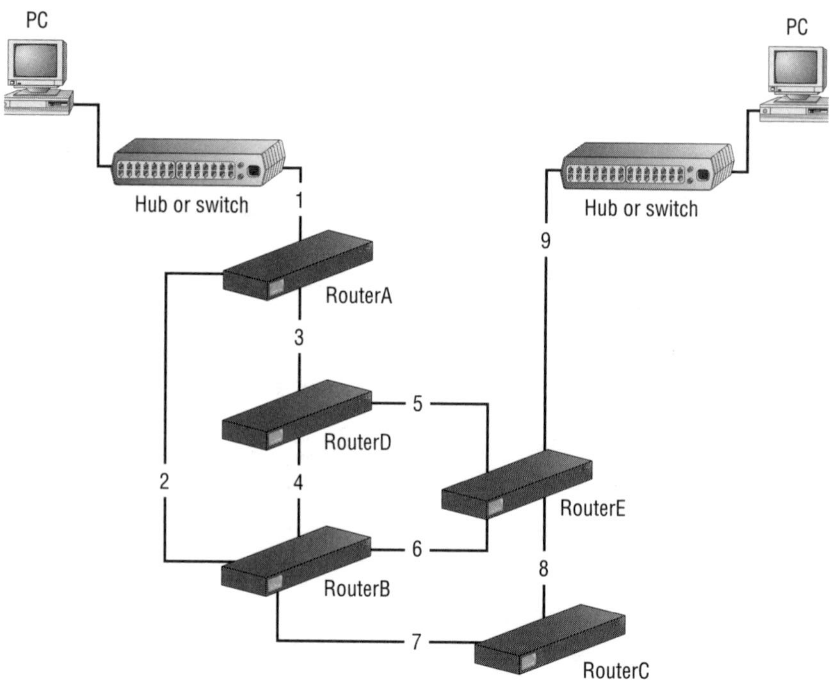

The following describes the Network layer process, as shown in Figure 1.7:

1. The sending PC sends a datagram to a PC located on Network 9.
2. RouterA receives the datagram and checks the destination network. RouterA forwards the packet based on its knowledge of where the network is located.
3. RouterB receives the packet and also checks the destination network. RouterB forwards this to RouterE after checking to find the best route to Network 9.
4. RouterE receives the packet, puts it in a frame with the hardware destination of the receiving PC, and sends out the frame.

Exam Essentials

The job of Cisco routers is routing. When taking the CCNA exam, you must have a fundamental understanding of routing.

Know how routers work at the Network layer. Routers create internetworks and route packets in an internetwork.

Understand when a packet is used and when a frame is used. A packet is put in a frame to be sent out on a LAN. Packets are used to send data between internetworks.

Key Terms and Concepts

Frame: A logical grouping of information sent as a Data Link layer unit over a transmission medium. The term *frame* often refers to the header and trailer, used for synchronization and error control, that surround the user data contained in the unit. The terms *cell, datagram, message, packet,* and *segment* are also used to describe logical information groupings at various layers of the OSI reference model and in various technology circles.

Packet: A logical grouping of information that includes a header containing control information and (usually) user data. The word *packets* is most often used to refer to Network layer units of data. The terms *datagram, frame, message,* and *segment* are also used to describe logical information groupings at various layers of the OSI reference model and in various technology circles.

Router: Network layer device that uses one or more metrics to determine the optimal path along which network traffic should be forwarded. Routers forward packets from one network to another based on Network layer information.

Routing: The process of finding a path to a destination host. Routing is very complex in large networks because of the many potential intermediate destinations a packet might traverse before reaching its destination host.

Sample Questions

1. When a router receives a packet destined for a host on a directly connected LAN and then forwards the packet in a frame, what are the source and destination hardware addresses within that frame? (Choose both correct answers.)

   A. Router interface connected to source network

   B. Router interface connected to destination network

   C. Host interface on source network

   D. Host interface on destination network

   Answer: B, D. The hardware addresses change at every hop. In this case, the source hardware address is that of the router interface connected to the destination network. The destination hardware address is that of the host connected to the destination network or LAN.

2. When a packet is sent between two devices on two different networks, what two addresses never change?

   A. Source MAC address

   B. Destination MAC address

   C. Source logical address

   D. Destination logical address

   Answer: C, D. Logical addresses do not change, but hardware addresses change at each hop.

CHAPTER 2

WAN Protocols

CCNA exam objectives covered in this chapter:

- **Differentiate between the following WAN services: Frame Relay, ISDN/LAPD, HDLC, & PPP.** *(pages 39 – 44)*
- **Recognize key Frame Relay terms and features.** *(pages 44 – 49)*
- **List commands to configure Frame Relay LMIs, maps, and subinterfaces.** *(pages 49 – 55)*
- **List commands to monitor Frame Relay operation in the router.** *(pages 55 – 61)*
- **Identify PPP operations to encapsulate WAN data on Cisco routers.** *(pages 61 – 65)*
- **State a relevant use and context for ISDN networking.** *(pages 65 – 67)*
- **Identify ISDN protocols, function groups, reference points, and channels.** *(pages 67 – 71)*
- **Describe Cisco's implementation of ISDN BRI.** *(pages 71 – 74)*

This chapter focuses on Cisco's WAN (wide-area network) support services. We will talk about Frame Relay terms and features, LMIs, and maps, and how to create subinterfaces. Then you will learn about the various steps and types of equipment a frame passes through as it makes its way along a Frame Relay network. We define each term as it is introduced.

You will also learn how to configure PPP encapsulation and HDLC. It is important to remember where the protocols for these are specified in relation to the OSI reference model.

At the end of the chapter we discuss ISDN networking, including protocols, function groups, reference points, and channels, as well as the difference between BRI and PRI.

Differentiate between the following WAN services: Frame Relay, ISDN/LAPD, HDLC, & PPP

In this chapter you will learn about Cisco's WAN support and how the different encapsulation methods relate to the OSI reference model.

You need to know how each encapsulation method works and be familiar with the protocols that each uses, both to pass the CCNA exam and to make good business decisions in a production environment. When taking the exam, having a clear understanding of the differences between the WAN services is extremely important.

Critical Information

This section covers the basics of Frame Relay, ISDN, HDLC, and PPP. You will learn how each protocol measures up to the OSI model and the functions of each encapsulation method.

Frame Relay

Frame Relay is a high-performance WAN protocol that operates at the Physical and Data Link layers of the OSI reference model. It was originally designed for use across ISDN (Integrated Services Digital Network) interfaces, but today it's also used over a variety of other network interfaces.

Popular opinion is that Frame Relay is faster and more efficient than X.25 because it assumes that error checking will be done through higher-layer protocols and application services. Frame Relay provides connection-oriented Data Link layer communication by using virtual circuits. A Frame Relay virtual circuit is a logical connection between two DTEs across a packet-switched network (PSN) and is identified by a Data Link Connection Identifier (DLCI). Figure 2.1 shows how Frame Relay matches up to the OSI reference model.

FIGURE 2.1: OSI reference model and the Frame Relay

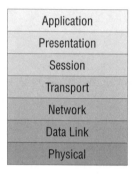

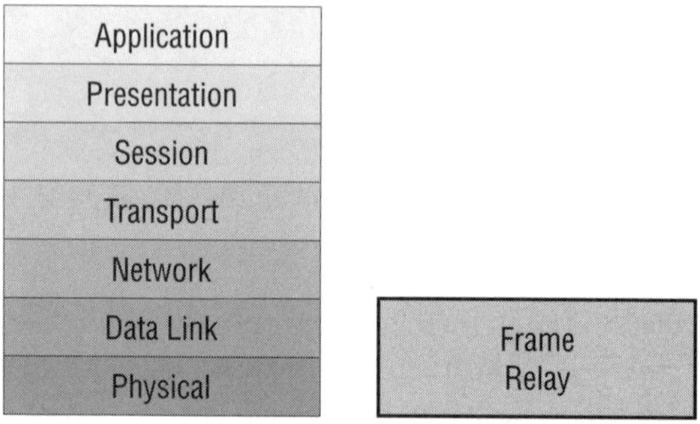

Application
Presentation
Session
Transport
Network
Data Link
Physical

ISDN/LAPD

ISDN (Integrated Services Digital Network) is a digital service designed to run over existing telephone networks. Being able to deliver a true digital service across your existing local loop is very cool indeed. ISDN can support both data and voice transmissions—a telecommuter's dream. But ISDN applications require bandwidth. Typical ISDN applications and implementations include high-speed image applications (such as Group IV facsimile), high-speed file transfer, videoconferencing, and multiple links into the homes of telecommuters.

ISDN is actually a set of communication protocols proposed by telephone companies. It allows them to carry a group of digital services that simultaneously convey data, text, voice, music, graphics, and video to end users, and it was designed to achieve this over the telephone systems already in place. The standards for ISDN encompass the OSI model's Physical, Data Link, Network, and Transport layers, as shown in Figure 2.2.

NOTE For more information on ISDN/LAPD, please refer to the Sybex *CCNA Study Guide.*

FIGURE 2.2: The OSI reference model and ISDN

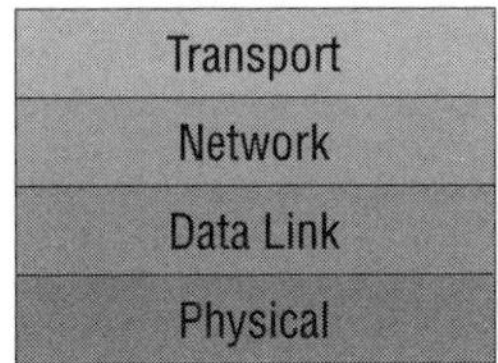

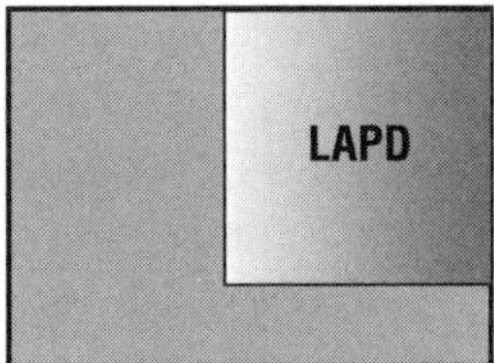

HDLC

The High-Level Data-Link Control protocol (HDLC) is a popular ISO-standard, bit-oriented, Data Link layer protocol that specifies an encapsulation method for data on synchronous serial data links. The International Organization for Standardization (ISO) modified SDLC (Synchronous Data Link Control), created by IBM, to come up with HDLC.

NOTE For more information on HDLC, read Chapter 11 of the Sybex *CCNA Study Guide.*

HDLC is the default encapsulation used by Cisco routers over synchronous serial links. Cisco's HDLC is proprietary—it won't communicate with any other vendor's HDLC implementation—but this is not unusual.

HDLC has both Physical layer and Data Link layer specifications, as shown in Figure 2.3.

PPP

Point-to-Point Protocol (PPP) is a Data Link protocol that can be used over either asynchronous (dial-up) or synchronous (ISDN) media. It uses LCP (Link Control Protocol) to build and maintain Data Link connections. LCP is packed with features, including:

- Authentication using either PAP (Password Authentication Protocol) or CHAP (Challenge-Handshake Authentication Protocol)

FIGURE 2.3: The OSI reference model and HDLC

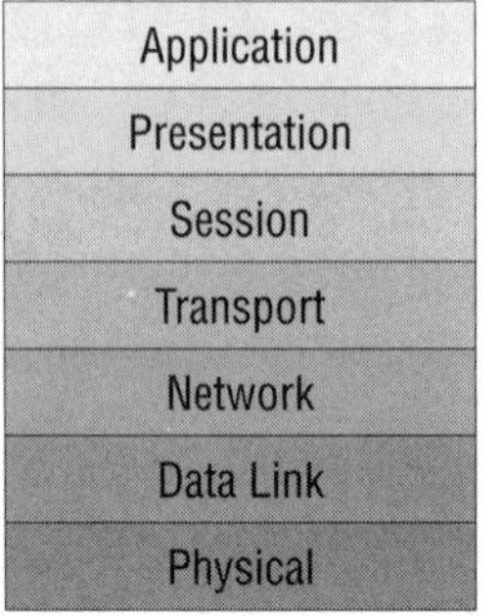

- Compression of data for transmission across media

These features weren't available in PPP's predecessor, SLIP (Serial Line Internet Protocol), so this is progress.

Another new feature is support for multiple protocols. SLIP supported only IP, but through NCP (Network Control Protocol), PPP supports IP, IPX, AppleTalk, DECnet, OSI/CLNS, and transparent bridging. NCP is actually a family of protocols, one for each Network layer protocol that is supported by PPP. Figure 2.4 shows PPP and the OSI model.

FIGURE 2.4: The OSI reference model and PPP

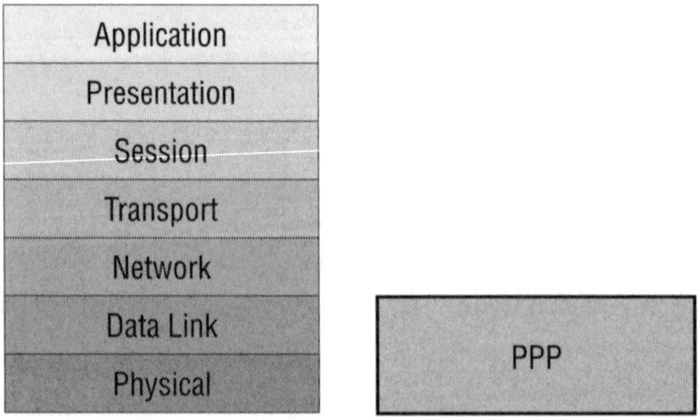

Application
Presentation
Session
Transport
Network
Data Link
Physical

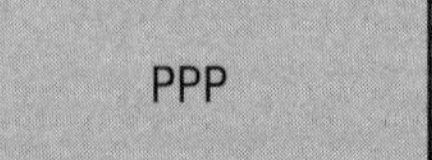

Exam Essentials

Have a clear understanding of the different WAN services and where they fit in the OSI model.

Know where each protocol stack is in relation to the OSI reference model. For the CCNA exam, it is crucial that you remember where each WAN protocol stack is used in relation to the OSI reference model.

Key Terms and Concepts

Frame Relay: A protocol, specified at the Physical and Data Link layers of the OSI model, that uses a PVC (Permanent Virtual Circuit).

HDLC: An acronym for High-Level Data-Link Control protocol, HDLC is a data encapsulation method specified at the Physical and Data Link layers of the OSI model. This is the default encapsulation method used on Cisco routers.

ISDN: A digital communication protocol that permits telephone networks to carry data and voice transmissions at higher speeds than typical analog transmission rates.

OSI: An acronym for Open Systems Interconnection, OSI was created by the International Organization for Standardization (ISO) to create a layered approach to interoperability between disparate systems.

PPP: A data encapsulation method that uses the Physical, Data Link, and Network layer specifications of the OSI model. PPP provides synchronous and asynchronous circuits.

Sample Questions

1. What is the default encapsulation for Cisco serial interfaces?

   A. PPP

B. Frame Relay

C. ISDN

D. HDLC

Answer: D. All Cisco routers use HDLC encapsulation by default on their serial interfaces.

2. Which statement is true of ISDN?

   A. You must have special cabling to use it.

   B. It can transmit voice and data.

   C. It can only transmit data.

   D. It can only transmit voice.

   Answer: B. ISDN can transmit voice and data at high speeds over standard telephone wires.

3. Which statement is true of Frame Relay?

   A. It uses Network layer protocols.

   B. It has been replaced by X.25.

   C. It uses a PVC at layer two.

   D. It's an encapsulation method used by NT routers.

   Answer: C. Frame Relay is a protocol specified at the Data Link layer. It generally uses PVCs.

Recognize key Frame Relay terms and features

The previous section introduced the Frame Relay protocol. In this section, we will discuss the terminology used for the various features within a Frame Relay network. You will learn how two internetwork devices communicate end-to-end through a Frame Relay cloud by using a DLCI number, DTE, DCE, demarcation (demarc), local loop, and PSE.

It is important to understand the difference between these devices and to know the terms used for them, both when you are working in a production environment and when you are studying for your CCNA exam. In a production environment, it will also be helpful if you can visualize how the frame traverses the internetwork; you'll have a better chance of troubleshooting problems.

Critical Information

To understand the terminology used in Frame Relay networks, first you need to know how the technology works. Figure 2.5 is labeled with the various terms used to describe different parts of a Frame Relay network.

FIGURE 2.5: Frame Relay technology and terms

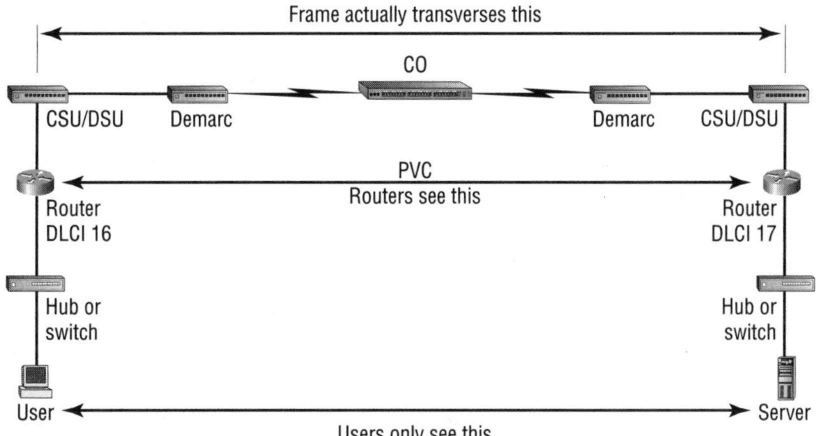

The basic idea behind Frame Relay is to allow users to communicate between two DTE (data terminal equipment) devices through DCE (data communication equipment). The users should not see the difference between connecting to and gathering resources from a local server and a server at a remote site connected with Frame Relay. Chances are that this connection will be slower than a 100Mbps

Ethernet LAN, but the difference in the connection should be transparent to the user.

Figure 2.5 illustrates everything that must happen in order for two DTE devices to communicate. Here is how the process works:

1. The user's network device sends a frame out on the local network. The hardware address of the router (default gateway) will be in the header of the frame.
2. The router picks up the frame, extracts the packet, and discards the frame. It then looks at the destination IP address within the packet and checks to see if it knows how to get to the destination network by looking in the routing table.
3. The router then forwards the data out the interface that it thinks can find the remote network. (If the router can't find the network in its routing table, it will discard the packet.) Since this will be a serial interface encapsulated with Frame Relay, the router puts the packet onto the Frame Relay network encapsulated within a Frame Relay frame. It will add the DLCI (Data Link Connection Identifier) number associated with the serial interface. DLCIs identify the type of virtual circuit—PVC, Permanent Virtual Circuit, or SVC, Switched Virtual Circuit—to the routers and switches participating in the Frame Relay network.
4. The Channel Service Unit/Data Service Unit (CSU/DSU) receives the digital signal and encodes it into the type of digital signaling that the switch at the Packet Switch Exchange (PSE) can understand. The PSE receives the digital signal and extracts the 1s and 0s from the line. The CSU/DSU is connected to a demarc installed by the service provider, and its location is the service provider's first point of responsibility (the last point on the receiving end). The demarc is typically just a RJ-45 jack installed close to the router and CSU/DSU.
5. The demarc is typically a twisted-pair cable that connects to the local loop. The local loop connects to the closest central office (CO), sometimes called a point of presence (POP). The local loop can connect using various physical mediums, but twisted-pair or fiber is very common.

6. The CO receives the frame and sends it through the Frame Relay "cloud" to its destination. This cloud can be dozens of switching offices—or more! The CO looks for the destination IP address and DLCI number. It typically can find the DLCI number of the remote device or router by looking up an IP-to-DLCI mapping. Frame Relay mappings are usually created statically by the service provider, but they can be created dynamically.
7. Once the frame reaches the switching office closest to the destination office, it is sent through the local loop. The frame gets to the demarc and then to the CSU/DSU. Finally, the router extracts the packet, or datagram, from the frame and puts it in a new LAN frame to be delivered to the destination host. Whew!

The user and the server do not need to know, nor should they know, everything that happens as the frame makes its way across the Frame Relay network. The remote server should be as easy to use as a locally connected resource.

Exam Essentials

There may be some questions specifically relating to WAN terms on the CCNA exam.

Understand where each of the terms is used in a Frame Relay network. Remember that a DTE is typically the router; the DCE is typically the CSU/DSU and switch located at the provider.

Key Terms and Concepts

Central Office (CO): The point at which the local loop gains access to the service provider's high-speed trunk lines. This is often referred to as a POP (point of presence).

Customer Premise Equipment (CPE): Refers to all wiring and equipment on the customer's side of the demarc.

Data Circuit-Terminating Equipment (DCE): Specific communications equipment, such as packet switches, that interface between a packet switching exchange (PSE) and DTE devices. DCEs are typically found in carrier facilities.

Data Link Connection Identifiers (DLCIs): Used to identify a Frame Relay virtual circuit. A Frame Relay service provider, like a telephone company, typically assigns DLCI values that are used by the Frame Relay protocol to distinguish between different virtual circuits on the network.

Data Terminal Equipment (DTE): End systems that communicate over an X.25 network (such as host systems, terminals, and PCs that belong to the individual subscriber) and that are present at the same site.

Demarcation (demarc): The boundary between the customer's in-house wiring and the service provider's wiring. This is the demarcation point, or the end of responsibility, for the service provider.

Local Loop: The wiring running from the demarc to the CO.

Packet Switching Exchange (PSE): Switches that constitute the majority of a carrier's network and handle the transfer of data between DTE devices via the X.25 packet-switched network.

Permanent Virtual Circuits (PVC): An established connection used for recurrent, steady data transfer.PVC sessions are continuously active, so DTEs can transmit data whenever necessary.

Switched Virtual Circuit (SVC): An SVC is a temporary connection used for intermittent data transfers. When using an SVC, DTE devices must establish, maintain, and then terminate a session every time they need to communicate.

Sample Questions

1. Which of the following are valid WAN terms?

   A. CPA

   B. CPE

   C. DTE

D. DCE

Answer: B, C, D. CPE (customer premise equipment), DTE (data terminal equipment), and DCE (data circuit-terminating equipment) are all valid Cisco WAN terms.

2. What is the local loop?

A. The link between the demarc and the DCE

B. The link between the demarc and the CO

C. The switch in the CO

D. The router at the CPE

Answer: B. The local loop is the connection between the demarcation location and the first switching office.

3. DTEs are usually:

A. CSU/DSU

B. PSE

C. Routers

D. demarc

Answer: C. Routers are DTE devices by default. However, remember that most devices can be configured to be either a DTE or DCE.

List commands to configure Frame Relay LMIs, maps, and subinterfaces

To prepare you for this portion of the CCNA exam, we will demonstrate how to configure a Cisco router to be used in a Frame Relay network. We will explain the steps for configuring a router to use the Frame Relay encapsulation, assigning a DLCI number, and choosing an LMI type. You will also learn how to create a subinterface and why you should use one. We will then finish the configuration by creating a Frame Relay mapping.

It's important to learn the commands and procedures for configuring a router for use on a Frame Relay network. Frame Relay is used in many production environments, and Cisco requires you to understand how to configure Frame Relay if you are going to be a CCNA.

Critical Information

When configuring Frame Relay on Cisco routers, the first thing you do is to specify it as an encapsulation on serial interfaces. There are only two encapsulation types: Cisco and IETF. Use these commands:

```
RouterA(config)#int s0
RouterA(config-if)#encapsulation frame-relay ?
 ietf Use RFC1490 encapsulation
 <cr>
```

Cisco is the default encapsulation unless you type **IETF**. Use the Cisco encapsulation when you are connecting two Cisco devices. Use the IETF (Internet Engineering Task Force) encapsulation when you are connecting a Cisco device to a non-Cisco device using Frame Relay.

Data Link Connection Identifiers

As discussed in previous sections, Frame Relay virtual circuits are identified by Data Link Connection Identifiers (DLCIs). Because many virtual circuits can be terminated on a multipoint Frame Relay interface, many DLCIs are affiliated with it. For the IP devices at each end of a virtual circuit to communicate, their IP addresses are mapped to DLCIs. This is so that a multipoint device can point out the appropriate destination virtual circuit on the Frame Relay network to each packet sent over the single physical interface.

Each DLCI can have a local meaning. In other words, two DTE devices connected via a virtual circuit use different DLCI values when referring to the same connection.

Here is an example that shows how to configure a DLCI number to an interface:

```
    RouterA(config-if)#frame-relay interface-dlci ?
    <16-1007> Define a DLCI as part of the current
    subinterface
RouterA(config-if)#frame-relay interface-dlci 16
```

Local Management Interface (LMI)

The Local Management Interface (LMI) was developed in 1990 by Cisco Systems, StrataCom, Northern Telecom, and Digital Equipment Corporation. The group became known as the "Gang-of-Four LMI," or "Cisco LMI." This "gang" took the basic Frame Relay protocol from the CCIT and added extensions to the protocol features that allowed internetworking devices to communicate easily with a Frame Relay network.

LMI messages provide information about the current DLCI values, the global or local significance of the DLCI values, and the status of virtual circuits. You will need to check with your Frame Relay provider to find out which LMI type to use. The default type is Cisco, but you may need to change to ANSI or Q.933A. You can display the three LMI types on your screen using the command shown here:

```
RouterA(config-if)#frame-relay lmi-type ?
 cisco
 ansi
 q933a
```

All standard LMI signaling formats are supported by the following:

ANSI: Annex D, defined by ANSI standard T1.617

ITU-T (Q933a): Annex A, defined by Q933a

Cisco: LMI, defined by the "Gang of Four" (default)

NOTE With Cisco IOS version 11.2 and above, the LMI type is auto-detected.

Subinterfaces

You can have multiple virtual circuits on a single serial interface and treat each virtual circuit as a separate interface, called a *subinterface*. Think of a subinterface as a hardware interface defined by the IOS software.

The advantage to using subinterfaces is that you can assign different Network layer characteristics to each subinterface and virtual circuit, such as IP routing on one virtual circuit and IPX on another. Define subinterfaces with the command `interface s0.subinterface number`, as shown in this example:

```
RouterA(config)#int s0.?
 <0-4294967295> Serial interface number
RouterA(config)#int s0.16 ?
 multipoint     Treat as a multipoint link
 point-to-point Treat as a point-to-point link
```

You can define a limitless number of subinterfaces on a given physical interface, keeping router memory in mind. In the above example, we chose to use subinterface 16 because that is the DLCI number of that interface. You can choose any number between 0 and 4294967295.

The two types of subinterfaces are point-to-point and multipoint. Point-to-point subinterfaces are used when a single virtual circuit connects one router to another. Multipoint subinterfaces are used when the router is at the center of a star of virtual circuits.

Mapping Frame Relay

As we explained earlier, in order for IP devices at the ends of virtual circuits to communicate, their addresses must be mapped to the DLCIs. There are two ways to make this mapping happen:

- Use the `frame relay map` command.
- Use the `inverse-arp` function.

For each packet sent out of a physical interface, mappings allow a multipoint device to identify a virtual circuit on the Frame Relay network.

This is an example program that uses the `frame relay map` command:

```
RouterA(config)#int s0.16 point-to-point
RouterA(config-if)#encap frame-relay ietf
RouterA(config-if)#no inverse-arp
RouterA(config-if)#ip address 172.16.30.1 255.255.255.0
RouterA(config-if)#frame-relay map ip 172.16.30.17 20
cisco broadcast
RouterA(config-if)#frame-relay map ip 172.16.30.18 30
broadcast
RouterA(config-if)#frame-relay map ip 172.16.30.19 40
```

Here's what we did: First we chose our subinterface and set the encapsulation to IETF. We then turned off `inverse arp` (IARP) and mapped three virtual circuits and their corresponding DLCI numbers. (IARP would map our DLCIs to IP addresses dynamically, as demonstrated below.) Notice that we specified Cisco encapsulation on the first virtual circuit. The other two virtual circuits will use the encapsulation type specified in the interface command (IETF). The `frame relay map` command is the only way to mix both Cisco and IETF encapsulation types. The `broadcast` keyword at the end of the `map` command tells the router to forward broadcasts for this interface to this specific virtual circuit.

Instead of putting in `map` commands for each virtual circuit, you can use the `inverse-arp` (IARP) function to perform dynamic mapping of the IP address to the DLCI number. In that case, your configuration program would look like this:

```
RouterA(config)#int s0.16 point-to-point
RouterA(config-if)#encap frame-relay ietf
RouterA(config-if)#ip address 172.16.30.1 255.255.255.0
```

Yes, this is a whole lot easier, but it's not as stable as using the `map` command. Why? Sometimes when you use the `inverse-arp` function, configuration errors occur, because virtual circuits can be insidiously and dynamically mapped to unknown devices.

TIP Frame Relay mapping isn't something an administrator would typically do. This process is usually performed at the switching office. Check with your provider before doing any Frame Relay configurations.

Exam Essentials

Review this section as often as needed for you to remember the different ways to configure a router for Frame Relay.

Understand how to configure Frame Relay on a Cisco router. It is crucial that you understand the difference between encapsulation, DLCI, LMI, and mappings.

Know how many encapsulation and LMI types Cisco supports. Cisco supports two encapsulation methods (Cisco and IETF) and three LMI types (Cisco, ANSI, and Q933a).

Key Terms and Concepts

DLCI: Data Link Connection Identifiers (DLCIs) are used in Frame Relay networks to keep track of virtual circuits.

Encapsulation: A method of encasing or wrapping data (packets) within a protocol that is understood on the link.

LMI: Local Management Interface (LMI) messages are used to provide three types of information—the current DLCI values, the global or local significance of the DLCI values, and the status of virtual circuits—to routers participating in the Frame Relay network.

Sample Questions

1. Which of the following is a valid command syntax to create a Frame Relay subinterface?

   A. `int s0.43569 point-to-point`

B. `int s0.16`

C. `int 16.s0 point-to-point`

D. `int s0 sub 16`

Answer: A. The way to configure a subinterface on your serial interface is with this syntax: `interface` *`[serial number]`* *`[point-to-point`* `or` *`multipoint]`*.

2. What are the LMI types supported by Cisco? (Choose all that apply.)

A. IETF

B. ANSI

C. Cisco

D. Q933a

Answer: B, C, D. Cisco supports three different LMI types: Cisco, ANSI, and Q933a.

3. What are the Frame Relay encapsulation types that Cisco supports? (Choose all that apply.)

A. ANSI

B. Q933a

C. Cisco

D. IETF

Answer: C, D. Cisco supports two encapsulation methods when running Frame Relay. Cisco is the default and IETF is used to connect Cisco equipment to other brands of routers.

List commands to monitor Frame Relay operation in the router

When you are working in a production environment that uses Frame Relay and while you are studying for the CCNA exam, this topic is an important one. You must have a fundamental understanding of not only how to configure Frame Relay but also the commands to monitor and troubleshoot Frame Relay.

Cisco Frame Relay support is stable and popular. If you want to work in a production environment, the ability to configure and maintain Frame Relay networks is sometimes a prerequisite to landing such a job. Knowing how to monitor and troubleshoot this protocol is a big part of that skill.

Critical Information

There are several ways to check the status of your interfaces and PVCs once you have Frame Relay encapsulation set up and running. Use the `show frame-relay ?` command at the router prompt to display all the commands you can use to view Frame Relay specifications:

```
Router#sh frame-relay ?
  ip        show frame relay IP statistics
  lapf      show frame relay lapf status/statistics
  lmi       show frame relay lmi statistics
  map       Frame-Relay map table
  pvc       show frame relay pvc statistics
  route     show frame relay route
  svc       show frame relay SVC stuff
  traffic   Frame-Relay protocol statistics
```

For monitoring purposes, the commands you'll be using are `show frame-relay pvc`, `show frame-relay lmi`, `show frame-relay traffic`, and `show interface`. Here's how to use each command:

- `show frame pvc` gives the statistics of your PVCs on all configured Frame Relay interfaces.
- `show frame lmi` displays the LMI statistics and the LMI type used on your Frame Relay network.
- `show frame-relay traffic` shows you the global Frame Relay statistics since the last time the router was booted.
- `show interface s0` displays your LMI information and DLCI type (local or switched), but not the DLCI number.

Necessary Procedures

This section runs through the commands that will help you monitor and troubleshoot a Frame Relay network.

show frame pvc

The `show frame pvc` command lists all configured PVCs and DLCIs. This command shows you the DLCI number configured for each interface, including subinterfaces. Also, you can see whether the router is configured as a switch or as a DTE (local). The output `DLCI USAGE=LOCAL` indicates that the router is used as a DTE (as in the example below); `DLCI USAGE=SWITCH` indicates that it's used as a switch.

```
RouterA#sh frame pvc

PVC Statistics for interface Serial0 (Frame Relay DTE)

DLCI = 16, DLCI USAGE = LOCAL, PVC STATUS = ACTIVE,
INTERFACE = Serial0.1

input pkts 50977876     output pkts 41822892   in bytes
                                               3137403144
 out bytes 3408047602  dropped pkts 5          in FECN
                                               pkts 0
 in BECN pkts 0        out FECN pkts 0         out BECN
                                               pkts 0
 in DE pkts 9393       out DE pkts 0
 pvc create time 7w3d,last time pvc status changed 7w3d

DLCI = 18, DLCI USAGE = LOCAL, PVC STATUS = ACTIVE,
INTERFACE = Serial0.3

input pkts 30572401     output pkts 31139837   in bytes
                                               1797291100
 out bytes 3227181474  dropped pkts 5          in FECN
                                               pkts 0
 in BECN pkts 0        out FECN pkts 0         out BECN
                                               pkts 0
 in DE pkts 28         out DE pkts 0
 pvc create time 7w3d,last time pvc status changed 7w3d
```

```
DLCI = 20, DLCI USAGE = LOCAL, PVC STATUS = ACTIVE,
INTERFACE = Serial0.5

input pkts 33059904     output pkts 33381448   in bytes
                                               2016627916
out bytes 4244863762    dropped pkts 6         in FECN
                                               pkts 0
in BECN pkts 0          out FECN pkts 0        out BECN
                                               pkts 0
in DE pkts 301          out DE pkts 0
pvc create time 7w3d,last time pvc status changed 3d02h
```

show frame-relay lmi

The show frame-relay lmi command displays information about the Local Management Interface (LMI). You can also see the LMI type the router has been configured to use.

```
    Router#sh frame-relay lmi
LMI Statistics for interface Serial0 (Frame Relay DTE)
LMI TYPE= ANSI
  Invalid Unnumbered info 0       Invalid Prot Disc 0
  Invalid dummy Call Ref 0        Invalid Msg Type 0
  Invalid Status Message 0        Invalid Lock Shift 0
  Invalid Information ID 0        Invalid Report IE Len 0
  Invalid Report Request 0        Invalid Keep IE Len 0
  Num Status Enq. Sent 0          Num Status msgs Rcvd 0
  Num Update Status Rcvd 0        Num Status Timeouts 0
```

show frame-relay traffic

The show frame-relay traffic command shows the ARP information since the last router reload.

```
Router#sh frame-relay traffic
Frame Relay statistics:
        ARP requests sent 10, ARP replies sent 0
        ARP request recvd 0, ARP replies recvd 0
```

show interface

You can also use the show interface command to check for LMI traffic. Note that you *cannot* see the DLCI number for an interface by using the show interface command. Instead you will see the encapsulation method and LMI information of the interface, including the LMI type. In the example shown below, the output DLCI 1023 does not indicate a DLCI number, but a virtual number the interface uses. You can see your DLCI numbers by using show frame pvc and show running-config.

```
RouterA#sh int s0
Serial0 is up, line protocol is up
 Hardware is HD64570
 MTU 1500 bytes, BW 1544 Kbit, DLY 20000 usec, rely
255/255, load 2/255
 Encapsulation FRAME-RELAY, loopback not set, keepalive
set (10 sec)
 LMI enq sent 451751, LMI stat recvd 451750, LMI upd
recvd 164, DTE LMI up
 LMI enq recvd 0, LMI stat sent 0, LMI upd sent 0
 LMI DLCI 1023 LMI type is CISCO frame relay DTE
 Broadcast queue 0/64, broadcasts sent/dropped 0/0,
interface broadcasts 8392947
 Last input 00:00:02, output 00:00:00, output hang never
 Last clearing of "show interface" counters never
 Input queue: 0/75/0 (size/max/drops); Total output
drops: 0
 Queueing strategy: weighted fair
 Output queue: 0/64/0 (size/threshold/drops)
   Conversations 0/19 (active/max active)
   Reserved Conversations 0/0 (allocated/max allocated)
 5 minute input rate 13000 bits/sec, 30 packets/sec
 5 minute output rate 16000 bits/sec, 28 packets/sec
   142390130 packets input, 5033149 bytes, 0 no buffer
   Received 0 broadcasts, 0 runts, 0 giants
   0 input errors, 0 CRC, 0 frame, 0 overrun, 0 ignored,
0 abort
   135137047 packets output, 709476803 bytes, 0 underruns
   0 output errors, 0 collisions, 7 interface resets
   0 output buffer failures, 0 output buffers swapped out
   0 carrier transitions
   DCD=up DSR=up DTR=up RTS=up CTS=up
```

Exam Essentials

It is just as crucial that you understand the ways to monitor a Frame Relay network as it is that you know how to configure one.

Remember which commands display your DLCI number and LMI type. The commands `show frame pvc` and `show running-config` display your DCLI number. The `show interface` and `show frame-relay lmi` commands give you the router's LMI and bandwidth information.

Key Terms and Concepts

Data Link Connection Identifiers (DLCIs): Used to identify a Frame Relay virtual circuit. A Frame Relay service provider, like a telephone company, typically assigns DLCI values that are used by Frame Relay to distinguish between different virtual circuits on the network.

Local Management Interface (LMI): LMI messages are used to provide three types of information to routers participating in the Frame Relay network: the current DLCI values, the global or local significance of the DLCI values, and the status of virtual circuits.

Permanent Virtual Circuits (PVC): An established connection used for recurrent, steady data transfer. PVC sessions are continuously active, so DTEs can transmit data whenever necessary.

Sample Questions

1. Which of the following statements is true regarding LMIs?

    A. They are not mandatory in all Frame Relay networks.

    B. They use DLCIs to track PVCs.

    C. The LMI type is auto-detected in IOS version 11.2.

D. Cisco supports four LMI types.

Answer: C. With IOS version 11.2 and above, the LMI type is auto-detected.

2. Which two commands show the LMI type configured on your router?

   A. `sh frame-relay dlci`

   B. `sh frame pvc`

   C. `sh frame lmi`

   D. `show interface`

   Answer: C, D. To see the LMI type configured on your router, use the `show frame lmi` and `show interface` commands.

3. Which command displays the DLCI number set on an interface?

   A. `sh int s0`

   B. `sh frame-relay dlci`

   C. `sh frame pvc`

   D. `sh frame-relay lmi`

   Answer: C. The `show interface` command will *not* show your DLCI number. `show frame pvc` and `sh run` give you the DLCI numbers for each interface.

Identify PPP operations to encapsulate WAN data on Cisco routers

Point-to-Point Protocol (PPP) was created to work with multiple protocols at the Network layer and to replace SLIP (Serial Line Internet Protocol), which could run only IP at the Network layer. This section covers Cisco support for PPP encapsulation.

The CCNA exam does not focus heavily on this subject, but you want to be prepared for anything. Besides, PPP is a great protocol and used in many different network environments. It is also non-proprietary, so it can work with many different vendors' equipment.

Critical Information

PPP can be used in asynchronous and synchronous networks. The steps for configuring PPP for synchronous networks on Cisco routers are covered in the "Necessary Procedures" section. Configuring PPP encapsulation on an interface is a fairly straightforward process.

Of course, in order for PPP encapsulation to work, it must be enabled on both interfaces that are connected to a serial line. Once you have PPP encapsulation enabled, you can verify that it's up and running with the `show interface` command.

Necessary Procedures

Here's how to configure routers for PPP encapsulation:

PPP Encapsulation

The first thing you need to do is to tell the router that the serial interface is using PPP encapsulation.

```
RouterA#config t
Enter configuration commands, one per line. End with
CNTL/Z.
RouterA(config)#int s0
RouterA(config-if)#encapsulation ppp
RouterA(config-if)#^Z
RouterA#
```

Once you have enabled PPP encapsulation, you should check to see that it's running correctly by using the `show interface` command.

show interface

The `show interface` command displays PPP statistics and other information that you may need.

In the sample output below, you can see that the connection has an encapsulation of PPP, and the sixth line indicates that LCP is open. Remember that LCP's job is to build and maintain connections. The eighth line indicates that IPCP, CDPCP, and ATCP are open. This shows the IP, CDP, and AppleTalk support from NCP. The seventh line reports that the router is listening for IPXCP.

```
RouterA#show int s0
Serial0 is up, line protocol is up
 Hardware is HD64570
 Internet address is 172.16.20.1/24
 MTU 1500 bytes, BW 1544 Kbit, DLY 20000 usec, rely
255/255, load 1/255
 Encapsulation PPP, loopback not set, keepalive set
(10 sec)
 LCP Open
 Listen: IPXCP
 Open: IPCP, CDPCP, ATCP
 Last input 00:00:05, output 00:00:05, output hang never
 Last clearing of "show interface" counters never
 Input queue: 0/75/0 (size/max/drops); Total output
drops: 0
 Queueing strategy: weighted fair
 Output queue: 0/1000/64/0 (size/max total/threshold/
drops)
   Conversations 0/2/256 (active/max active/max total)
   Reserved Conversations 0/0 (allocated/max allocated)
  5 minute input rate 0 bits/sec, 0 packets/sec
  5 minute output rate 0 bits/sec, 0 packets/sec
   670 packets input, 31845 bytes, 0 no buffer
   Received 596 broadcasts, 0 runts, 0 giants,
0 throttles
   0 input errors, 0 CRC, 0 frame, 0 overrun, 0 ignored,
0 abort
   707 packets output, 31553 bytes, 0 underruns
```

```
     0 output errors, 0 collisions, 18 interface resets
     0 output buffer failures, 0 output buffers swapped out
  21 carrier transitions
     DCD=up DSR=up DTR=up RTS=up CTS=up
```

Exam Essentials

The CCNA exam generally does not contain many questions relating to PPP protocols, but as always you should be prepared.

Remember how the PPP protocols fit within the OSI layers. It is important to remember how all WAN protocols are related to the OSI reference model, not just PPP. PPP is defined at the Data Link layer (layer two).

Key Terms and Concepts

PPP: Point-to-Point Protocol (PPP) is a data encapsulation method that uses the Physical, Data Link, and Network layer specifications of the OSI model. PPP provides synchronous and asynchronous circuits.

SLIP: An acronym for Serial Line Interface Protocol, SLIP is the predecessor to PPP. It can only use TCP/IP and does not provide authentication.

Sample Questions

1. What does PPP stand for?

   A. Please Pass my Protocol

   B. Point-to-Protocol Point

   C. Point-to-Point Protocol

   D. Protocol used in a Point-to-Point network

   Answer: C. Point-to-Point Protocol.

2. What protocol does PPP use to support multiple Network layer protocols?

   A. NCP (Network Control Protocol)

   B. LCP (Link Control Protocol)

   C. NCP (Network Chosen Protocol)

   D. LCP (Lat Control Protocol)

   Answer: A. NCP is actually a family of protocols, one for each Network layer protocol that is supported by PPP.

State a relevant use and context for ISDN networking

Integrated Services Digital Network (ISDN) is a very popular type of network, if you can get it. ISDN provides enough bandwidth to allow voice and data transmission at fast speeds, making it very useful for telecommuters. The problem with ISDN is that it is not available everywhere.

Another nice thing about this technology is that it allows digital services over standard telephone cabling. However, the reason that it is not available everywhere is that some types of telephone cabling cannot support the encoding necessary to transmit large amounts of data.

To pass this portion of the CCNA exam, make sure you understand the purpose of ISDN and its advantages.

Critical Information

ISDN (Integrated Services Digital Network) is a digital service designed to run over existing telephone networks. Because it can support both data and voice transmissions, ISDN is perfect for the users on your network who telecommute. But ISDN applications require bandwidth. Typical ISDN applications and implementations include high-speed image applications (such as Group IV facsimile), high-speed file transfer, videoconferencing, and multiple links into homes of telecommuters.

ISDN is actually a set of communication protocols and standards devised by telephone companies that define the hardware and call setup schemes for end-to-end digital connectivity. With it they can provide digital services that simultaneously convey data, text, voice, music, graphics, and video to end users, all while using the telephone systems that are already in place. ISDN is referenced by a suite of ITU-T standards that encompass the OSI model's Physical, Data Link, and Network layers.

ISDN supports virtually every upper-layer network protocol (IP, IPX, AppleTalk, and so on), and you can choose PPP, HDLC, or LAPD as your encapsulation protocol.

Exam Essentials

Cisco wants you to know the reasons that network administrators would want to use ISDN.

Remember the different services that ISDN can run. ISDN can run both voice and data services over existing telephone lines.

Key Terms and Concepts

ISDN: A digital communication protocol that permits telephone networks to carry data and voice transmissions at higher speeds than typical analog transmission rates.

ITU-T: An acronym for International Telecommunication Union Telecommunication Standardization Sector. This group creates international standards for internetworks and telecommunications.

OSI: An acronym for Open Systems Interconnection, OSI was created by the International Organization for Standardization (ISO) to create a layered approach to interoperability between disparate systems.

Sample Questions

1. Which of the following can be transmitted with ISDN?

   A. Voice

   B. Data

   C. Music

   D. Video

   E. All of the above

   Answer: E. ISDN can support all of these types of data and more.

2. Which of the following is a good reason to use ISDN?

   A. You need constant data streams.

   B. When you need to have constant connections to multiple locations.

   C. Your network uses off-brand routers.

   D. Your network users need high-speed voice and data capability.

   Answer: D. Cisco considers ISDN a high-speed connection. Measured against a 28.8K or 56K dial-up connection, this is true.

Identify ISDN protocols, function groups, reference points, and channels

People in the networking industry tend to use a lot of acronyms and other lingo to describe basic things. The parts of ISDN are no exception. In this section we define some of these terms and the features they describe.

The components we describe are really the nuts and bolts of ISDN, which are very important for you to understand both when you are setting up an ISDN connection and studying for the CCNA exam.

Critical Information

This section focuses on ISDN and how Cisco views its protocols, function groups, reference points, and channels.

ISDN Protocols

ISDN protocols are defined by the ITU-T. Here are three diverse ISDN protocols whose function is specified by their first letter:

- *E* protocols apply to ISDN on an existing telephone network.
- *I* protocols deal with concepts, terminology, and services.
- *Q* protocols pertain to switching and signaling.

Function Groups

Function groups connecting to the ISDN network are known as *terminals*. These come in two types:

- TE1 (Terminal Endpoint Device type 1) is a BRI (Basic Rate Interface) that understands ISDN standards. (BRI will be covered in detail in the next section of this chapter.)
- TE2 (Terminal Endpoint Device type 2) predates ISDN standards. To use a TE2, you have to use a terminal adapter (TA) to generate BRI signals for a Cisco router interface.

ISDN Reference Points

ISDN uses four different reference points to define logical interfaces between functional groupings such as TAs and NT1s. They are as follows:

- *R* defines the reference point between non-ISDN equipment and a TA.

- *S* defines the reference point between user terminals and an NT2.
- *T* defines the reference point between NT1 and NT2 devices.
- *U* defines the reference point between NT1 devices and line-termination equipment in a carrier network. (This type of reference point is only used in North America where the NT1 function isn't provided by the carrier network.)

ISDN Channels

There are two types of channels used in BRI ISDN: B and D. Here's what each one does:

- B, or bearer, channels have a 64Kbps capacity. They can be used for voice or data. Two B channels in a BRI can be combined for a total of 128Kbps.
- D, or data, channels are used for call signaling or clocking. This type of channel has a 16Kbps capacity.

NOTE To learn more about ISDN and channels, read the Sybex *Advanced Cisco Router Configuration (ACRC) Study Guide.*

Exam Essentials

To pass this portion of the exam, you'll need to remember the terminology used for ISDN features, as well as how the various parts function.

Understand the different protocols used in ISDN. The Q protocol specifies switching and signaling. E protocols apply to ISDN on an existing telephone network. I protocols deal with concepts, terminology, and services.

Know the difference between a B channel and a D channel. A BRI uses 2 B channels and one D channel. Each B channel is 64Kbps; a D channel is 16Kbps.

Key Terms and Concepts

BRI: Basic Rate Interface (BRI) is an ISDN interface composed of two B channels and one D channel for circuit-switched communication of voice, video, and data.

ISDN: A digital communication protocol that permits telephone networks to carry data and voice transmissions at higher speeds than typical analog transmission rates.

ITU-T: International Telecommunication Union Telecommunication Standardization Sector. This group creates international standards for internetworks and telecommunications.

OSI: An acronym for Open Systems Interconnection, OSI was created by the International Organization for Standardization (ISO) to create a layered approach to interoperability between disparate systems.

Reference Point: Used to define logical interfaces in ISDN.

Sample Questions

1. What does an R reference point define?

   A. The reference point between non-ISDN equipment and a TA

   B. The reference point between ISDN equipment and a BRI

   C. The reference point between ISDN equipment and a PRI

   D. The reference point between non-ISDN equipment and an NA1

   Answer: A. R reference points are used when connecting ISDN to a router interface other than a BRI or PRI.

2. When protocols begin with the letter *Q*, what does that specify?

   A. Switching and signaling

   B. Existing telephone service

   C. Concepts, terminology, and services

D. Quality ISDN service

Answer: **A.** To read about switching and signaling in ISDN, look for the specifications and protocols that begin with *Q*.

Describe Cisco's implementation of ISDN BRI

BRI (Basic Rate Interface) is very popular in the U.S. because it provides 128Kbps transmission at a good price. BRI is not the best choice for large, steady data streams, but it works well for bursts of data.

Understanding what ISDN BRI offers will be helpful for you when comparing possible network solutions for your business requirements and when you take the CCNA exam.

Critical Information

ISDN Basic Rate Interface service (BRI, also known as 2B+1D) provides two B (bearer) channels and one D (data) channel. The BRI B-channel service operates at 64Kbps and carries data, while the BRI D-channel service operates at 16Kbps and usually carries control and signaling information. The D-channel signaling protocol spans the OSI reference model's Physical, Data Link, and Network layers. BRI also provides framing control for a total bit rate of up to 192Kbps.

When configuring ISDN BRI, you will need to obtain SPIDs (Service Profile Identifiers); you should have one SPID for each B channel and two for BRI. SPIDs can be thought of as the telephone number of each B channel. The ISDN device gives the SPID to the ISDN switch, which then allows the device to access the network for BRI or PRI service. If an ISDN device doesn't have an SPID, many IDSN switches won't allow it to place a call on the network.

Necessary Procedures

In order to use ISDN with a Cisco router, you need to purchase either a Network Termination 1 (NT1) or an ISDN modem. If your router has a BRI interface, you're all set. Otherwise, you can use one of your router's serial interfaces—if you can get a hold of a TA (terminal adapter). A router with a BRI interface is called a TE (Terminal Endpoint 1), and one that requires a TA is called a TE2 (Terminal Endpoint 2).

ISDN supports virtually every upper-layer network protocol (IP, IPX, AppleTalk, etc.), and you can choose PPP, HDLC, or LAPD as your encapsulation protocol.

NOTE When configuring ISDN, you'll need to know the type of switch that your service provider is using, because each manufacturer has a proprietary protocol for signaling. To see which switches your router will support, use the `isdn switch-type ?` command in global configuration mode.

For each ISDN BRI interface, you need to specify the SPIDs by using the `isdn spid1` and `isdn spid2` interface subcommands. Here's an example:

```
RouterA#config t
Enter configuration commands, one per line. End with
CNTL/Z.
RouterA(config)#isdn switch-type basic-dms100
RouterA(config)#int bri0
RouterA(config-if)#encap ppp
RouterA(config-if)#isdn spid1 775456721
RouterA(config-if)#isdn spid2 775456722
```

The encapsulation is PPP; ISDN specifies this method, used to establish the digital phone call.

Exam Essentials

Review this section until you fully understand what BRI is and what terminology is associated with it.

Remember the different protocols used within a BRI. A BRI uses two B channels of 64Kbps each and one D channel of 16Kbps.

Key Terms and Concepts

BRI: Basic Rate Interface. ISDN interface composed of two B channels and one D channel for circuit-switched communication of voice, video, and data.

ISDN: A digital communication protocol that permits telephone networks to carry data and voice transmissions at higher speeds than typical analog transmission rates.

ITU-T: International Telecommunication Union Telecommunication Standardization Sector. Creates standards internationally for internetworks and telecommunications.

OSI: An acronym for Open Systems Interconnection, OSI was created by the International Organization for Standardization (ISO) to create a layered approach to interoperability between disparate systems.

Reference Point: Used to define logical interfaces in ISDN

Sample Questions

1. Which of these statements about a BRI is true?

   A. It uses two D channels of 16Kbps and one B channel of 64Kbps.

   B. It uses two B channels of 64Kbps and one D channel of 16Kbps.

C. It uses one D channel of 64Kbps and two B channels of 16Kbps.

D. It uses one B channel of 16Kbps and two D channels of 64Kbps.

Answer: B. A BRI uses two B channels and one D channel.

2. What command can you use to set the ISDN switch type on a BRI interface?

   A. `switch`

   B. `isdn-switch`

   C. `isdn switch-type`

   D. `switch-type`

   Answer: C. The command `isdn switch-type` is used to set the switch type on a BRI interface.

CHAPTER 3

IOS

Cisco exam objectives covered in this chapter:

- **Log into a router in both user and privileged modes.** *(pages 77 – 81)*
- **Use the context-sensitive help facility.** *(pages 81 – 85)*
- **Use the command history and editing features.** *(pages 85 – 88)*
- **Examine router elements (RAM, ROM, CDP, show).** *(pages 89 – 98)*
- **Manage configuration files from the privileged exec mode.** *(pages 98 – 102)*
- **Control router passwords, identification, and banner.** *(pages 103 – 113)*
- **Identify the main Cisco IOS commands for router startup.** *(pages 113 – 120)*
- **Enter an initial configuration using the `setup` command.** *(pages 120 – 124)*
- **Copy and manipulate configuration files.** *(pages 125 – 129)*
- **List the commands to load Cisco IOS software from: flash memory, a TFTP server, or ROM.** *(pages 129 – 137)*
- **Prepare to backup, upgrade, and load a backup Cisco IOS software image.** *(pages 137 – 139)*
- **Prepare the initial configuration of your router and enable IP.** *(pages 139 – 146)*

All of the test objectives covered in this chapter are useful. You can use all of the commands we review here in your production network. To truly learn and understand these commands, you need hands-on experience. Practice the commands over and over again before you take the CCNA exam and before trying them on a production network. As you practice, pay close attention to the details of what a command is really doing and the information it can provide.

This chapter starts with the basics: how to log on to a router and the two different modes that a router provides. You will then learn how to use the question mark to access help when using Cisco commands. The command history and editing features will be talked about in detail, as well as the different types of memory a Cisco router uses.

One of the most useful topics we'll discuss is how to set your router passwords, banners, and identification. After that, we'll cover what happens when a router boots up and which files it uses to boot. You will learn how to view these files and copy them.

Cisco routers can be configured manually or with a setup routine. We will go through both methods in this chapter. You will also learn how to copy and restore a Cisco IOS.

This chapter is dedicated to the Cisco IOS (Internetworking Operating System). It will help you learn hands-on techniques for configuring a router.

Log into a router in both user and privileged modes

You can connect to a router from different sources, but what you do once you are connected is determined by how you log on to the router.

You first log in to user mode and then can change to privileged mode. It is important to remember how to log on to both modes and the different commands that can be run in both modes.

When configuring your Cisco routers in a production environment, you can use these two different modes to allow some users to configure the router and others only to view statistics.

Critical Information

Cisco routers are configured from the user interface, which you can run either from the console port on the router or by telnetting in to the router from another host through any router interface. You can also connect a modem to the auxiliary port and dial in to the router for console access.

The Exec Command Interpreter

Cisco IOS software has a command interpreter called the Exec. The Exec first interprets the command you type and then executes the operation you've commanded. (You have to log in to the router before an Exec command can be entered.)

The Exec has two levels of access: user and privileged. These two levels, sometimes referred to as *modes,* serve as security for access into the different levels of commands.

User Mode

User mode is used for ordinary tasks like checking the router's status, connecting to remote devices, making temporary changes to terminal settings, and viewing basic system information. But in this mode, your view of the router's configuration and your troubleshooting capabilities are very limited.

Privileged Mode

This mode is used to change the configuration of the router. (From here, you can access the configuration mode discussed next.) The commands in privileged mode include all those in user mode, plus those used to set operating system parameters, get detailed information on the router's status, test and run debug operations, and access global configuration modes.

Necessary Procedures

There are very few procedures involved in logging in, but they are important to know both when you configure a Cisco router and when you take the CCNA exam.

Connecting a Console Cable and Logging In to User Mode

The first way to attach to a router and log in is to attach a console cable to the console port of the router. Once this is done, you will be asked to press Enter to continue.

If a user mode password is assigned, you will have to enter this password before gaining access to user mode. If no password is assigned, you will be greeted with a `Router>` prompt. The > prompt indicates that you are in user mode:

```
Bob con0 is now available
Press RETURN to get started.
User Access Verification
Password:
Bob>
```

Logging On to Privileged Mode

Once you are in user mode, you can enter privileged mode by typing **enable**. Type **disable** to return to user mode, as in this example (note that the password does not appear on the screen):

```
Bob>enable
Password:
Bob#disable
Bob>
```

Exam Essentials

On a Cisco router, practice logging in to user and privileged mode.

Know the difference between user and privileged modes. You cannot see the router configuration in user mode. You can both view the router configuration and change it in privileged mode.

Remember how to log in to a router in both modes. When you connect a console cable to a router, you are prompted with this message: `Press Return to continue`. At this point, you must enter a user-mode password if one is assigned. You can then type **enable** to enter privileged mode. You will be prompted for a password if one is assigned.

Key Terms and Concepts

Exec: Cisco IOS software command interpreter.

Privileged Mode: This mode is used to view and change the configuration of the router.

User Mode: User mode is used for ordinary tasks like checking the router's status.

Sample Questions

1. If you connect a console cable to a router, what happens?

   A. You are prompted for a user-mode password if required.

   B. You are prompted for a privileged-mode password if required.

   C. You are prompted to press Enter and then prompted to enter a user-mode password if required.

   D. You are automatically put into user mode.

Answer: C. Once you connect to a router through the console connection, you are prompted to press Enter. You will then be prompted for a user-mode password if required. If no password is assigned, you will automatically be put into user mode.

2. In which of the following modes can you see the router's running configuration?

   A. Exec

   B. User

   C. Privileged

   D. Config

   Answer: C. Only in privileged mode can you see the router's configuration.

3. What command do you use to go to privileged mode? What command do you type to go back to user mode?

   A. `user, enable`

   B. `enable, user`

   C. `priv, confg`

   D. `enable, disable`

   Answer: D. To go to privileged mode, you type **enable**. To go back to user mode, type **disable**.

Use the context-sensitive help facility

Some of the commands used to configure and administrate a Cisco router can be hard to remember. By using the context-sensitive help facility, you can get either the next possible command or a list of commands that start with a certain letter.

Understanding how to use the help screens can save you from calling Cisco technical support or looking up information in the Cisco router documentation every time you need to make a router configuration change.

Critical Information

You can access a help screen for any command by typing a question mark (?) after the command. This will give you a list of the commands available. You can then choose the next command in the command string and type a question mark again to get the next command, and so on until you have the complete command string.

For example, if you need to set the clock on your router, but you don't know what the commands are, you could type **clock ?**. You must leave one space between the command `clock` (or another command) and the question mark, or your query won't work. In this example, the next command is `set`; you would type **set** and then a space and a question mark to get the next command, and so on until you have the complete command string.

Suppose you need to know all the commands that start with *cl* because you can't remember the command you need. You can type **cl?** to see all the commands that start with *cl*. Notice that there is no space between the letters and the question mark. This tells the Exec to give you all the commands that start with *cl*.

TIP We can't stress this enough: Hands-on experience here is very important. Practice going through the help screens over and over again.

Necessary Procedures

To master the help features Cisco provides, you need to practice using question mark commands on a Cisco router. The following example shows how to set the router time using the help screens. Notice the difference between typing **clock ?** and **cl?**.

```
Router#cl?
clear  clock
Router#clock ?
```

Notice the space between **clock** and **?**. You could also type **clo ?**.

```
  set  Set the time and date
```

This tells you the next command is `set` and that this command is used to set the date and time. This form of help is called *command syntax help* because it tells you which keywords or arguments are required to continue with a command.

Next, type **clock set ?**

```
Router#clock set ?
  hh:mm:ss  Current Time (hh:mm:ss)
```

Notice that doing this has given you even more information on how to set the clock. Now type in **clock set 10:29:30 ?**

```
Router#clock set 10:29:30 ?
  <1-31>  Day of the month
  MONTH   Month of the year
```

The router responds by giving you a message that it wants information about the day and month. So you need to type in more information, as in this example:

```
RouterB#clock set 10:29:30 23 5
                              ^
% Invalid input detected at '^' marker
```

Notice that if you type a number (5, in this case) instead of the name of the month (May), you receive a `% Invalid input` message. The router is very clear about what it considers invalid input—it includes a caret symbol (^) to indicate where the error is in the command.

To continue, type in **clock set 10:29:30 23 May ?**

```
Router#clock set 10:29:30 23 May ?
  <1993-2035>  Year
```

Okay, the router accepted May and now wants you to specify the year. So, to finish this command, type in **clock set 10:29:30 23 May 1999.**

Exam Essentials

Cisco believes that accessing the context-sensitive help facilities is an important enough skill to test on the exam. They think that if you can use the help screens, you might not call them for every little problem.

Know the different ways to use the question mark. There are two different ways to use the question mark to gain help when administrating your router. You can type **cl?**, for example, which will give you all the commands that start with *cl*. Another option is to type **clock ?**, which gives you the next argument or command available.

Key Terms and Concepts

Context-Sensitive Help: This form of help can also be called *command syntax help* because it tells you which keywords or arguments are required to continue with a command.

Sample Questions

1. If you type **cl ?** and receive an ambiguous command, what should you do?

   A. Type **help cl**.

   B. Type **cl help**.

   C. Type **cl?**.

   D. Type **cl ?**.

   Answer: C. Only answer C is correct. Entering **cl?** will give you all the commands that start with *cl*. If you type **cl ?** and receive an ambiguous command, that means there is more than one command that starts with *cl*.

2. If you want to set the system clock but don't know the command string, what command should you use?

   A. `cl?`

   B. `cl ?`

   C. `clock?`

   D. `clock ?`

   Answer: D. Typing **clock ?** (notice the space) will give you the next command in the string.

Use the command history and editing features

The user interface comes with an advanced editing feature that can help you type in repetitive commands. This feature helps administrators configure routers efficiently. The command history and editing features do not change the configuration in any way; their only purpose is to make things easier for the administrator.

Critical Information

First of all, you can turn off the advanced editing features at any time by typing the command **terminal no editing**. You can re-enable terminal editing by entering **terminal editing**.

Using the advanced editing features is completely up to the administrator configuring the router. None of the advanced editing feature commands are mandatory in any configuration—unless you are taking the CCNA exam, of course!

The chart below describes the different commands used to edit and review the command history.

Command	Purpose
Ctrl+A	Move to the beginning of the command line
Ctrl+E	Move to the end of the command line
Ctrl+F (or right arrow)	Move forward one character
Ctrl+B (or left arrow)	Move back one character
Ctrl+P (or up arrow)	Repeat previous command entry
Ctrl+N (or down arrow)	Repeat most recent command
Esc+B	Move backward one word
Esc+F	Move forward one word
`Router> show history`	Show command buffer
`Router> terminal history size`	Set command buffer size
`Router> terminal no editing`	Disable advanced editing features
`Router> terminal editing`	Re-enable advanced editing

Another helpful editing feature is Tab, which completes an entry for you. For example, you could type in **sh run** and then press the Tab key:

```
Router#sh run [Tab]
 Router#sh running-config
```

The router finishes typing in **sh running-config** for you. Remember to use Tab for those long commands.

Exam Essentials

Practice running the advanced editing features on a Cisco router. Memorize the different commands and what they do.

Remember how to turn off and on advanced editing features. The commands `terminal no editing` and `terminal editing` turn off and on the advanced editing features.

Get hands-on experience using the different editing commands. You must remember the editing commands for the exam. The best way to do this is to practice on a router.

Key Terms and Concepts

Advanced Editing: Cisco's way of creating shortcuts. These key combinations are mostly old Unix commands.

show: Command used from the Cisco command prompt to display configurations and statistics.

Terminal: The console used in Cisco routers is sometimes referred to as a *terminal.*

Sample Questions

1. To put your cursor at the beginning of the line, what command should you use?

   A. Ctrl+P

   B. Ctrl+A

   C. Shift+Esc

   D. Ctrl+N

   Answer: B. Hold down the Control key and press A to move the cursor to the beginning of the line.

2. If you want to disable the advanced editing features on a Cisco router, what command should you use?

   A. `no advanced editing`

   B. `no terminal editing`

   C. `terminal no editing`

   D. `advanced no editing`

   Answer: C. `terminal no editing` is the command to turn off Cisco's advanced editing features. To turn it back on, type **terminal editing.**

3. What command will move your cursor to the end of the line?

   A. Ctrl+E

   B. Ctrl+N

   C. Ctrl+F

   D. Shift+Home

   Answer: A. By holding down the Control key and pressing E, you can move your cursor to the end of the line.

4. Which of the following key presses can be used to see the last command entered at the router?

   A. Ctrl+N

   B. Ctrl+P

   C. The up arrow

   D. Shift+Esc

   Answer: B, C. Either pressing the up arrow or holding down the Control key and pressing P will give you the last command entered.

Examine router elements (RAM, ROM, CDP, show)

For this exam objective you must understand the difference between RAM, ROM, and flash. It is important when studying for the CCNA exam to be able to explain the difference between types of memory and the files stored in each piece of memory. This is also good to know when working in a production environment for troubleshooting and maintenance purposes.

We will also cover a Cisco proprietary protocol called Cisco Discovery Protocol. This allows an administrator to gather information about locally attached routers and switches. This can be used in a production environment to help an administrator gather information about the internetwork, for example if the previous network administrator was fired or quit and destroyed or never created a network topology map. Cisco wants to be sure you understand what information you can gather with CDP and includes questions regarding this on the exam.

Critical Information

These are the different types of memory used in a Cisco router:

- ROM is used by the router to store the bootstrap startup program, operating system software, and Power-On Self-Test (POST). ROM chips are installed in sockets on the router's motherboard so that they can be replaced or upgraded. The IOS included in the ROM is a scaled-down, and usually older, version.
- Flash is basically an erasable, reprogrammable ROM that holds the operating system image and microcode. It allows you to "flash" the router and perform upgrades without removing and replacing chips on the motherboard. Flash is retained even when the router is turned off.

- RAM (random access memory) provides caching and packet buffering, plus information like routing tables, which will be explained in more detail in Chapter 6. RAM is used to hold the running operating system when the router is powered on; it is cleared when the router is reset or powered off.
- NVRAM, an acronym for nonvolatile RAM, stores the router's startup configuration file. NVRAM retains its information even when the router is rebooted or shut down.

Files Stored in Memory

These are the files stored in the different types of memory defined above:

- `startup-config`
- `running-config`
- Cisco IOS

startup-config

The startup configuration file (`startup-config`) is held in NVRAM. When the router is started, the file is accessed and placed into DRAM (sometimes just referred to as RAM). Type **show startup-config** to see the configuration.

```
RouterB#sh startup-config
Using 661 out of 32762 bytes
!
version 11.0
service udp-small-servers
service tcp-small-servers
!
hostname RouterB
!
enable secret 5 $1$jMYk$21eDXo8XXwrBiVm5RR9wN.
enable password password
!
!
```

```
interface Ethernet0
 ip address 172.16.30.1 255.255.255.0
!
interface Serial0
 ip address 172.16.20.2 255.255.255.0
 no fair-queue
 clockrate 56000
!
interface Serial1
 ip address 172.16.40.1 255.255.255.0
 clockrate 56000
```

running-config

The running configuration file is the configuration from NVRAM placed in DRAM at startup. By typing **config terminal** (**config t** will also work), you open the file for updating; any changes you make will amend the running-config file. When you're happy with the new configuration, copy it to startup-config as shown here:

```
Router#copy running-config startup-config
Building configuration...
[OK]
```

You can also view the running configuration file at any time by typing **show running-config**. However, you do not have to type in the full commands. You can abbreviate commands, as long as they are unique. For example, to carry out the command show running-config, you can type simply **sh run**. For show startup-config, you can type **sh start**. For copy running-config startup-config, you can type **copy run start**.

Cisco IOS

Flash holds the router's Internetworking Operating System, or IOS. You can see the IOS currently stored in flash by typing **sh flash**.

The show flash command (or sh flash) displays your flash memory and reveals both the size of your files and the amount of free flash memory.

```
Router#sh flash

System flash directory:
File  Length   Name/status
  1   3612396  igs-i-l.110-16
[3612460 bytes used, 4776148 available, 8388608 total]
8192K bytes of processor board System flash (Read ONLY)
```

Cisco Discovery Protocol (CDP)

The proprietary protocol CDP allows you to access configuration information on other routers with a single command. When you run the Subnetwork Access Protocol (SNAP) at the Data Link layer, two devices running different Network layer protocols can still communicate and learn about each other. This includes all LANs and most WANs.

CDP starts by default on any Cisco router version 10.3 or newer and discovers neighboring Cisco routers running CDP by doing a Data Link broadcast. It doesn't matter which protocol is running at the Network layer.

Once CDP has discovered a router, it can display information about the upper-layer protocols such as IP and IPX. A router caches the information it receives from its CDP neighbors. Anytime a router receives updated information that a CDP neighbor has changed, it discards the old information in favor of the new broadcast.

Necessary Procedures

To get a more thorough understanding of the commands for viewing and saving the router's configuration, see the following section on the privileged Exec mode exam objective. Here we'll run through the CDP commands.

Running CDP Commands

The commands to display the results of the CDP broadcast can be viewed by connecting a PC to the console port of a router that's configured to run CDP on its interfaces—but you can see only the directly connected routers. To see a remote router, you would have to telnet into that router to get CDP information. This is because CDP information is sent out in a SNAP frame, which cannot be routed.

You can type in **show cdp** to see the update and holdtime frequency, as shown here:

```
Router#sh cdp
Global CDP information:
        Sending CDP packets every 60 seconds
        Sending a holdtime value of 180 seconds
```

The `cdp timer` command is used to change the frequency of the CDP broadcasts.

```
Router(config)#cdp ?
  holdtime  Specify the holdtime (in sec) to be sent in
packets
  timer     Specify the rate at which CDP packets are
sent (in sec)
  run


Router(config)#cdp timer 90
Router(config)#exit
```

Type **sh cdp ?** at the privileged mode prompt to display a list of commands available on the router.

```
RouterB#sh cdp ?
  entry       Information for specific neighbor entry
  interface   CDP interface status and configuration
  neighbors   CDP neighbor entries
  traffic     CDP statistics
  <cr>
```

Type **sh cdp int** to see both the interface information and the default encapsulation used by the interface. This command also displays the timers—60 seconds for an update and 180 seconds for holdtime in this case:

```
RouterB#sh cdp int
```

```
Ethernet0 is up, line protocol is up, encapsulation is
ARPA
  Sending CDP packets every 60 seconds
  Holdtime is 180 seconds
Serial0 is up, line protocol is up, encapsulation is
HDLC
  Sending CDP packets every 60 seconds
  Holdtime is 180 seconds
Serial1 is up, line protocol is up, encapsulation is
HDLC
  Sending CDP packets every 60 seconds
  Holdtime is 180 seconds
```

The `sh cdp entry` command will give you the CDP information received from all routers if you use an asterisk (*) or the CDP information for a specific router if you type the router name.

```
RouterB#sh cdp entry ?
  *     all CDP neighbor entries
  WORD  Name of CDP neighbor entry
  <cr>

RouterB#sh cdp entry RouterA
-------------------------
Device ID: RouterA
Entry address(es):
  IP address: 172.16.20.1
Platform: cisco 2500,  Capabilities: Router
Interface: Serial0,  Port ID (outgoing port): Serial0
Holdtime : 130 sec

Version :
Cisco Internetwork Operating System Software
IOS (tm) 3000 Software (IGS-I-L), Version 11.0(18),
RELEASE SOFTWARE (fc1)
Copyright (c) 1986-1997 by cisco Systems, Inc.
Compiled Mon 01-Dec-97 18:09 by jaturner
```

The `show cdp neighbors` command reveals the information being exchanged among neighbors.

```
RouterB#sh cdp neighbors
Capability Codes: R - Router, T - Trans Bridge, B -
Source Route Bridge, S - Switch, H - Host, I - IGMP, r
- Repeater

Device ID  Local Intrfce Holdtme Capability Platform Port ID
RouterC    Ser 1         158     R          2500     Ser 0
RouterA    Ser 0         150     R          2500     Ser 0
```

For each neighbor, the following information is displayed:

Neighbor Device ID: The name of the neighbor router that this router exchanges CDP information with

Local Interface: The interface on which this neighbor is heard

Holdtime: Decremental holdtime, in seconds

Capability: Router's capability code—R for router, S for switch, etc.

Platform: What type of device the neighbor is

Port ID: The interface of the remote neighbor router you receive CDP information from

The `sh cdp neighbor detail` command displays the same data as well as the information you would get with the `sh cdp entry` command.

```
RouterB#sh cdp neighbor detail
-------------------------
Device ID: RouterC
Entry address(es):
  IP address: 172.16.40.2
Platform: cisco 2500,  Capabilities: Router
Interface: Serial1,  Port ID (outgoing port): Serial0
Holdtime : 123 sec

Version :
Cisco Internetwork Operating System Software
```

```
IOS (tm) 3000 Software (IGS-I-L), Version 11.0(18),
RELEASE SOFTWARE (fc1)
Copyright (c) 1986-1997 by cisco Systems, Inc.
Compiled Mon 01-Dec-97 18:09 by jaturner

-------------------------
Device ID: RouterA
Entry address(es):
  IP address: 172.16.20.1
Platform: cisco 2500,  Capabilities: Router
Interface: Serial0,  Port ID (outgoing port): Serial0
Holdtime : 174 sec

Version :
Cisco Internetwork Operating System Software
IOS (tm) 3000 Software (IGS-I-L), Version 11.0(18),
RELEASE SOFTWARE (fc1)
Copyright (c) 1986-1997 by cisco Systems, Inc.
Compiled Mon 01-Dec-97 18:09 by jaturner
```

The `sh cdp traffic` command reveals the number of packets sent and received among neighbors.

```
RouterB#sh cdp traffic
CDP counters :
       Packets output: 206, Input: 202
       Hdr syntax: 0, Chksum error: 0, Encaps failed: 0
       No memory: 0, Invalid packet: 0, Fragmented: 0
```

Exam Essentials

You'll need to know the different types of memory and what is stored in each memory location. For related information, see the following exam objective regarding privileged Exec mode.

Remember the CDP commands. Know how to change the frequency of the broadcast timer, which is done with the `cdp timer` command. Also, remember what output is displayed when you use the `show cdp neighbor` command.

Key Terms and Concepts

CDP: An acronym for Cisco Discovery Protocol, CDP is a proprietary Cisco protocol that uses a SNAP frame to gather information about locally attached routers and switches.

DRAM: Short for dynamic random access memory, DRAM is usually referred to simply as RAM. This type of memory does not keep the information stored when the device (router) is rebooted or powered down.

Flash: ROM used to store the Cisco IOS.

NVRAM: An acronym for nonvolatile random access memory, NVRAM is used to store the router's startup configuration file. This type of memory does not lose its data when the router is rebooted.

Sample Questions

1. With which of these commands can you change the frequency of your CDP broadcasts?

   A. `cdp frequency`

   B. `timer cdp`

   C. `cdp timer`

   D. `timer broadcast cdp`

   Answer: C. Use the `cdp timer` command to change the frequency of CDP broadcasts.

2. What type of output does the `sh cdp nei` command display? (Choose all that apply.)

   A. Port ID

B. Local interface

C. Capability

D. Device ID

E. Holdtime

F. Platform

G. Logical address

Answer: A, B, C, D, E, F. All of these except logical address are displayed when you use `show cdp neighbor` (`sh cdp nei`). To display the logical address of neighbor devices, type **sh cdp entry** *.

Manage configuration files from the privileged exec mode

This exam objective covers the commands that can be run from privileged Exec mode. The commands Cisco is interested in here are those used for starting and saving configurations. This section builds on the commands introduced in the previous section.

Notice where these commands can be run from and where the files to be managed are stored.

Critical Information

Cisco has new commands to help administrators manage configuration files from privileged Exec mode. Below is a list of the commands used to start and save configurations on Cisco routers.

Command	Purpose
`show startup-config`	Shows the configuration that will be loaded when the router boots.

Command	Purpose
`show running-config`	Shows the configuration that's currently loaded into RAM and running.
`copy running-config startup-config`	Copies the configuration stored in running RAM to backup or NVRAM.
`copy startup-config running-config`	Copies the configuration stored in NVRAM to running RAM.
`erase startup-config`	Erases the configuration in the router's NVRAM and lands it right back into the initial configuration dialog. (Don't try this one at work!)
`reload`	Reboots the router and reloads the startup configuration into memory.
`setup`	Starts the initial configuration dialog.

Necessary Procedures

It is time to run through all of the commands that can help you manage the configuration files. One of the things you should notice when running these commands is that none of them is run from configuration mode (`config t`), all are run from the privileged mode prompt (`Router#`).

show startup-config

Below is the output of the command `sh start` (`show startup-config`) when no configuration has been saved to NVRAM. This is a bad thing to see on a Monday morning!

```
Router#sh start
%% Non-volatile configuration memory has not been set
up or has bad checksum
```

show running-config

This command will show you the router configuration that is currently loaded in RAM and running. If you typed **config t**, you would be changing this file. The output below was cut for brevity.

```
Router#sh run
Building configuration...

Current configuration:
!
version 11.2
```

copy running-config startup-config

This command copies the running configuration file into NVRAM or `startup-config`. This will completely erase the existing `startup-config` file and replace it with the `running-config` file.

```
Router#copy run star
Building configuration...
[OK]
```

copy startup-config running-config

The `copy startup-config running-config` command is used to copy the configuration from NVRAM into running RAM. You can use this if you changed your configuration but had problems with the new setup. Note that this command just appends anything in the `startup-config` that is not in the `running-config`. It doesn't overwrite anything.

```
Router#copy start run
Building configuration...
[OK]
```

erase startup-config

The `erase startup-config` command shown below is used to erase the configuration in NVRAM. If you used the command `sh start` after erasing the NVRAM configuration, you would get an error message as shown earlier in this section. You also would be put into setup mode when you rebooted your router.

```
Router#erase start
[OK]
```

reload

The `reload` command reboots the router.

```
Router#reload
Proceed with reload? [enter]
```

setup

The `setup` command puts you into setup mode regardless of what your configuration is set at.

```
Router#setup

         --- System Configuration Dialog ---

At any point you may enter a question mark '?' for
help.
Use ctrl-c to abort configuration dialog at any prompt.
Default settings are in square brackets '[]'.
Continue with configuration dialog? [yes/no]:
```

Exam Essentials

To prepare for the test, be sure to practice on a router using the commands covered in this section.

Remember which file is stored in which memory location. Remember that NVRAM holds the startup configuration file and DRAM holds the running configuration file. Flash is used to hold the Cisco IOS.

Know the difference between the commands. You must have a thorough understanding of the different commands. For example, you should know that `copy star run` will copy `startup-config` into running RAM.

Key Terms and Concepts

DRAM: Short for dynamic random access memory, DRAM is usually referred to simply as RAM. This type of memory does not keep the information stored when the device (router) is rebooted or powered down.

Flash: ROM used to store the Cisco IOS.

NVRAM: An acronym for nonvolatile random access memory, NVRAM is used to store the router's startup configuration file. This type of memory does not lose its data when the router is rebooted.

Sample Questions

1. To save your configuration, what command should you use?

   A. `copy star run`

   B. `copy tftp run`

   C. `copy run start`

   D. `save config`

   Answer: C. The `copy run start` command overwrites any configuration stored in NVRAM (`startup-config`).

2. To view the configuration that will load when a router reboots, what command should you use?

   A. `show running-config`

   B. `sh run`

   C. `show startup-config`

   D. `write term`

   Answer: C. The `show startup-config` command displays the contents of the configuration stored in NVRAM.

Control router passwords, identification, and banner

This is a great exam objective. Not only is it important that you understand everything that you read here for the CCNA exam, but these are probably the most helpful commands to use when configuring a router for the first time. They can also be the most fun.

The key to understanding this objective is practice. You must practice these commands on Cisco routers to get a full understanding of what Cisco is asking. Also, for security's sake, you should be able to set your passwords!

Critical Information

This section covers the different passwords used in Cisco routers, how to set various banners, and ways to identify Cisco routers.

Routing Passwords

There are five different types of passwords used in securing Cisco routers: enable secret, enable, virtual terminal, auxiliary, and console. These are their functions:

- The enable secret password is a one-way cryptographic secret password used in versions 10.3 and up. It takes precedence over the enable password when it exists. You can configure this password either when setting up your router or at any time after that.
- The enable password is used when there is no enable secret and when you are using older software and some boot images. It's manually encrypted by the administrator. You can set this up within setup mode or anytime after that.

- The virtual terminal password (VTY) is used for Telnet sessions into the router. You can change the VTY at any time, but it must be specified or you won't be able to telnet into the router. You can specify this type of password during setup or anytime after that.
- The auxiliary password is used to set a password for the auxiliary port. This port is used to connect a modem to a router for remote console connections. This can only be set up manually.
- The console password is used to set the console port password. It can only be set up manually. This sets up a password for anyone that connects directly to your router's console port.

Banners

There are four types of banners used in Cisco routers, which are set with the following commands:

- `banner exec`
- `banner incoming`
- `banner login`
- `banner motd`

All of the banner commands use the delimiting character of your choice—a pound sign (#), for example. Note that you cannot use the delimiting character within the banner message, only in the command.

banner exec

The `banner exec` command is used when an Exec process is created. An Exec process is created when either a line is activated or a VTY (Telnet) connection is made.

When a user connects to the router, the MOTD (message of the day) banner appears before the login prompt. After the user successfully logs in to the router, the Exec banner will be displayed if the type of connection is VTY.

banner incoming

The `banner incoming` command is used when a host on the network connects to the router for a reverse Telnet session. These sessions can display MOTD banners and incoming banners, but they do not display Exec banners.

When a user connects to the router, the MOTD banner appears before the login prompt. After the user successfully logs in to the router, the incoming banner will be displayed if the connection is a reverse Telnet login.

`banner login`

The `banner login` command is used to display a message before the prompt for a username and password.

When a user connects to the router, the MOTD banner (if configured) appears first, followed by the login banner and login prompts. After the user successfully logs in to the router, the Exec banner or incoming banner will be displayed, depending on the type of connection.

`banner motd`

The MOTD banner, configured with the `banner motd` command, is the first message displayed when any user connects to the router.

After the user logs in, the Exec banner or incoming banner will be displayed, depending on the type of connection.

Router Identification

A router's identifying information consists of two things: its hostname and its interface.

Hostname

You can change the name your router displays by using the `hostname` command. For example, to change the name of a router to RouterC, you would type **hostname RouterC**.

Interfaces

The interfaces, also known as ports, on Cisco 2500 routers are referred to as Serial0, Serial1, and Ethernet0 and are considered fixed configurations. When you are in configuration mode, you can type in S0, S1, and E0 to reference these ports. If you were using Token Ring, you would use T0; if you used FDDI, you would use F0.

If the device is modular, like a Catalyst 5000 switch, the interfaces are numbered using the syntax *type slot/port*. For example, to configure a port on a 5000 switch for Ethernet card 4, port 2, you would type **e 4/2**.

Cisco 7000 and 7500 series routers have cards called VIP, or Versatile Interface Processor. These can have one or two slots for each port adapter, and each port adapter can have a number of interfaces.

The numbering syntax is *type slot/port number adapter/port*. For example, if you wanted to configure a port on the third Ethernet VIP card, first port (0), second Ethernet interface, you would type **e 2/0/1**.

These are some other commands that can be used within an interface configuration:

Shutdown: To change the administrative state of a router interface to either up or down, use the `shutdown` command. This will turn the administrative state of the interface down. The `no shutdown` command turns the administrative state of an interface up.

Description: You can also add a description or text line to an interface by using the `description` command. This lets you document your interfaces for administrative purposes. For example, you can add circuit numbers to your serial links.

Host Table

You can configure your router to resolve IP addresses to hostnames, which can be configured on each router like a host's table in Unix, or you can use a DNS server to resolve names. That way, you don't have to remember IP addresses and you can connect to a remote router by using its hostname. To configure your routers to use hostnames, use the `ip host` command. To display all the hostnames and the related IP addresses that your router knows about, you can use the `sh hosts` command (both `sh hosts` and `sh host` work).

Necessary Procedures

You need to practice some commands. This section reviews the processes for setting passwords and the MOTD banner, setting the hostname, and setting the identification of an interface using the `description` command.

Setting Passwords

The following examples show how to set Cisco router passwords. Of course, you can choose your own passwords in place of the ones used in the examples.

Enable Secret

To set the enable secret password, type the following commands:

```
Router#config t
Enter configuration commands, one per line.  End with
CNTL/Z.
Router(config)#enable secret todd
Router(config)#^Z
```

Enable Password

To set the enable password, type the following commands:

```
Router#config t
Enter configuration commands, one per line.  End with
CNTL/Z.
Router(config)#enable password todd
The enable password you have chosen is the same as your
enable secret.
This is not recommended.  Re-enter the enable password.
Router(config)#enable password lammle
Router(config)#^Z
```

Notice that if you type the same password as the enable secret, you get a warning message. If, despite the warning, you chose the same password again, the router would accept it—but neither the secret nor enable passwords would work. Can you say password recovery?

Virtual Terminal Password

To set your VTY password, type the following commands:

```
Router#config t
Enter configuration commands, one per line.  End with
CNTL/Z.
Router(config)#line vty 0 4
Router(config-line)#login
Router(config-line)#password todd
Router(config-line)#^Z
```

The command `line vty 0 4` specifies the number of Telnet sessions allowed in the router. You can also set up a different password for each line by typing **line vty** *port number*. The login command tells the router to prompt for a password. If no login command is used, users can gain access via the VTY port without being prompted for a password.

Auxiliary Password

To set the auxiliary password, use the following commands:

```
Router#config t
Enter configuration commands, one per line.  End with
CNTL/Z.
Router(config)#line aux 0
Router(config-line)#login
Router(config-line)#password todd
Router(config-line)#^Z
```

Console Password

Finally, to set the console password, use these commands:

```
Router(config)#line con 0
Router(config-line)#login
Router(config-line)#password todd
Router(config-line)#^Z
```

Configuring Banners

Now practice configuring a message of the day (MOTD) banner.

Message of the Day (MOTD)

You can add a message of the day (MOTD) banner that will be displayed whenever anyone logs in to your Cisco router. The command is `banner motd #`. You must start the banner with a delimiting character of your choice. Here's an example:

```
Router(config)#banner motd #
Enter TEXT message.  End with the character '#'.
If you are not authorized to be in Acme.com router, log
out immediately!
# [enter]
RouterC(config)#end
```

The output for this example will look like this when users either telnet in to the router or connect to a console port:

```
Router con0 is now available


Press ENTER to get started.


If you are not authorized to be in Acme.com router, log
out immediately!


User Access Verification
Password:
```

This output shows an example of what you'd see when connecting to your router's console port. It tells you that the router is available, and then to press Enter to get started. You will see the MOTD banner and then be asked for the user mode password, if one is configured.

Changing Router Identification

You can change the name your router displays by using the `hostname` command. For example, to change the name of a router to RouterC, type the following commands:

```
Router#config t
Enter configuration commands, one per line.  End with
CNTL/Z.
```

```
Router(config)#hostname RouterC
RouterC(config-line)#^Z
```

Notice that there is no space in the command `hostname`.

Building a Host Table

To build a host table on your router, type the following commands:

```
RouterB#config t
Enter configuration commands, one per line.  End with
CNTL/Z.
RouterB(config)#ip host ?
  WORD  Name of host

RouterB(config)#ip host RouterC ?
  <0-65535>  Default telnet port number
  A.B.C.D    Host IP address (maximum of 8)

RouterB(config)#ip host RouterC 172.16.40.2
RouterB(config)#^Z
RouterB#
```

Typing **ip host ?** displayed the help screen, which prompted you to enter the name of the host. After entering **RouterC ?** you saw the next help screen, which told you to give the IP address of the host and an optional number to set when telnetting. The default port is 23. Notice that you can have up to eight IP addresses for the hostname. For this example, you entered the IP address 172.16. 40.2; remember, you can use any interface address.

After you've entered the commands above, your host table should look like this:

```
RouterB#sh hosts
Default domain is not set
Name/address lookup uses domain service
Name servers are 255.255.255.255
```

```
Host      Flags        Age   Type  Address(es)
RouterC   (perm, OK)   0     IP    172.16.40.2
RouterA   (perm, OK)   0     IP    172.16.20.1
RouterB#
```

Exam Essentials

To be successful on the CCNA exam, practice all the commands in this section over and over again.

Remember how to set your passwords. Make sure you know the difference between enable, enable secret, virtual terminal (VTY), console, and auxiliary passwords.

Know the difference between the banners. Practice setting banners and notice where they show up when you log in to the router.

Read about and memorize the identification terms and commands. Routers use interface terms s0 and e0 for serial 0 and Ethernet 0. Switches have many physical ports on one card. To configure a 7000 router with a VIP card, use the *type slot/port number adapter/port* syntax.

Set your router name. Be sure you know how to set a hostname. Remember that the command `hostname` is one word.

Practice building a host table. You can build a host table to resolve names on your Cisco router by entering **ip host *hostname IP address***.

Key Terms and Concepts

Host Table: A type of table that originated in old Unix networks. It is a simple way of providing name-to-IP address translation.

Versatile Interface Processor (VIP): The new Versatile Interface Processor (VIP) cards double the performance and port density of Cisco 7000 and 7500 series routers. On the Cisco 7500 series with distributed switching and dual Route Switch Processors (RSPs), VIPs can scale performance from 500,000 to more than 1 million packets per second (pps).

VTY: Virtual terminal (VTY) is a term from the old IBM days. It referred to a dumb terminal that connected into a mainframe network and asked the mainframe to process data.

Sample Questions

1. To change the name on a router, what command should you use?

   A. `config t, change name SF`

   B. `config t, host name SF`

   C. `config t, prompt SF`

   D. `config t, hostname SF`

   Answer: D. The `hostname` command is one word.

2. To set a MOTD, which of the following is correct?

   A. `config t, motd banner #`

   B. `banner motd $`

   C. `config t, banner motd &`

   D. `config t, banner #`

   Answer: C. Only answer C is correct. You can use any delimiting character you choose.

3. Which of the following commands will change your console password?

   A. `config t, enable password bob`

   B. `config t, line console password bob`

   C. `config t, line console 0, login, password bob`

   D. `config t, line con 0, password login bob`

   Answer: C. The login command is not required, but it is used to tell the router to ask for a console password.

4. Which of the following syntax examples is correct to configure a 7000 router with a VIP card?

   A. *port adapter/card slot/port*

   B. *type slot/port number adapter/port*

   C. *slot type/port port/adapter*

   D. *type port/card*

   Answer: B. To configure a 7000 router with a VIP card, use the syntax *type slot/port number adapter/port.*

5. Which of the following will change your enable secret password?

   A. `config t, enable password bob`

   B. `config t, enable secret password bob`

   C. `config t, enable secret, login, password bob`

   D. `config t, enable secret bob`

   Answer: D. Do not use the word *password* in the argument.

Identify the main Cisco IOS commands for router startup

The same commands used in the objective "Examine router elements (RAM, ROM, CDP, `show`)" are used in this objective also. We won't go over those commands again, but you will learn some new commands.

When a router is booted and it is connected to a live network, it will try and autoinstall itself. We will go through the steps of autoconfiguration.

As with the other topics covered in this chapter, be sure to get the hands-on experience that you can only get when sitting in front of a router. The CCNA exam will test you on the output of the different commands and what happens when the router is booted.

Critical Information

The commands `copy run star`, `copy star run`, `sh run`, etc. are all part of this objective. Review the section above on the objective "Examine router elements (RAM, ROM, CDP, `show`)" to make sure you understand the commands and their output.

In addition to those commands, there are a few others that are important to understand both for the test and for configuring routers in a production environment:

`show interface`: Provides general information about an interface, including the IP address and subnet mask

`show ip interface`: Gives you a look at the IP parameters on an interface

`show protocol`: Displays the protocols and addresses running on your router

`show ip protocol`: Gives you information on which routing protocols are running on your router (RIP, IGRP, etc.) and what their parameters are

We will go over these commands in more detail in the "Necessary Procedures" section.

Cisco AutoInstall Procedure

The Cisco AutoInstall procedure lets you configure your routers automatically and remotely over the network. It's typically used when you need to set up a router in a remote office where either there is no MIS staff or the staff has very limited knowledge and experience.

For you to be able to configure a router automatically, the router must be connected to your LAN or WAN through one of its interfaces. The router can be configured through its Ethernet, Token Ring, FDDI, or any serial interfaces.

The router will act as a BootP (bootstrap protocol) workstation and connect to an existing router that is acting as a BootP or RARP (reverse address resolution protocol) server. The existing router will be used to give the new router its IP address and point the new router to the TFTP server by way of its helper address.

A helper address is defined on a router to forward UDP broadcasts to a server; in this case, a TFTP broadcast will be forwarded to a TFTP server. The helper address can also be used to forward DHCP requests to a DHCP server.

After the BootP server (the one with the existing router) gives the new router its IP address, the new router will look for a DNS server to resolve the IP address to its hostname. The router configuration will then be downloaded from the TFTP server to the new router.

These steps outline the procedure a new router takes when trying to download a configuration from a TFTP server:

1. Upon bootup, the new router sends out a BootP request for an IP address, and it takes the first IP address received from a BootP server.
2. After it has received an IP address, the new router attempts to resolve the IP address to a hostname, whether from the TFTP server or a DNS server. If the hostname is resolved from the TFTP server, the TFTP server sends a file named `network-confg`, which contains the new hostname of the router. The `network-confg` file contains commands that apply to all routers and terminal servers on the network.
3. After the hostname is resolved, the router requests a configuration file from the TFTP server that contains the configuration information named `hostname-confg`. The `hostname-confg` file contains commands that apply to one router in particular. If the TFTP server can't send the `hostname-confg` file, it sends out a generic file named `router-config`. At that point, you have to telnet in to the new router and make the necessary configurations manually. This `hostname-confg` file can also be referred to as the host config file type. However, the router will only look for a file named `hostname-confg`.
4. The TFTP server sends this file to the new router. The new router then loads it into `running-config`.

Necessary Procedures

This section expands on the commands from the objective "Examine router elements (RAM, ROM, CDP, show)." It also covers the commands `sh interface`, `sh ip interface`, `sh protocol`, and `sh ip protocol`.

Using `show interface`

`show interface` (`sh int`) displays the hardware interfaces installed on a router as well as their status. It begins with the first interface and continues through the rest. For example, you can type **sh int e0** to see the status of that particular interface.

```
Router#sh int
Ethernet0 is up, line protocol is down
```

The lines that follow show the hardware address and other information about the connection. (The output shown here was cut for brevity.)

```
  Hardware is Lance, address is 00e0.1ea9.c418 (bia
00e0.1ea9.c418)
  Internet address is 172.16.30.1 255.255.255.0
  MTU 1500 bytes, BW 10000 Kbit, DLY 1000 usec, rely
128/255, load 1/255
  Encapsulation ARPA, loopback not set, keepalive set
(10 sec)
  ARP type: ARPA, ARP Timeout 4:00:00
  Last input never, output 0:00:01, output hang never
  Last clearing of "show interface" counters never
  Output queue 0/40, 0 drops; input queue 0/75, 0 drops
  5 minute input rate 0 bits/sec, 0 packets/sec
  5 minute output rate 0 bits/sec, 0 packets/sec
     0 packets input, 0 bytes, 0 no buffer
     Received 0 broadcasts, 0 runts, 0 giants
     0 input errors, 0 CRC, 0 frame, 0 overrun, 0
ignored, 0 abort
     0 input packets with dribble condition detected
```

```
    384 packets output, 23049 bytes, 0 underruns
    384 output errors, 0 collisions, 1 interface
resets, 0 restarts
    0 output buffer failures, 0 output buffers swapped
out
```

Using show ip interface

This command displays the usability status of interfaces configured with IP. The usability status, as defined by Cisco, is an interface through which the software can send and receive packets. If the interface hardware is usable, it is then marked as up. If both ends of the communication link are up, then the line protocol will display up.

```
Router#sh ip int
Ethernet0 is up, line protocol is up
  Internet address is 172.16.10.1/24
  Broadcast address is 255.255.255.255
  Address determined by setup command
  MTU is 1500 bytes
  Helper address is not set
  Directed broadcast forwarding is enabled
  Outgoing access list is not set
  Inbound  access list is not set
```

The command output was cut for brevity.

Using show protocol

The show protocol command (sh prot) details which protocols are configured on the router. In the sample output below, you can see that only the IP protocol is configured on interfaces e0, s0, and s1.

```
Router#sh prot
Global values:
  Internet Protocol routing is enabled
Ethernet0 is up, line protocol is down
  Internet address is 172.16.30.1 255.255.255.0
Serial0 is down, line protocol is up
  Internet address is 172.16.20.2 255.255.255.0
```

```
Serial1 is down, line protocol is up
  Internet address is 172.16.40.1 255.255.255.0
```

Using show ip protocol

To see more detail on the protocols on your system, use the `show ip protocol` command (`sh ip prot`). Notice in the sample output below that the routing protocol RIP is being used. The `sh ip protocol` command also displays the current state of the active routing protocols. This is a helpful command to use when you are troubleshooting routers that are sending or receiving bad routing information.

```
RouterC#sh ip prot
Routing Protocol is "rip"
  Sending updates every 30 seconds, next due in 22
seconds
  Invalid after 180 seconds, hold down 180, flushed
after 240
  Outgoing update filter list for all interfaces is
not set
  Incoming update filter list for all interfaces is
not set
  Redistributing: rip
  Routing for Networks:
    172.16.0.0
  Routing Information Sources:
    Gateway         Distance      Last Update
    172.16.40.1          120      0:00:02
  Distance: (default is 120)
```

Exam Essentials

Practice using each of the commands covered in this section on your router.

Notice the output the commands give you. In addition to the commands themselves, you need to remember the output of the various commands. Which commands show you the IP address of your interfaces? Which command displays the routing protocol that is running on your router?

Remember the steps and files needed when running AutoInstall. The router will boot up and try to find its IP address. Once that is accomplished, it will try to resolve its hostname. After the hostname is resolved, it will search for its specific configuration by looking for the `hostname-config` file.

Key Terms and Concepts

AutoInstall: The process the router uses to try to configure itself when connected to a live network.

`hostname-config`: File used in autoconfiguring to give a router its specific configuration after the `network-config` file has given the router its global configuration and the hostname has been resolved. This is sometimes referred to as the *host config* file type.

`network-config`: File that contains the new hostname of the router. The `network-config` file contains commands that apply to all routers and terminal servers on the network.

Sample Questions

1. After a router boots with AutoInstall, it first tries to resolve its hostname. What file does it load next to get its specific configuration?

   A. `router-config`

   B. `hostname-config`

   C. `network-config`

   D. `startup-config`

   Answer: B. After a router resolves its hostname, it searches for its specific configuration by looking for the `hostname-config` file. This file can reside on a TFTP server.

2. Which of the following commands will show you the hardware address of Ethernet 0?

   A. `sh ip protocol`

   B. `sh int`

   C. `sh ip int`

   D. `sh prot`

   Answer: B. Only `show interface` will show you the hardware address of an interface.

3. Which of the following commands will show you the routing protocol configured on your router?

   A. `sh int`

   B. `sh ip int`

   C. `sh prot`

   D. `sh ip prot`

   Answer: D. Only `sh ip protocol` will show you the routing protocol(s) configured on your router.

Enter an initial configuration using the setup command

If you use the commands `write erase` or `erase startup-config` and then either reload your router or power it off and on, you'll see the system configuration dialog screen. You can also type **setup** within privileged mode to get the dialog screen at any time, which can be helpful in configuring your router.

For this section of the exam, you'll need to know how to configure a router using the `setup` command. The `setup` command can be helpful, but it is not necessarily one you'll use in a production environment. It may prompt you for commands that you don't use in your internetwork, which can be tedious. When going through this section, notice the difference between setting your router up manually and using the `setup` command, including which prompts you see in the second alternative.

Critical Information

Let's take a look at what happens when you type **erase startup-config** and then reboot your router.

setup

If you erase the `startup-config` file and reboot your router, you will see the following dialog upon bootup:

```
Notice: NVRAM invalid, possibly due to write erase.
         --- System Configuration Dialog ---
At any point you may enter a question mark '?' for
help.
Use CTRL-c to abort configuration dialog at any prompt.
Default settings are in square brackets '[]'.
Would you like to enter the initial configuration
dialog? [yes][enter]
```

Press Enter at the `[yes]` prompt to continue with the configuration and see how the router responds:

```
First, would you like to see the current interface
summary? [yes][enter]

Any interface listed with OK? value "NO" does not have
a valid configuration
Interface  IP-Address  OK? Method   Status  Protocol
Ethernet0  unassigned  NO  not set  up      down
Serial0    unassigned  NO  not set  up      down
Serial1    unassigned  NO  not set  up      down
```

```
Configuring global parameters:
```

By pressing Enter at the [yes] prompt to view the current interface summary, you're assured that the POST (Power-On Self-Test) has found all the interfaces.

In this case, you have two serial ports and one Ethernet port. They aren't okay (see the NO not set next to them?), because they aren't set up yet. They're designated as unassigned. The router now wants the name of the router you're trying to configure, which is RouterA in this example. Enter that now and then press Enter. The router responds with this dialog:

```
Enter host name [Router]: RouterA
The enable secret is a one-way cryptographic secret used
instead of the enable password when it exists.
Enter enable secret: todd
The enable password is used when there is no enable
secret
and when using older software and some boot images.
Enter enable password: password
  Enter virtual terminal password: password2
  Configure SNMP Network Management? [yes]: n
  Configure IP? [yes][enter]
Configure IP? [yes][enter]
    Configure IGRP routing? [yes]: n
    Configure RIP routing? [no]: [enter]

Configuring interface parameters:

Configuring interface Ethernet0:
  Is this interface in use? [yes][enter]
  Configure IP on this interface? [yes][enter]
    IP address for this interface: 172.16.10.1
    Number of bits in subnet field [0]: 8
    Class B network is 172.16.0.0, 8 subnet bits; mask
is 255.255.255.0
```

```
Configuring interface Serial0:
  Is this interface in use? [yes]:[enter]
  Configure IP on this interface? [yes]:[enter]
  Configure IP unnumbered on this interface?
[no]:[enter]
    IP address for this interface: 172.16.20.1
    Number of bits in subnet field [8]:[enter]
    Class B network is 172.16.0.0, 8 subnet bits; mask
is 255.255.255.0

Configuring interface Serial1:
  Is this interface in use? [yes]: n
```

Notice that we had you type **no** (or **n** for no) to the routing commands like RIP and IGRP. Also notice that for the subnet mask, you were to enter 8 for the number of bits. The router doesn't count the default masks in the number of bits, so even though you set the number of bits to eight, the subnet mask will still be realized as 255.255.255.0. The third byte is the only one used for subnetting.

After you answer no to configuring Serial1, the router shows the configuration it created. It then asks if you want to save the configuration:

```
Use this configuration? [yes/no]:y
```

Type **y** for yes, and then press Enter. The router saves the configuration to NVRAM.

Exam Essentials

For the CCNA exam, it is important to know the difference between the commands that can be entered by using the `startup` command and the commands that can only be entered manually.

Remember which passwords are set when using the *setup* command. When you run the `setup` command, the password types you must enter are enable secret, enable, and VTY.

Key Terms and Concepts

IGRP: Newer Cisco proprietary distance vector routing algorithms used in dynamic routing

RIP: Old distance vector algorithm used to update neighbor routers about known networks

Setup: Mode used to help an administrator configure a router

Sample Questions

1. When you are in privileged mode, which of the following statements is true?

   A. You can do a reload to enter setup mode.

   B. You can type **erase running-config** and then do a reload to enter setup mode.

   C. You can type **setup** to enter setup mode.

   D. If you type **erase star**, you will automatically be prompted with setup commands.

   Answer: C. There are two ways to enter setup commands. You can type **erase star** and then reboot the router or you can type **setup** at any time at the privileged mode prompt.

1. In setup mode, which passwords must you enter? (Choose three.)

   A. Console

   B. Enable

   C. Enable secret

   D. VTY

   Answer: B, C, D. When entering setup mode commands, you are prompted for the enable, enable secret, and VTY passwords.

Copy and manipulate configuration files

As an administrator, and to pass the CCNA exam, you need to know how to back up configuration files in places other than NVRAM. Whenever you are going to make a configuration change, it is good practice to copy the original configuration first to a TFTP host before making any changes.

In this section, we demonstrate how to copy a configuration file from a TFTP host and load it into running RAM. You will then learn commands to back up the configuration from the router to a TFTP host.

Critical Information

Earlier in this chapter, we reviewed how to use the `copy startup-config running-config` and `copy running-config startup-config` commands. Those commands are used for manipulating and copying configuration files, which is the focus of this section.

However, since those commands were demonstrated previously, here we will talk only about copying and manipulating configuration files between Cisco routers and a TFTP host.

There are a couple ways of copying the configuration files between a Cisco router and a TFTP host and back again. The first command is `config net`. This is used to copy a configuration from a TFTP host into running RAM. You cannot use this command to copy the configuration into NVRAM.

The second command for copying a configuration file is simply `copy`. You can use this a few different ways. First, you can use it to copy a configuration file from a TFTP host into running RAM, or you can use it to copy files from a TFTP host into NVRAM. These commands are `copy tftp run` or `copy tftp star`.

You can also use the `copy` command to copy the configuration from either `running-config` or `startup-config` to a TFTP host by using the commands `copy run tftp` or `copy star tftp`.

Necessary Procedures

Let's take a look at the different ways of copying the router configuration between a router and a TFTP host.

Using `config net`

The `config net` command is not as useful in production networks as the `copy tftp run` command (discussed below). Basically, all it does is copy a configuration file stored on a TFTP host into running RAM. When using `config net`, you must supply the IP address or hostname of the network TFTP host.

```
Router#config net
Host or network configuration file [host]? [enter]
Address of remote host [255.255.255.255]? 172.16.10.1
Name of configuration file [router-confg]? RouterA-confg
Configure using RouterA-confg from 172.16.10.1?
[confirm] [enter]
Loading RouterA-confg
```

Using `copy run tftp`

You can copy the router's current configuration from a router to a TFTP server by typing **copy running-config tftp**. Doing this gives you a backup of the router configuration and allows you to run the configuration from this server. You can also configure the router by making your changes to the configuration file stored on the TFTP server; when you're happy with the new configuration, copy the file to the router by using the `copy tftp running-config` command (`copy run tftp`).

```
RouterC#copy run tftp
Remote host []? 172.16.10.1
```

```
Name of configuration file to write [routerc-confg]?
[enter]
Write file routerc-confg on host 172.16.10.1? [confirm]
[enter]
Building configuration...
OK
```

Notice that by default Cisco adds `–confg` to the end of the router's hostname to create a default filename. When configuring an IOS device from a TFTP server, the device's default method is to try to load a file with the name of the device followed by the string `–confg`.

Using copy `tftp run`

To copy a configuration from a TFTP host to a router, use the `copy tftp run` or `copy tftp star` commands.

```
Router#copy tftp run
Host or network configuration file [host]? [enter]
Address of remote host [255.255.255.255]? 172.16.10.1
Name of configuration file []? detroit-confg [enter]
Configure using detroit-confg from 172.16.10.1?
[confirm] [enter]
Loading detroit-confg ..from 172.16.10.1 (via
Ethernet0): !
[OK - 717/32723 bytes]
Detroit#
```

Notice in this example that the hostname of the router changed immediately after the configuration file was loaded; this happened because the configuration file was loaded directly into DRAM. You would need to use a `copy run star` command at this point.

Exam Essentials

For the exam, remember the differences between DRAM (RAM), NVRAM, and the TFTP host and the ways configuration files are copied to and from each one.

Know how to copy a configuration file from a TFTP host. The commands to copy a configuration file from a TFTP host to a router are `config net`, `copy tftp run`, and `copy tftp star`.

Know how to copy a configuration file to a TFTP host. The commands to copy a configuration file from a router to a TFTP host are `copy run tftp` and `copy star tftp`.

Key Terms and Concepts

Flash: Basically an erasable, reprogrammable ROM that holds the operating system image and microcode. It allows you to "flash" the router and perform upgrades without removing and replacing chips on the motherboard. Flash is retained even when the router is turned off.

NVRAM: Nonvolatile RAM that stores the router's startup configuration file. NVRAM retains its information even when the router is rebooted or shut down.

RAM: Provides caching and packet buffering, plus information like routing tables, which will be explained in more detail in Chapter 6. RAM is used to hold the running operating system when the router is powered on; it is cleared when the router is reset or powered off.

ROM: Used by the router to store the bootstrap startup program, operating system software, and Power-On Self-Test (POST). ROM chips are installed in sockets on the router's motherboard so that they can be replaced or upgraded.

Sample Questions

1. To copy a configuration stored on a TFTP host and make it a `startup-config` file, what command should you use?

   A. `copy tftp flash`

   B. `config net`

C. `copy star run`

D. `copy tftp start`

E. `copy tftp run`

Answer: D. The only command that copies the configuration from a TFTP host to NVRAM is `copy tftp startup-config` (`copy tftp start`).

2. If you want to back up your `running-config`, what two commands are valid?

A. `copy run star`

B. `copy run tftp`

C. `copy star tftp`

D. `config net`

Answer: A, B. Copying the configuration into NVRAM (startup) and to a TFTP host are both considered backing up the `running-config`.

List the commands to load Cisco IOS software from: flash memory, a TFTP server, or ROM

The Cisco IOS can be loaded into a Cisco router from many sources. The default source for the Cisco IOS depends mainly on hardware, but the Cisco IOS is typically loaded from EEPROM (Electronic Erasable Programmable Read Only Memory), also known as *flash memory*. You can use other sources, such as a TFTP server, or the router can use a fallback routine.

Remember that flash memory holds the binary executable IOS image known as the Cisco IOS. Do not confuse this with the router configuration held in NVRAM. The IOS image is the binary program that parses and executes the configuration, while the IOS configuration tells the device its current configuration.

For this exam objective you need to learn how to back up and restore a Cisco IOS. This is also important to know in production environments so that you can back up and upgrade your router to a new version of IOS.

Critical Information

You can copy the contents of flash (the Cisco IOS) to a TFTP server by typing **copy flash tftp.** This copy can serve as a backup version of the Cisco IOS; it can also be used to verify that the copy in flash is the same as the original file. You can restore the Cisco IOS, or upgrade it, by typing **copy tftp flash.**

The router Exec will understand what you are trying to do by the way you word the command. For example, if you type **copy tftp run,** it will look for a Cisco configuration on a TFTP host to copy a configuration into running RAM. If you include the word *flash* in the command, the router knows you are referring to a Cisco IOS and not a configuration.

Fallback

You can specify sources in which the router should look for the Cisco IOS software to create a fallback in case one configuration doesn't load or if you just want the Cisco IOS to load from a TFTP server. To have your router load the Cisco IOS from a TFTP server, use the following command string:

```
boot system TFTP ios_filename TFTP_ipaddress
```

Remember, there are three places a Cisco router can look for a valid Cisco IOS: flash, a TFTP server, or ROM. You can change the spot where a Cisco router looks for the IOS by adding boot commands in the configuration. The default action is defined by the Configuration Register setting and is normally set to load the first file found in flash memory.

```
RouterC(config)#boot ?
```

```
  bootstrap   Bootstrap image file
  buffersize  Specify the buffer size for netbooting a
config file
  host        Router-specific config file
  network     Network-wide config file
  system      System image file

RouterC(config)#boot system ?
  WORD   System image filename
  flash  Boot from flash memory
  mop    Boot from a Decnet MOP server
  rcp    Boot from a server via rcp
  rom    Boot from rom
  TFTP   Boot from a TFTP server
```

The following command lines will cause your router to try the other alternatives if the flash configuration doesn't come up:

```
boot system flash ios_filename
boot system TFTP ios_filename TFTP_address
boot system rom
```

The three examples above show how you can enter multiple boot commands for fallback purposes. The router will try to load from flash, then from a TFTP server, and finally from ROM. Here's a brief description of each option:

- Flash allows you to copy a system image without physically changing EEPROM. Flash memory is not vulnerable to network failures that can occur when loading system images from a TFTP server.
- A TFTP server is best used as a backup in case flash memory gets corrupted or lost.
- If flash memory is corrupted and a TFTP server can't load the image for some reason, booting from ROM is the final bootstrap option in software. Typically this lacks the protocols, features, and configurations of full Cisco IOS software.

WARNING The **boot system rom** command is no longer valid in IOS 11.3. (The command has been changed to **boot system flash bootflash**.) Remember, however, that this test is based on 11.2 IOS; the boot command is valid in that IOS and thus is included on the test.

Necessary Procedures

In this section, you can work through the examples given to practice backing up a Cisco IOS to a TFTP host and then restoring it.

Using copy flash tftp

Start with a ping from your router to your TFTP server to ensure that IP connectivity is working from the router that is targeted to copy the flash over to your TFTP host. After you've verified connectivity, the flash can be copied to your TFTP server, as shown in this example:

```
RouterC#ping 172.16.10.2
Type escape sequence to abort.
Sending 5, 100-byte ICMP Echos to 172.16.10.2, timeout
is 2 seconds:
.!!!!
Success rate is 80 percent (4/5), round-trip min/avg/
max = 1/2/4 ms
RouterC#copy flash tftp
System flash directory:
File  Length   Name/status
  1   3621884  igs-i-l.110-18.bin
[3621948 bytes used, 572356 available, 4194304 total]
Address or name of remote host [255.255.255.255]?
172.16.10.2
Source file name? igs-i-l.110-18.bin
Destination file name [igs-i-l.110-18.bin]?
Verifying checksum for 'igs-i-l.110-18.bin' (file #
1)...  OK
```

```
Copy 'igs-i-l.110-18.bin' from Flash to server
  as 'igs-i-l.110-18.bin'? [yes/no]y
!!!!!!!!!!!!!!!!!!!!!!!!!!!!!!!!!!!!!!!!!!!!!!!!!!!!!!!
!!!!!!!!!!!!!!!!!!!!!!!!!!!!!!!!!!!!!!!!!!!!!!!!!!!!!!!
!!!!!!!!!!!!!!!!!!!!!!!!!!!!!!!!!!!!!!!!!!!!!!!!!!!!!!!
!!!!!!!!!!!!!!!!!!!!!!!!!!!!!!!!!!!!!!!!!!!!!!!!!!!!!!!
!!!!!!!!!!!!!!!!!!!!!!!!!!!!!!!!!!!!!!!!!!!!!!!!!!!!!!!
!!!!!!!!!!!!!!!!!!!!!!!!!!!!!!!!!!!!!!!!!!!!!!!!!!!!!!!
!!!!!!!!!!!!!!!!!!!!!!!!!!!!!!!!!!!!!!!!!!!!!!!!!!!!!!!
!!!!!!!!!!!!!!!!!!!!!!!!!!!!!!!!!!!!!!!!!!!!!!!!!!!!!!!
!!!!!!!!!!!!!!!!!!!!!!!!!!!!!!!!!!!!!!!!!!!!!!!!!!!!!!!
!!!!!!!!!!!!!!!!!!!!!!!!!!!!!!!!!!!!!!!!!!!!!!!!!!!!!!!
!!!!!!!!!!!!!!!!!!!!!!!!!!!!!!!!!!!!!!!!!!!!!!!!!!!!!!!
!!!!!!!!!!!!!!!!!!!!!!!!!!!!!!!!!!!!!!!!!!!!!!!!!!!!!!!
!!!!!!!!!!!!!!!!!!!!!!!!!!!!!!!!!!!!!!!!!!
Upload to server done
Flash copy took 0:21:53 [hh:mm:ss]
RouterC#
```

If you tried this example, you probably noticed that it took almost 22 minutes to download the flash through a simulated WAN network. Keep this in mind when backing up your files from remote locations.

Using `copy tftp flash`

You can copy from a TFTP server to flash anytime by typing **copy tftp flash.** This command is very useful for downloading new versions of the Cisco IOS to your router.

```
RouterC#copy tftp flash
                           ****  NOTICE  ****
Flash load helper v1.0
This process will accept the copy options and then
terminate
the current system image to use the ROM based image for
the copy.
Routing functionality will not be available during that
time.
If you are logged in via telnet, this connection will
terminate.
Users with console access can see the results of the
copy operation.
                           ---- ******** ----
```

```
Proceed? [confirm] [enter]

System flash directory:
File  Length   Name/status
  1   3621884  igs-i-l.110-18.bin
[3621948 bytes used, 572356 available, 4194304 total]
Address or name of remote host [172.16.10.1]? [enter]
Source file name? igs-i-l.110-18.bin
Destination file name [igs-i-l.110-18.bin]?
Accessing file 'igs-i-l.110-18.bin' on 172.16.10.2...
Loading igs-i-l.110-18.bin from 172.16.10.2 (via
Serial0): ! [OK]

Erase flash device before writing? [confirm] [enter]
Flash contains files. Are you sure you want to erase?
[confirm] [enter]

Copy 'igs-i-l.110-18.bin' from server
 as 'igs-i-l.110-18.bin' into Flash WITH erase? [yes/no]y

%SYS-5-RELOAD: Reload requested
%FLH: igs-i-l.110-18.bin from 172.16.10.2 to flash ...
System flash directory:
File  Length   Name/status
  1   3621884  igs-i-l.110-18.bin
[3621948 bytes used, 572356 available, 4194304 total]
Accessing file 'igs-i-l.110-18.bin' on 172.16.10.2...
Loading igs-i-l.110-18.bin from 172.16.10.2 (via
Serial0): ! [OK]
Erasing device... eeeeeeeeeeeeeeee ...erased
Loading igs-i-l.110-18.bin from 172.16.10.2 (via
Serial0):
!!!!!!!!!!!!!!!!!!!!!!!!!!!!!!!!!!!!!!!!!!!!!!!!!!!!!!!
!!!!!!!!!!!!!!!!!!!!!!!!!!!!!!!!!!!!!!!!!!!!!!!!!!!!!!!
!!!!!!!!!!!!!!!!!!!!!!!!!!!!!!!!!!!!!!!!!!!!!!!!!!!!!!!
!!!!!!!!!!!!!!!!!!!!!!!!!!!!!!!!!!!!!!!!!!!!!!!!!!!!!!!
!!!!!!!!!!!!!!!!!!!!!!!!!!!!!!!!!!!!!!!!!!!!!!!!!!!!!!!
!!!!!!!!!!!!!!!!!!!!!!!!!!!!!!!!!!!!!!!!!!!!!!!!!!!!!!!
```

```
[OK - 3621884/4194304 bytes]

Verifying checksum...  OK (0xC248)
Flash copy took 0:21:34 [hh:mm:ss]
%FLH: Re-booting system after download
```

After confirming a few entries, you're asked if it's okay to erase the entire contents of flash memory. The program asks the question because there's rarely room for more than one flash file. However, if there is room, you can have many different versions loaded in flash.

Each `e` in the output stands for *erase,* and each exclamation point (`!`) indicates that one UDP segment has been successfully transferred. The router must be rebooted to load the new image on a 2500 series router, because the currently running IOS image is in flash memory. Use `show flash` to verify that the size matches that of the original file.

Exam Essentials

For the exam, remember the difference between ROM, TFTP, and flash.

Practice copying a Cisco IOS to a TFTP server and back again. You need to understand the output of backing up and restoring a Cisco IOS. The only way to do this is to practice and look closely at the output of the commands.

Understand the process of the fallback routine. Know the commands associated with fallback and their parameters. For example, you must know that when you type in **boot system tftp**, you need to add the Cisco IOS filename and IP address of the TFTP server.

Key Terms and Concepts

Flash: Basically an erasable, reprogrammable ROM that holds the operating system image and microcode. It allows you to "flash" the router and perform upgrades without removing and replacing chips on the motherboard. Flash is retained even when the router is turned off.

NVRAM: Nonvolatile RAM that stores the router's startup configuration file. NVRAM retains its information even when the router is rebooted or shut down.

RAM: Provides caching and packet buffering, plus information like routing tables, which will be explained in more detail in Chapter 6. RAM is used to hold the running operating system when the router is powered on; it is cleared when the router is reset or powered off.

ROM: Used by the router to store the bootstrap startup program, operating system software, and Power-On Self-Test (POST). ROM chips are installed in sockets on the router's motherboard so that they can be replaced or upgraded.

Sample Questions

1. To copy a Cisco IOS to your router, what command should you use?

   A. `copy tftp flash`

   B. `copy flash tftp`

   C. `copy tftp run`

   D. `copy run tftp`

   Answer: **A.** The correct command for copying a Cisco IOS to a router is `copy tftp flash`.

2. If you wanted to boot a Cisco IOS named Alpha from your tftp host, which of the following is the correct command?

   A. `(config-if)boot system tftp Alpha 172.16.10.1`

   B. `(config)boot system tftp 172.16.10.1 Alpha`

   C. `(config-if)copy tftp flash Alpha 172.16.10.1`

   D. `(config) boot system tftp Alpha 182.16.10.1`

   Answer: D. You use the `boot system` command from global configuration mode, not the interface configuration. Also, the syntax is *boot system tftp/IOS filename/IP address of TFTP host.*

Prepare to backup, upgrade, and load a backup Cisco IOS software image

What Cisco is checking in this section of the exam is that you have actual hands-on experience logging in to a Cisco router, copying the router's IOS software to a TFTP host, and then restoring the IOS file.

For background information, review the previous section, which covered the objective "List the commands to load Cisco IOS software from flash memory, a TFTP server, or ROM." Practice on a TFTP host uploading a new IOS (software image) or backing up an old IOS image.

Critical Information

You must have a fundamental understanding of where the Cisco IOS is stored on the Cisco router. IOS is typically found and loaded in flash memory, also known as EEPROM. However, the Cisco IOS can also be loaded from a TFTP host and ROM, as shown in the previous objective.

Exam Essentials

It is important to practice these commands on Cisco routers if possible.

Remember the difference between where a configuration is stored on a router and where the Cisco IOS is stored. The Cisco IOS is typically stored and loaded from flash memory. The router's configuration is typically stored and loaded from NVRAM.

Know the commands for copying and restoring the IOS. Review the section above on the objective "List the commands to load Cisco IOS software from flash memory, a TFTP server, or ROM," which covered all the commands for copying and restoring a Cisco IOS.

Remember the context for booting a Cisco IOS from a TFTP host. To load a Cisco IOS named Alpha when the router boots, for example, this is a sample command string: `boot system tftp Alpha 172.16.10.1`.

Key Terms and Concepts

Flash: Basically an erasable, reprogrammable ROM that holds the operating system image and microcode. It allows you to "flash" the router and perform upgrades without removing and replacing chips on the motherboard. Flash is retained even when the router is turned off.

IOS: Internetworking Operating System (IOS) is the router kernel designed by Cisco to providing routing functions and the interface.

NVRAM: Nonvolatile RAM that stores the router's startup configuration file. NVRAM retains its information even when the router is rebooted or shut down.

RAM: Provides caching and packet buffering, plus information like routing tables, which will be explained in more detail in Chapter 6. RAM is used to hold the running operating system when the router is powered on; it is cleared when the router is reset or powered off.

ROM: Used by the router to store the bootstrap startup program, operating system software, and Power-On Self-Test (POST). ROM chips are installed in sockets on the router's motherboard so that they can be replaced or upgraded.

Sample Questions

1. To copy a Cisco IOS to a TFTP server, what command is valid?

   A. `copy start tftp`

   B. `copy tftp run`

   C. `copy flash tftp`

   D. `copy flash net`

   Answer: C. To copy your Cisco IOS to a TFTP server, use the `copy flash tftp` command.

2. If you copy your IOS to a TFTP server, what parameters are required? (Choose two.)

   A. Flash size

   B. TFTP IP address

   C. IOS filename

   D. TFTP directory

   Answer: B, C. To copy your IOS to a TFTP server, you would use the command `copy flash tftp` plus the IP address of the TFTP host and source filename.

Prepare the initial configuration of your router and enable IP

This section pulls together a lot of the commands you have learned throughout this chapter. It is important that you know how to configure a router manually and that you know all the commands associated with enabling IP on a router. When working in a production network or studying for the exam, practicing these commands is essential.

In this section, you will learn how to configure a router manually, starting with a minimal configuration and adding the commands for connecting two routers together with a WAN simulator cable.

Critical Information

To manually configure a router, you need to get into configuration mode, which can be accessed only from within privileged mode. In configuration mode, you have access to configuration commands that will allow you to configure the router as a whole, as well as to view other configuration modes.

Type **config** and then press Enter. The router prompts you with the following options:

```
Router#config
Configuring from terminal, memory, or network
[terminal]?
```

`Config terminal` (or `config t`) executes configuration commands from the terminal. From a console port or Telnet session, you can make changes to your router. Press Ctrl+Z to end the session and return to the console prompt. This will change the configuration file in running RAM, known as `running-config`.

```
Router#config t
Enter configuration commands, one per line.  End
with CRTL/Z.
Router(config)#^Z
```

`Config memory (config mem)` executes configuration commands stored in NVRAM; this copies the `startup-config` file to `running-config`.

`Config network (config net)` is used to retrieve router configuration information from a network TFTP server. This copies the configuration from a TFTP host to running RAM.

```
Router#config net
Host or network configuration file [host]? [enter]
Address of remote host [255.255.255.255]?172.16.10.1
Name of configuration file [router-confg]?RouterA-confg
Configure using RouterA-confg from 172.16.10.1?
[confirm] [enter]
Loading RouterA-confg
```

Manual Configuration

When a router comes up without a startup configuration file, it will go into setup mode. If you want to skip the automatic setup, you can press Ctrl+C at any time, then type **config t** to get into configuration mode. Here's an example of a manual configuration:

```
router#config t
Enter configuration commands, one per line.  End with
CNTL/Z.
router(config)#int e0
router(config-if)#description LAN Link to Sales
router(config-if)#ip address 172.16.50.1 255.255.255.0
router(config-if)#no shutdown
router(config-if)#int s0
router(config-if)#description WAN Link to SF
router(config-if)#ip address 172.16.40.2 255.255.255.0
router(config-if)#no shutdown
router(config-if)#exit
router(config)#hostname RouterC
RouterC(config)#enable ?
last-resort  Define enable action if no TACACS servers
respond
  password     Assign the privileged level password
  secret       Assign the privileged level secret
  use-tacacs   Use TACACS to check enable passwords
RouterC(config)#enable password simple1
```

```
RouterC(config)#enable secret todd
RouterC(config)#line vty 0 4
RouterC(config-line)#login
RouterC(config-line)#password telnettome
RouterC(config)#banner motd #
Enter TEXT message.  End with the character '#'.
If you are not me, then why are you here?
#
RouterC(config-line)#^Z
RouterC#
```

In this example, we typed **config t** and then chose interface Ethernet0 by typing **int e0**. We typed in the description, IP address, and subnet mask and then, to configure serial0 (s0), put in the relevant description, IP address, and mask. Notice that the complete IP address and mask need to be entered on one line.

That done, we changed the hostname of the router and typed **enable ?** to get the syntax to change passwords. We then entered passwords for the enable password, enable secret, and VTY (Telnet) ports. We entered **line vty 0 4** to specify the number of Telnet ports defined; this number can be displayed by typing **sh running-config.** The bottom of the configuration shows the number of VTY ports available (0 through 4):

```
!
line con 0
line aux 0
 transport input all
line vty 0 4
password telnettome
 login
!
end
```

There is now one more password to enter: the console password. This is used when your terminal is directly connected to the console.

```
RouterC(config)#line console 0
RouterC(config-line)#login
```

```
RouterC(config-line)#password iamdirectlyconnected
RouterC(config-line)#^Z
```

Notice that the con 0 password shows in the configuration output:

```
line con 0
 password iamdirectlyconnected
 login
line aux 0
 transport input all
line vty 0 4
 password telnettome
 login
!
```

DTE/DCE Cable

If you have connected a Cisco DTE/DCE (Data Terminal Equipment/Data Communication Equipment) cable, and you are simulating a WAN link between routers, you need to add a clock source.

By default, Cisco routers are DTE devices, but when you have routers connected together to simulate a WAN link, you can define a serial interface as a DCE device. Because Cisco routers use synchronous communications, which means a clock is required and is usually supplied from an external source, you need to add the `clock rate` command to the DCE serial ports on your routers. Why? Because you don't have a CSU/DSU that would normally handle the clocking on the line for you. You must specify the clock rate command on the DCE interfaces to simulate a clocking source. You should also specify the `bandwidth` command, because it's used by some routing protocols like IGRP to make routing decisions. If you are using RIP or static routing, the `bandwidth` command will not help.

To configure your router to enable clocking, you would type in the following commands:

```
RouterB#config t
Enter configuration commands, one per line.  End with
CNTL/Z.
```

```
RouterB(config)#int s0
RouterB(config-if)#clock rate ?
        Speed (bits per second)
  1200
  2400
  4800
  9600
  19200
  38400
  56000
  64000
  72000
  125000
  148000
  250000
  500000
  800000
  1000000
  1300000
  2000000
  4000000
<300-8000000>    Choose clock rate from list above

RouterB(config-if)#clock rate 56000
RouterB(config-if)#bandwidth ?
  <1-10000000>  Bandwidth in kilobits
RouterB(config-if)#bandwidth 56
RouterB(config-if)#int s1
RouterB(config-if)#clock rate 56000
RouterB(config-if)#bandwidth 56
RouterB(config-if)#^Z
```

Exam Essentials

As with many of the topics in this chapter, it's best to get hands-on experience. Run through all the commands you learned in this section and throughout the chapter.

Remember the commands to configure your router. Practice going to different interfaces and setting IP addresses. Remember that the IP address and mask are configured on the same line. Also set your passwords, banner, and hostname. Set your router to do name resolution with the `ip host` command.

Remember when to use the *`clock rate`* command and how to set your clock rate. The `clock rate` command is two words. Practice setting the clock rate on your DCE interfaces.

Key Terms and Concepts

`bandwidth`: A command used in Cisco routers to set the amount of availability of a link. This command only works if a dynamic routing protocol (EIGRP, for example) is running that can use the bandwidth of a link to help make routing decisions.

`clock rate`: A command used in Cisco routers to set the clocking used on a line. Typically the clock will be provided by the provider or CDU/DSU.

Sample Questions

1. Which command is valid for adding an IP address to router interface e0?

   A. `int e0, ip address 172.16.10.1, 255.255.255.0`

   B. `int e0, ip address 172.16.10.1 255.255.255.0`

C. `ip address 172.16.10.1`

D. `ip address 172.16.10.1 255.255.255.0`

Answer: B. The `ip address` command is used to add an IP address to an interface. The IP address and mask are typed on the same line.

2. What is the command used to simulate a CSU/DSU device connected to your router?

A. `clockrate`

B. `bandwidth`

C. `clock rate`

D. `band width`

Answer: C. On an interface connected with a DCE cable, use the `clock rate` command.

3. If you wanted to change your `running-config` file, which of the following commands would you use?

A. `config net`

B. `config mem`

C. `configure terminal`

D. `copy star run`

Answer: C, D. `config t` and `copy star run` can both be used to modify `running-config`.

4

Network Protocols

Cisco exam objectives covered in this chapter:

- **Monitor Novell IPX operation on the router.** *(pages 149 – 158)*
- **Describe the two parts of network addressing, then identify the parts in specific protocol address examples.** *(pages 158 – 165)*
- **Create the different classes of IP addresses [and subnetting].** *(pages 166 – 176)*
- **Configure IP addresses.** *(pages 176 – 180)*
- **Verify IP addresses.** *(pages 180 – 187)*
- **List the required IPX address and encapsulation type.** *(pages 187 – 190)*
- **Enable the Novell IPX protocol and configure interfaces.** *(pages 191 – 198)*
- **Identify the functions of the TCP/IP transport-layer protocols.** *(pages 199 – 203)*
- **Identify the functions of the TCP/IP network-layer protocols.** *(pages 203 – 207)*
- **Identify the functions performed by ICMP.** *(pages 208 – 211)*
- **Configure IPX access lists and SAP filters to control basic Novell traffic.** *(pages 212 – 220)*

In this chapter you will learn about Internetworking Protocol Exchange (IPX) and Internet Protocol (IP) addressing as well as IP subnetting. It is very important to understand that we will not teach you the basics of subnetting an IP address, but will cover only the information needed to pass the CCNA exam. We assume that you have at least some basic background in TCP/IP and subnetting. If not, read Chapters 3 and 4 in the Sybex *CCNA Study Guide*. That will give you the background needed to comprehend the protocols, addressing, and subnetting exam objectives discussed in this chapter.

Because many of the exam objectives covered here specifically refer to IPX, much of the material in this chapter will focus on Novell systems. Novell created NetWare, a client/server operating system (OS), in the early 1980s. The company then created its own protocol stack to work with the NetWare OS. This protocol stack included a routed protocol called Internetwork Protocol Exchange (IPX), defined at the Network layer of the OSI reference model.

We start off by introducing the commands needed to monitor IPX in a Cisco routed environment. We will then move on to the addressing of networks and hosts in both an IP and IPX internetwork. The next three sections cover IP addressing, subnetting, and configuring, as well as how to verify IP addressing on a Cisco router.

We continue with IPX by introducing the different LAN encapsulation methods and how to configure IPX on a Cisco router. Next you will learn about the protocols specified by the DOD (Department of Defense) at the Internet and Host-to-Host layers. The last exam objective covered is how to filter an IPX network using access lists.

The material covered in this chapter is important to know both so that you can work successfully in a production environment and prepare well for the CCNA exam. You will learn processes that are essential to properly configure Cisco routers in an IP and IPX network. Keep in mind that all of the topics in this chapter are important and that you will be tested on your understanding of them.

Monitor Novell IPX operation on the router

In this section, you will learn how to monitor IPX on an internetwork. You will learn a variety of commands that you can use at a Cisco router. With the correct commands, you can find out if the routers are seeing the NetWare servers on your network, read the IPX routing table, check the IPX traffic on a network, and find the IPX address of your Cisco router interfaces.

Whether you are working in a Novell environment or studying for the CCNA exam, your comprehension of these commands is crucial for success. It is also important that you understand the output that each command shows.

Critical Information

Once you have IPX configured and running, as explained in the objective "Enable the Novell IPX protocol and configure interfaces" later in this chapter, you have several ways to verify and track that the router is communicating correctly. The most frequently used commands are described briefly here and in more detail in the "Necessary Procedures" section:

- The `show ipx servers` command is a lot like the `display servers` command in NetWare; it displays the contents of the SAP table in the Cisco router, so you should see the names of all SAP services in the output. Remember that if the router doesn't have entries for remote servers in its own SAP table, local clients will never see those servers. So if you notice servers missing from the output, double-check your IPX network addresses and encapsulation settings.
- The `show ipx route` command displays the IPX routing table entries that the router knows about. The router reports networks to which it is directly connected, then reports networks that it has learned of since the router has come online.
- `show ipx traffic` gives you a summary of the number and type of IPX packets received and transmitted by the router. This command shows both the IPX Routing Information Protocol (RIP) and Service Advertising Protocol (SAP) update packets.
- `show ipx interface` returns detailed information such as the IPX address for the interface, hardware address, and encapsulation type. It is important to remember that the `show interface` command will not give you the IPX address of the interface.
- The `show protocol` command is the only other command that shows the IPX addresses for a router's interfaces.

- `debug ipx` displays IPX as it's running through the internetwork. It's noteworthy that you can see the IPX RIP and SAP updates with this command, but be careful—it can consume precious CPU cycles if you don't use it wisely.
- With extended `ping`, you can ping IPX nodes and interfaces to test for IPX connectivity.

Necessary Procedures

In this section we will demonstrate how to use each of the commands described above. It is important to remember the type of output each command returns.

show ipx servers

The `show ipx servers` command displays all the NetWare services collected by the Cisco routers. These are sent out every 60 seconds by each NetWare device that has a network service. Keep in mind that a Microsoft Windows workstation with Client Services for NetWare installed will broadcast its services (shares) every 60 seconds just as a NetWare server does.

```
RouterA#sh ipx servers
Codes: S - Static, P - Periodic, E - EIGRP, N - NLSP,
H - Holddown, + = detail
9 Total IPX Servers

Table ordering is based on routing and server info

Type Name         Net       Address              Port Route Hops Itf
P    4 BORDER1    350ED6D2.0000.0000.0001:0451 2/01  1    Et0
P    4 BORDER3    12DB8494.0000.0000.0001:0451 2/01  1    Et0
P    107 BORDER1  350ED6D2.0000.0000.0001:8104 2/01  1    Et0
P    107 BORDER3  12DB8494.0000.0000.0001:8104 2/01  1    Et0
P    26B BORDER   350ED6D2.0000.0000.0001:0005 2/01  1    Et0
P    278 BORDER   12DB8494.0000.0000.0001:4006 2/01  1    t0
P    278 BORDER   350ED6D2.0000.0000.0001:4006 2/01  1    Et0
P    3E1 BORDER1  350ED6D2.0000.0000.0001:9056 2/01  1    Et0
P    3E1 BORDER3  12DB8494.0000.0000.0001:9056 2/01  1    Et0
```

show ipx route

The `show ipx route` command shows the IPX routing table in the Cisco router. By default, IPX uses the RIP routing protocol to find all routes in a network. The `C` in the output represents directly connected networks, and the `R` stands for RIP found networks.

```
RouterA#sh ipx route
Codes: C - Connected primary network,    c - Connected
secondary network, S - Static, F - Floating static, L -
Local (internal), W - IPXWAN, R - RIP, E - EIGRP, N -
NLSP, X - External, A - Aggregate, s - seconds, u - uses


6 Total IPX routes. Up to 1 parallel paths and 16 hops
allowed.


No default route known.


C       2100 (NOVELL-ETHER),  Et0
C       2200 (HDLC),          Se0
C       2300 (SAP),           Et0.100
c       3200 (HDLC),          Se0
R       4100 [07/01] via  2200.00e0.1ea9.c418, 13s, Se0
R       5200 [13/02] via  2200.00e0.1ea9.c418, 13s, Se0
```

show ipx traffic

The `show ipx traffic` command displays the RIP and SAP (services broadcasted) information that has been sent and received by the router. (The output shown here was cut for brevity.)

```
RouterA#sh ipx traffic
System Traffic for 0.0000.0000.0001 System-Name:
RouterA
Rcvd:   15 total, 0 format errors, 0 checksum errors, 0
bad hop count, 0 packets pitched, 15 local destination,
0 multicast
Bcast:  10 received, 249 sent
Sent:   255 generated, 0 forwarded
        0 encapsulation failed, 0 no route
```

```
SAP:     1 SAP requests, 0 SAP replies, 0 servers
         0 SAP Nearest Name requests, 0 replies
         0 SAP General Name requests, 0 replies
         0 SAP advertisements received, 0 sent
         0 SAP flash updates sent, 0 SAP format errors
RIP:     1 RIP requests, 0 RIP replies, 6 routes
         8 RIP advertisements received, 230 sent
         12 RIP flash updates sent, 0 RIP format errors
Echo:    Rcvd 0 requests, 5 replies
         Sent 5 requests, 0 replies
         0 unknown: 0 no socket, 0 filtered, 0 no helper
         0 SAPs throttled, freed NDB len 0
Watchdog:
         0 packets received, 0 replies spoofed
Queue lengths:
         IPX input: 0, SAP 0, RIP 0, GNS 0
         SAP throttling length: 0/(no limit), 0 nets
pending lost route reply
```

show ipx interface

This command gives you the interface settings. Notice that the output below shows the IPX address for the interface, the encapsulation method (Novell-ether, or 802.3), the delay of the line, RIP and SAP size and delay, and more. (Note that this sample output was cut for brevity.)

```
RouterA#sh ipx int e0
Ethernet0 is up, line protocol is up
  IPX address is 2100.0000.0c8d.5c9d, NOVELL-ETHER [up]
  Delay of this IPX network, in ticks is 1 throughput 0
link delay 0
  IPXWAN processing not enabled on this interface.
  IPX SAP update interval is 1 minute(s)
  IPX type 20 propagation packet forwarding is disabled
  Incoming access list is not set
  Outgoing access list is not set
  IPX helper access list is not set
```

```
  SAP GNS processing enabled, delay 0 ms, output filter
list is not set
  SAP Input filter list is not set
  SAP Output filter list is not set
  SAP Router filter list is not set
  Input filter list is not set
  Output filter list is not set
  Router filter list is not set
  Netbios Input host access list is not set
  Netbios Input bytes access list is not set
  Netbios Output host access list is not set
  Netbios Output bytes access list is not set
  Updates each 60 seconds, aging multiples RIP: 3 SAP: 3
  SAP interpacket delay is 55 ms, maximum size is 480
bytes
  RIP interpacket delay is 55 ms, maximum size is 432
bytes
```

show protocol

This command returns the routed protocols configured on your router as well as the address and encapsulation configured on each interface.

```
RouterA#sh prot
Global values:
  Internet Protocol routing is enabled
  IPX routing is enabled
Ethernet0 is up, line protocol is up
  Internet address is 172.16.10.1/24
  IPX address is 2200.0000.0c8d.4b8e (Novell-ether)
Serial0 is up, line protocol is up
  Internet address is 172.16.20.1/24
  IPX address is 2300.0000.0c8d.5c9d (HDLC)
Serial1 is administratively down, line protocol is down
```

debug ipx

The debug command shows real-time updates for an IPX network. Notice in the output below all the options that you can use with the debug ipx command. For monitoring purposes, you'll want to use the routing command. Use the undebug command to turn off this program.

```
RouterA#debug ipx ?
  compression     IPX compression
  eigrp           IPX EIGRP packets
  ipxwan          Novell IPXWAN events
  nlsp            IPX NLSP activity
  packet          IPX activity
  redistribution  IPX route redistribution
  routing         IPX RIP routing information
  sap             IPX Service Advertisement information
  spoof           IPX and SPX Spoofing activity
RouterA#debug ipx routing ?
  activity  IPX RIP routing activity
  events    IPX RIP routing events
RouterA#debug ipx routing act
IPX routing debugging is on
RouterA#
IPXRIP: update from 2200.00e0.1ea9.c418
    5200 in 2 hops, delay 13
    4100 in 1 hops, delay 7
IPXRIP: positing full update to 2100.ffff.ffff.ffff via
Ethernet0 (broadcast)
IPXRIP: src=2100.0000.0c8d.5c9d,
dst=2100.ffff.ffff.ffff, packet sent
    network 5200, hops 3,  delay 14
    network 4100, hops 2,  delay 8
    network 2300, hops 1,  delay 2
    network 3200, hops 1,  delay 2
    network 2200, hops 1,  delay 2
IPXRIP: positing full update to 3200.ffff.ffff.ffff via
Serial0 (broadcast)
```

```
IPXRIP: src=3200.0000.0c8d.5c9d,
dst=3200.ffff.ffff.ffff, packet sent
    network 5200, hops 3,  delay 19
    network 4100, hops 2,  delay 13
    network 2300, hops 1,  delay 7
    network 2200, hops 1,  delay 7
    network 2100, hops 1,  delay
RouterA#undebug ipx routing act
IPX routing debugging is off
```

Extended ping

After entering **ping** at the router prompt, you can ping by protocols other than the popular IP ping. For example, here's how you can ping for IPX:

```
RouterA#ping
Protocol [ip]: ipx
Target IPX address: 5200.0000.0c3f.1d86
Repeat count [5]:[enter]
Datagram size [100]: [enter]
Timeout in seconds [2]: [enter]
Verbose [n]: [enter]
Novell Standard Echo [n]: y
Type escape sequence to abort.
Sending 5, 100-byte IPX Novell Echoes to
5200.0000.0c3f.1d86, timeout is 2 seconds:!!!!!
Success rate is 100 percent (5/5), round-trip min/avg/
max = 4/7/12 ms
```

Exam Essentials

You need to remember what output each command displays.

Practice these commands on your Cisco router. We cannot stress this enough: Practice, practice, practice.

Remember the output each command gives you. When practicing the commands on your Cisco router, pay close attention to the output each command displays.

Key Terms and Concepts

debug: A command used to display real-time network updates on a console.

Extended `ping`: Program that allows you to specify arguments in the ping command. This is useful when you want to ping other protocols besides IP.

IP (Internet Protocol): A protocol specified at the Internet layer of the Department of Defense (DOD) model. Used to route packets through an internetwork and for network addressing.

IPX (Internetworking Packet Exchange): A protocol stack developed by Xerox, which they called XNS. Novell copied the protocol and called it IPX. It is used for routing packets through an internetwork and for network addressing.

`ping`: An acronym for Packet Internet Groper, `ping` is used to test IP connectivity between two IP hosts on an internetwork.

RIP (Routing Information Protocol): A distance vector routing protocol that is used to update routing tables dynamically.

SAP (Service Advertising Protocol): A Novell protocol defined at the Application layer of the OSI model and used to advertise network services on an internetwork.

Sample Questions

1. Which of the following commands displays the IPX address on an interface?

   A. `sh int`

   B. `sh ip int`

   C. `sh ipx int`

   D. `sh proto`

   Answer: C, D. The commands `show ipx interface` and `show protocol` will display the IPX address of a Cisco router interface.

2. Which command displays all the NetWare servers found by your Cisco router?

   A. `sh ipx servers`

   B. `display server`

   C. `show servers`

   D. `display routers`

   Answer: A. The command `show ipx servers` is similar to the command `display servers` on a NetWare console.

3. Which command displays the IPX routing table?

   A. `sh protocol`

   B. `sh ip route`

   C. `show ipx route`

   D. `show route`

   Answer: C. `show ipx route` displays the IPX routing table built in a Cisco router. It is important to remember that each protocol has its own routing table.

Describe the two parts of network addressing, then identify the parts in specific protocol address examples

In this section you will learn how to read addresses on both IP and IPX hosts in an internetwork. We will cover how IP addressing works in an internetwork and how different classes of networks were created especially for organizations of different sizes. It is important to know how to read an IP address, including which part of the first octet describes the network and which part describes the hosts.

You will also learn how IPX addresses are created and how to read the network and host information they convey.

When working in a network environment or taking the CCNA exam, you are expected to understand the basics of IP and IPX addressing.

Critical Information

In this section we will take a look at both IP and IPX network addressing.

IP Network Addressing

An IP address is made up of 32 bits of information. These bits are divided into four sections containing one byte (eight bits) each. These sections are referred to as *octets*. There are three methods for depicting an IP address:

- Dotted-decimal, as in 130.57.30.56
- Binary, as in 10000010.00111001.00011110.00111000
- Hexadecimal, as in 82 39 1E 38

All of these examples represent the same IP address. Dotted-decimal is the most common style used.

The network address uniquely identifies each network. Every machine on the same network shares that network address as part of its IP address. In the IP address 172.16.30.56, for example, 172.16 is the network address.

The node address is assigned to, and uniquely identifies, each machine on a network. This part of the address must be unique because it identifies a particular, individual machine—as opposed to a network, which identifies a group of machines. This number can also be referred to as a *host address*. In the IP address 172.16.30.56, for example, .30.56 is the node address.

The designers of the Internet decided to create classes of networks based on network size. For the small number of networks possessing a very large number of nodes, they created the Class A network. At the other extreme is the Class C network, reserved for the numerous networks with a small number of nodes. The class distinction for networks between very large and very small is predictably called the Class B network. How an IP address is subdivided into a network and node address is determined by the class designation of one's network. Table 4.1 provides us with a summary of the three classes of networks, which will be described in much more detail throughout this chapter.

TABLE 4.1: Summary of the Three Classes of Networks

Class	Format	Leading bit pattern	Decimal range*	Maximum networks	Maximum nodes per network
A	Net.Node. Node.Node	0	1–127	127	16,777,214
B	Net.Net. Node.Node	10	128–191	16,384	65,534
C	Net.Net. Net.Node	110	192–223	2,097,152	254

***first byte of network address**

Some IP addresses are reserved for special purposes and shouldn't be assigned to nodes by network administrators. Table 4.2 lists the members of this exclusive club and why they're included in it.

TABLE 4.2: Reserved IP Addresses

Address	Function
Network address of all 0s	Interpreted to mean "this network or segment."
Network address of all 1s	Interpreted to mean "all networks."
Network 127	Reserved for loopback tests. Designates the local node and allows that node to send a test packet to itself without generating network traffic.
Node address of all 0s	Interpreted to mean "this node."

TABLE 4.2: Reserved IP Addresses *(cont.)*

Address	Function
Node address of all 1s	Interpreted to mean "all nodes" on the specified network; for example, 128.2.255.255 means "all nodes" on network 128.2 (Class B address).
Entire IP address set to all 0s	Used by Cisco routers to designate the default route.
Entire IP address set to all 1s (same as 255.255.255.255)	Broadcast to all nodes on the current network; sometimes called an "all 1s broadcast."

Class A Networks

In a Class A network, the first byte is assigned to the network address, and the three remaining bytes are used for the node addresses. The Class A format is:

```
Network.Node.Node.Node
```

For example, in the IP address 49.22.102.70, 49 is the network address and 22.102.70 is the node address. Every machine on this particular network would have the distinctive network address of 49.

Class A network addresses are a byte long, with the first bit of that byte reserved (see Table 4.1) and the seven remaining bits available for manipulation. This means that the maximum number of Class A networks that can be created would be 128. Why? Because each of the seven bit positions can either be a 0 or a 1, thus the total is 2^7, or 128. But to complicate things further, it was also decided that the network address of all 0s (0000 0000) would be reserved to designate the default route (see Table 4.2). This means the actual number of usable Class A network addresses is 128 minus 1, or 127.

The range of network addresses for a Class A network is 1 through 127. Table 4.2 shows us that another Class A number in that reserved club is number 127. This revelation technically brings the total down to 126.

Each Class A network has three bytes (24-bit positions) for the node address of a machine. That means there are 2^{24}—or 16,777,216—unique combinations, and therefore precisely that many possible unique node addresses for each Class A network. Because addresses with the two patterns of all 0s and all 1s are reserved, the actual maximum usable number of nodes for a Class A network is 2^{24} minus 2, which equals 16,777,214.

Class B Networks

In a Class B network, the first two bytes are assigned to the network address, and the remaining two bytes are used for node addresses. This is the format:

```
Network.Network.Node.Node
```

For example, in the IP address 172.16.30.56, the network address is 172.16 and the node address is 30.56.

If a network address could be any two bytes of eight bits each, there would be 2^{16} unique combinations. But the Internet designers decided that all Class B networks should start with the binary digits 1 and 0. This leaves 14 bit positions to manipulate; therefore there are 16,384 (2^{14}) unique Class B networks. If you see a network address with the first byte in the range of decimal 128 to 191, you know it's a Class B network.

A Class B network has two bytes to use for node addresses. This is 2^{16} minus the two reserved patterns (all 0s and all 1s), for a total of 65,534 possible node addresses for each Class B network.

Class C Networks

The first three bytes of a Class C network are dedicated to the network portion of the address, with only one byte remaining for the node address. This is the format:

```
Network.Network.Network.Node
```

In the example IP address 192.168.100.102, the network address is 192.168.100 and the node address is 102.

In a Class C network, the first three bit positions are always the binary 110. The calculation—3 bytes, or 24 bits, minus 3 reserved positions—leaves 21 positions. There are therefore 2^{21}, or 2,097,152, possible Class C networks. You can identify an address as Class C if the first byte is between 192 and 223.

Each unique Class C network has one byte to use for node addresses. This leads to 2^8, or 256, minus the two reserved patterns of all 0s and all 1s, for a total of 254 node addresses for each Class C network.

IPX Network Addressing

IPX addresses use 80 bits, or 10 bytes, of data. As with TCP/IP addresses, they are hierarchical and divided into a network and node portion. The first four bytes always represent the network address, and the last six bytes always represent the node address. There are no Class A, B, or C distinctions in IPX addressing—the network and node portions of the address are always the same length.

Just as it is with IP network addresses, the network portion of the IPX address is assigned by administrators and must be unique on the entire IPX internetwork. However, here is the great part about IPX: Node addresses are automatically assigned to every node. In most cases, the MAC address of the machine is used as the node portion of the address. This offers several notable advantages over TCP/IP addressing. Since client addressing is dynamic (automatic), you don't have to run Dynamic Host Configuration Protocol (DHCP) or manually configure each individual workstation with an IPX address. Also, since the hardware address (defined at the Data Link layer) is included as part of the software address (defined at the Network layer), there's no need for a TCP/IP ARP equivalent in IPX.

As with TCP/IP addresses, IPX addresses can be written in several formats. Most often, they're written in hexadecimal (hex) format, such as 00007C80.0000.8609.33E9.

The first eight hex digits in this example (00007C80) represent the network portion of the address; the remaining 12 hex digits (0000.8609.33E9) represent the node portion and are the MAC address of the workstation. When referring to the IPX network, it's a common IPX custom to drop leading 0s. This done, the example network address above would simply be referred to as IPX network 7C80. The node portion is commonly divided into three sections of four hex digits divided by periods, as shown above.

Exam Essentials

By working with routers and workstations, you can get a good idea of how IP and IPX addressing works.

Remember the difference between Class A, B, and C IP addresses. The syntax for a Class A IP address is *net.node.node.node*. Class A network addresses start with a number between 1 and127. The syntax for a Class B IP address is *net.net.node.node*. Class B network addresses start with a number from 128 to 191. The syntax for a Class C IP address is *net.net.net.node*. Class C network addresses start with a number between 192 and 223.

Remember the IPX address format. The syntax for an IPX address is *net.node.node.node*. There are no class distinctions and no other syntax types for IPX addresses.

Key Terms and Concepts

IP (Internet Protocol): A protocol specified at the Internet layer of the Department of Defense (DOD) model. Used to route packets through an internetwork and for network addressing.

IPX (Internetworking Packet Exchange): A protocol stack developed by Xerox, which they called XNS. Novell copied the protocol and called it IPX. It is used for routing packets through an internetwork and for network addressing.

Network: A collection of computers that are tied together with some type of network medium in order to share resources.

Node: A network device attached to a network. A node can be a PC, printer, Macintosh, Unix workstation, fax server, etc.

Sample Questions

1. Which statements are true regarding the following IPX address: 7c89.0000.3456.1234? (Choose two.)

   A. 7c89.0000 is the network number.

   B. 3456.1234 is the node number.

   C. 7c89 is the network number.

   D. 0000.3456.1234 is the node number.

   Answer: C, D. The syntax of an IPX address is *network.node.node.node*.

2. Which of the following statements are true regarding the following IP address: 172.16.10.1?

   A. 172.16.10 is the network number.

   B. 10.1 is the node number.

   C. 1 is the node number.

   D. 172.16 is the network number.

   Answer: B, D. You must remember that Class A networks start with 1-127, Class B addresses start with 128-191, and Class C addresses start with 192-223. However, 127 is invalid to use as a network number. The number 172.16.10.1 is a Class B address. In a Class B address, the numbering scheme is *net.net.node.node*.

3. Which of the following statements are true regarding the following IP address: 192.168.10.1?

   A. 192.168.10 is the network number.

   B. 10.1 is the node number.

   C. 1 is the node number.

   D. 192.168 is the network number.

   Answer: A, C. The number 192.168.10.1 is a Class C address. In a Class C address, the numbering scheme is *net.net.net.node*.

Create the different classes of IP addresses [and subnetting]

After reading through the previous section, you should understand the different classes of IP addresses. Now we will cover how to create subnets and how to find valid subnets within a subnet. In the next section, you will learn to apply the valid subnets and hosts to a Cisco router interface.

Subnetting is network procreation. It is the act of creating little subnetworks from a single, large parent network. An organization with a single network address can have a subnet address for each individual physical network. Each subnet is still part of the shared network address, but it also has an additional identifier denoting its individual subnetwork number. This identifier is called a *subnet address.*

Let's make one thing clear here: This book will not teach you how to subnet a network. We will teach you the essential subnetting facts that you need to know and understand to pass the CCNA exam. For a complete understanding of addressing and subnetting, we urge you to read Chapter 4 of the Sybex *CCNA Study Guide.*

This section covers Class B and C subnetting. It is important to be able to subnet Class B and C addresses quickly and easily.

NOTE Unfortunately, you are not allowed to use the Windows calculator during the CCNA exam.

Critical Information

As discussed previously, a Class C IP network uses the first three bytes (24 bits) to define the network address. This leaves eight bits (one byte) to address hosts. If you want to create a subnet, your options are limited because of the small number of bits available.

Table 4.3 shows all the available subnets with a Class C network address. Notice the absence of the 128 subnet mask (one bit). Cisco follows the Request For Comments (RFCs), which specify that subnet bits can't all be on or off at the same time. If you had only one subnet bit, then all of your bits would either be on or off, which is not allowed.

TIP You should memorize this table and write it down on the scratch paper given to you at test time. You are not allowed to take anything into the testing center with you, but you can write anything down on paper before you start your exam.

TABLE 4.3: Subnet Masks Available for a Class C Network

Subnet Mask	Length of Subnet Mask (bits)	Number of Subnets	Number of Hosts per Subnet
255.255.255.252	30	62	2
255.255.255.248	29	30	6
255.255.255.240	28	14	14
255.255.255.224	27	6	30
255.255.255.192	26	2	62

Class B

In a Class B network, subnetting is done exactly the same as it is with Class C networks except that you have more host bits. Notice in Table 4.4, which shows the different subnet masks available for a Class B network, that the number of hosts increases as the number of bits used for subnetting decreases and vice versa.

TABLE 4.4: Subnet Masks Available for a Class B Network

Subnet Mask	Length of Subnet Mask (bits)	Number of Subnets	Number of Hosts per Subnet
255.255.255.252	30	16,382	2
255.255.255.248	29	8190	6
255.255.255.240	28	4094	14
255.255.255.224	27	2046	30
255.255.255.192	26	1022	62
255.255.255.128	25	510	126
255.255.255.0	24	254	254
255.255.254.0	23	126	510
255.255.252.0	22	62	1022
255.255.248.0	21	30	2046
255.255.240.0	20	14	4094
255.255.224.0	19	6	8190
255.255.192.0	18	2	16,382

It is important to remember that subnet bits can extend to more than eight bits, or one octet.

Let's talk about the 255.255.255.128 mask used in a Class B network. You must remember that the first two octets are not used for subnetting or addressing of hosts, only for network IDs. This leaves the last two octets in a Class B network available for administrators to create subnets and hosts. In the mask 255.255.255.128, there are nine bits for creating subnets and seven bits for addressing of hosts within those subnets. The 128 is valid in the fourth octet because there are 9 bits available, and only one bit has to be turned on for a subnet to be valid.

255.128 would give us the calculation:

2^9–2=510 subnets

2^7–2=126 hosts per subnet

256–255=1 (for the third octet)

256–128=128 (for the fourth octet)

This means the third octet can be any number between 1 and 255, but the fourth octet gets a little tricky. There is only one subnet bit, so it can be either off or on. If it is turned on, the subnet in the fourth octet has a value of 128. If the subnet bit is off, the value of the subnet is 0.

This gives us two subnets in the fourth octet:

172.16.10.0: Valid hosts will be in the range 1 through 126. 127 is the broadcast address.

172.16.10.128: Valid hosts are between 129 and 254. 255 is the broadcast address.

The IPCalc program shown here illustrates how this works:

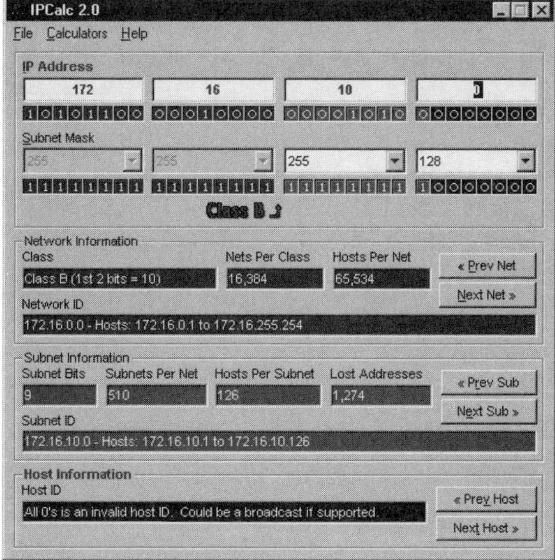

As you can see, there are nine bits turned on for subnetting. The ninth bit (or fourth octet) does not have the subnet bit on. The subnet is therefore 172.16.10.0. Notice that the host bits have no bits on, which is invalid. This means the host bit range must start with an octet value of 1.

This IPCalc screen shows the host bits all turned on and 172.16.10.127 as the broadcast address for subnet 0:

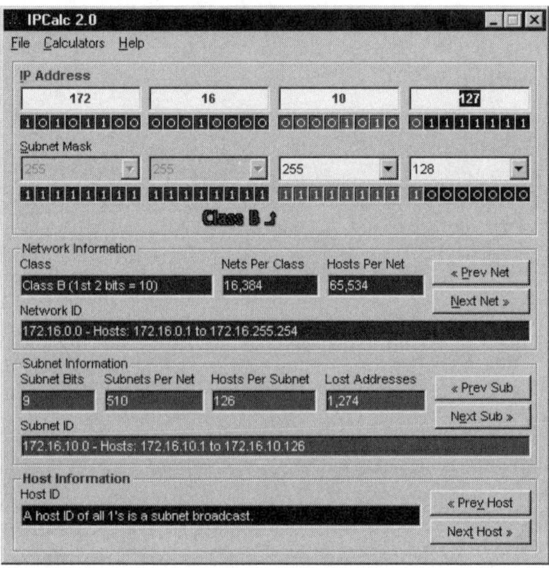

The next example shows the 128 subnet bit on. The value of the octet is 128, but no host bits are turned on. This means the first valid host must be 129. The subnet address is 172.16.10.128.

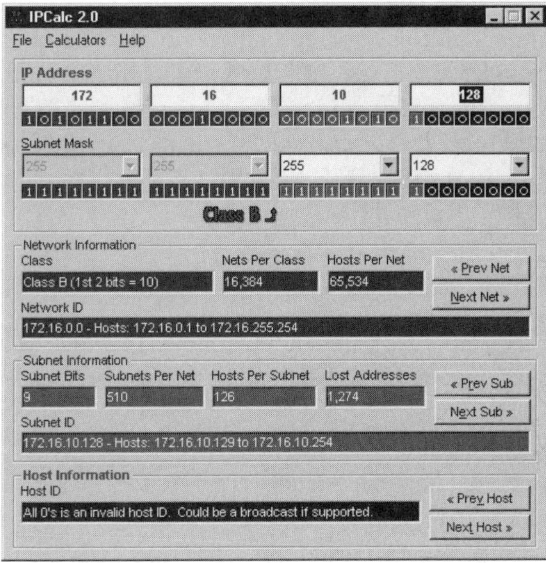

The final example shows the host bits all on for subnet 172.16.10.128 which is the broadcast address for that subnet, 172.16.10.255.

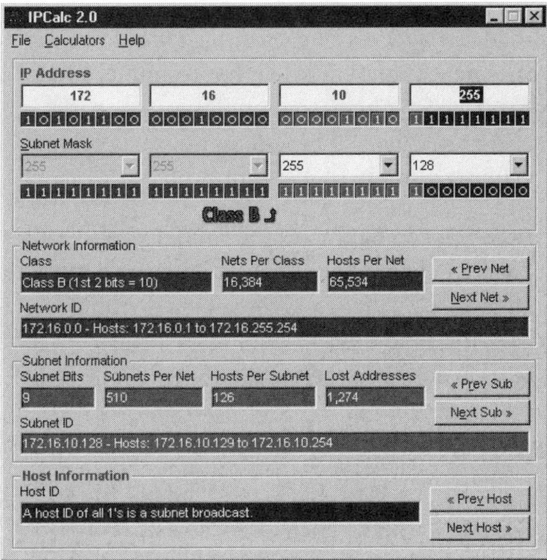

Broadcast Addresses

It is important to be able to find the broadcast address in a subnet. The broadcast address is all the host bits turned on for that subnet. However, the easiest way to find a broadcast address is to figure out the valid subnets. For example, if you have an IP network address of 192.168.50.0 with a 255.255.255.248 mask, your valid subnets would be calculated this way:

256–248=8

Thus 8 is your base number, or variable. You add the base number to itself until you reach the subnet mask number:

8+8=16

16+8=24

and so on to generate the following series:

32, 40, 48, 56, 64, 72, 80, 88, 96, 104, 112, 120, 128, 136, 144, 152, 160, 168, 176, 184, 192, 200, 208, 216, 224, 232, 240

The broadcast address of each subnet would be the number just before the next subnet number. For example, subnet 8 would have a broadcast of 15. Subnet 16 would have a broadcast address of 23, subnet 24 would have a broadcast address of 31, subnet 32 would have a subnet address of 39, and so on.

From here you can figure out the valid hosts for each subnet by using the numbers between the subnet number and the broadcast address. For example, the valid hosts for subnet 8 would be 9 through14. For subnet 16, the valid hosts would be 17 through 22. For subnet 24, the valid hosts would be 25 through 30.

Number of Bits in a Mask

When referring to Veritable Length Subnet Masks (VLSMs), the IP addresses and masks can be written as 172.16.10.3/24. This means the mask is 24 bits long, or 255.255.255.0. This is an industry standard.

However, when using Setup mode to configure your router, the subnet mask is referred to as bits used to create subnets. For example, the 172.16.10.3/24 really only uses eight bits to create subnets with, so 8 would be the number you enter in the router when prompted for subnet mask bits.

When taking the CCNA exam, you will be asked questions that refer to a large number of subnet bits. The writers of the test want you to refer only to the bits used in creating subnets. For example, if you get a question about a 20-bit subnet mask, you must add 20 bits to the default mask of a Class A, B, or C network. The first thing you should do is write out the mask. A 20-bit mask in a Class A network would be 255.255.255.240. The default mask is 255, and 20 bits would be 255.255.240. You could not add 20 bits to a default Class B or C network. A Class B network only has 16 bits available and a Class C only has 8 bits available.

For the exam, remember not to try to figure out the number of subnets, but only the number of host bits available. In the above example, only four bits are available for creating hosts. That means there are 14 hosts per subnet.

Exam Essentials

You must know how to subnet an IP network. This exam objective is featured in many questions on the CCNA test.

Understand how to find the valid hosts in a subnet. The best way to do this is to use the equation 256 minus the subnet mask. For example, if you have a 240 mask, you would use the equation of 256–240. The result, 16, is your first subnet and your base number, or interval. Keep adding the base number to itself until you reach the value of the subnet mask. The valid hosts are the numbers between the subnets.

Understand how to find a broadcast address in a subnet. Once you find the valid subnets, you can find the valid hosts, which are the numbers between the subnets minus the broadcast address, which is the last number in the host range. For example, in a 240 mask the first subnet is 16 and the second subnet is 32. That means the valid hosts are 17 through 20, with 31 being the broadcast address for that subnet.

Key Terms and Concepts

Class B: Address class used to differentiate between a network and node within an IP address. The syntax is *net.net.node.node.*

Class C: Address class used to differentiate between a network and node within an IP address. The syntax is *net.net.net.node.*

IP Address: Network address assigned to a node on a network. Used to send and receive packets or datagrams on an internetwork.

IPCalc: Program written by Progression Inc. to help with complex IP calculations. This program can be found online at `http://www.progession-inc.com`.

Subnetting: The breaking up of an IP network address into smaller networks.

Sample Questions

1. With an IP address of 172.16.10.16 and a mask of 255.255.255.128, what are the class of address, subnet address, and broadcast address?

   A. Class C, 172.16.10.0, 172.16.10.128

   B. Class B, 172.16.10.0, 172.16.10.255

   C. Class B, 172.16.10.0, 172.16.10.127

   D. Class B, 172.16.10.0, 172.16.10.126

   Answer: C. 172.16.10.0 is the subnet number because the fourth octet has a value of 16. That is in the range from 0 to 127, and 128 is the next subnet. Therefore 172.16.10.127 is the broadcast address.

2. If you have a 22-bit subnet mask, how many subnets and hosts per subnet do you have?

   A. 4,194,302 subnets, 2 hosts

   B. 4,194,302 subnets, 4 hosts

   C. 8,190 subnets, 4,096 hosts

   D. 16,382 subnets, 14 hosts

   Answer: A. A 22-bit subnet mask added onto the default Class A mask is 255.255.255.255.252. That only leaves you two host bits, or two hosts per subnet. Remember that the best way to solve these kinds of problems on the CCNA exam is to look only for the number of host bits.

3. If you have an IP address of 192.168.10.42 with a 255.255.255.224 mask, what are your valid hosts?

   A. 10.1 to 10.254

   B. 10.33 to 10.64

   C. 10.33 to 10.62

   D. 10.33 to 10.63

   Answer: C. A 224 subnet mask gives you six subnets, each with 30 hosts. The valid subnets are 256–224=32, 64, 96, etc. The 42 in the last octet is in the 32 subnet. Since 32 is the subnet and 63 is the broadcast for that subnet, the valid hosts are 33 through 62.

4. If you have an IP address of 172.16.30.10 with a 255.255.252.0 subnet mask, what are the class of address, subnet address, and broadcast address?

   A. Class A, 172.16.28.0, 172.16.31.255

   B. Class B, 172.16.28.0, 172.16.31.127

   C. Class B, 172.16.28.0, 172.16.31.254

   D. Class B, 172.16.28.128, 172.16.31.254

   Answer: C. With a 255.255.252.0 mask, you have six bits for subnets. Your valid subnets are 256–252=4, 8, 12, 16, 20, 24, 28, 32, 36, etc. The third octet is 30, which is in the 28 subnet range. However, you need the fourth octet for host addressing. So your valid range is 28.1 through 31.254, and 31.255 is the broadcast address. 172.16.28.0 is the subnet address.

Configure IP addresses

In this section you can take what you learned from the last objective and apply that to your Cisco routers. It is imperative that you can create a subnet mask to meet a given business requirement and that you can apply that mask to an internetwork.

The information covered here is the basics of IP routing and addressing. You need to understand how to create a subnet mask regardless of the type of environment you are working in (Cisco, Bay, 3Com) or even what test you are taking (Cisco, Novell, NT).

Critical Information

This section covers the steps for applying a subnet mask to meet a business requirement. As discussed in the previous section, the IP addressing scheme used for subnets is referred to as *subnetting*. Before you implement subnetting, you need to determine your current requirements and plan for future conditions. Follow these guidelines:

1. Determine the number of required network IDs.
   - One for each subnet
   - One for each wide area network connection
2. Determine the number of required host IDs per subnet.
   - One for each TCP/IP host
   - One for each router interface

3. Based on the number of required host IDs you determined in Step 2, create the following:
   - One subnet mask for your entire network
   - A unique subnet ID for each physical segment
   - A range of host IDs for each subnet

Necessary Procedures

Now you can practice applying a business requirement to a Cisco router. Imagine that you have been hired to install a Cisco router in a company that has two 10BaseT Ethernet LANs and three WAN links connecting three branch offices, each with eight people. The local Ethernet LANs will never be used by more than 10 people each. You have acquired the Cisco router with two Ethernet interfaces and three serial interfaces for the WAN links.

Your job is to come up with an addressing scheme for the company and apply it to the Cisco routers. You are told that you have to use a Class C network address of 192.168.10.0.

Reading the business requirements, you can see that you need eight subnets, each with a maximum of twelve hosts. If you created a mask of 255.255.255.224, that would only give you six subnets, but you would have thirty valid addresses per subnet. You need more subnets and fewer hosts per subnet. A mask of 255.255.255.240 will give you four bits for subnetting (14 subnets) and four bits for host addressing (14 hosts per subnet). What are the valid subnets and hosts? They are calculated as follows:

> 256–240=16, 32, 48, 64, 80, 96, 112, 128, 144, 160, 176, 192, 208, 224

As you already know, the valid hosts are the numbers between the subnets, minus the subnet number and the broadcast addresses. Figure 4.1 shows how to apply the subnets to a router with the valid host addresses.

FIGURE 4.1: Applying a subnet mask to your network

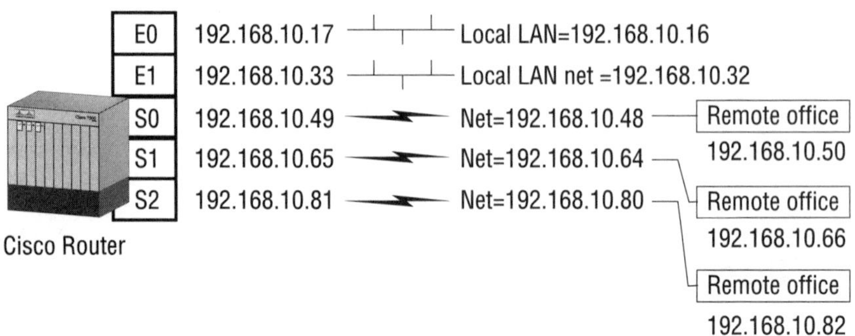

You can use a configuration such as this to apply the valid hosts to the local Cisco router:

```
RouterA#config t
RouterA#(config)int e0
RouterA#(config-int)ip address 192.168.10.17
255.255.255.240
RouterA#(config-int)no shut
RouterA#(config-int)int e1
RouterA#(config-int)ip address 192.168.10.33
255.255.255.240
RouterA#(config-int)no shut
RouterA#(config-int)int s0
RouterA#(config-int)ip address 192.168.10.49
255.255.255.240
RouterA#(config-int)no shut
RouterA#(config-int)int s1
RouterA#(config-int)ip address 192.168.10.65
255.255.255.240
RouterA#(config-int)no shut
RouterA#(config-int)int s2
RouterA#(config-int)ip address 192.168.10.81
255.255.255.240
RouterA#(config-int)no shut
```

Now, you could have used any IP address that is valid in the subnet you wanted your router interface to participate in; in this example, we chose to use the first available address in each subnet. Also, there are many other commands to configure your serial and LAN interfaces with, but here we are only demonstrating how to apply a valid IP address scheme to a router.

Exam Essentials

It is important to know how to add an IP address to a Cisco router.

Remember the commands to add an IP address to a Cisco router. To configure a Cisco router with an IP address, use the `ip address` command in an interface configuration.

Understand how to find the valid host addresses in a subnet. You need to be able to determine your valid hosts; use the equation 256–*[subnet mask]* to get your base number and first subnet. Keep adding the base number to itself until you reach the subnet mask value. The valid hosts are the numbers in between the subnets minus the broadcast address.

Key Terms and Concepts

IP Address: Network address assigned to a node on a network. Used to send and receive packets or datagrams on an internetwork.

Subnet mask: Used in configuring an IP address on a network node to determine the subnet in which the node is located.

Subnetting: The breaking up of an IP network address into smaller networks.

Sample Questions

1. You need to apply a subnet mask of 255.255.255.248. How many subnets and hosts per subnet do you have?

   A. 254 subnets, 254 hosts

   B. 4,094 subnets, 14 hosts

C. 524,286 subnets, 30 hosts

D. 30 subnets, 6 hosts

Answer: D. Remember to look only for the host bits in a question like this. You have only 3 host bits, or 6 hosts per subnet.

2. You need to come up with a subnet mask for your company. Which factors should you consider? (Choose all that apply.)

A. The traffic on the LAN

B. The location of the servers

C. The number of users in each LAN

D. The number of WAN links

Answer: C, D. You need to consider the number of users in each subnet as well as the number of subnets you need. The subnets include the LAN and WAN links.

Verify IP addresses

This section covers the different IP tools available to verify IP addresses. We will talk about Telnet, `ping`, and `trace`. These are tools that are included in all Internet Protocol (IP) stacks.

It is important to understand what each tool can do for you when working in an internetworking environment. These tools, if used correctly, can help you identify where a problem exists in an IP internetwork. When studying for the CCNA exam, be sure to remember the output that each command displays.

Critical Information

Once you have your routers configured, there are some basic IP tools to test connectivity between two TCP/IP hosts. To perform basic testing on your internetwork, you can follow the layers of the OSI reference model. Start by telnetting to a remote router. This way you'll know that all layers (upper and lower) are working.

These are the basic tools you can use, to be discussed in more detail below:

- Telnet, short for Terminal Emulation protocol, is included in the TCP/IP (DOD) suite of protocols. It provides remote terminal connection services. Telnet is the best tool for checking TCP/IP connectivity between devices because it uses specifications from all layers of the OSI reference model. However, in order for you to telnet into a host device, the device must be running a Telnet daemon.
- `ping` (Packet Internet Groper) is a testing or diagnostic tool used to check IP connectivity between two IP devices. `ping` uses ICMP echo requests and echo replies defined at the Network layer of the OSI reference model. The `ping` command isn't just used for IP networks; it can be used with almost any type of Network-layer protocol, including IPX, AppleTalk, Apollo, VINES, and DECnet.
- Trace Route, or `trace`, is used to test IP connectivity in an internetwork. `trace` is used at the Network layer and uses TTL (Time to Live) to discover routes to remote destinations; it's similar to the `ping` command. The `trace` command will start out by sending a TTL of 1. This will cause the first router to receive the packet and send back an error. It keeps sending new probes with incrementing TTL, with each packet reaching one hop further than the last, until it understands the complete path, distance, and time between each router.

Necessary Procedures

This section demonstrates how to use the commands used to test connectivity between routers.

Telnet

You can easily use Telnet from any Windows workstation by opening a DOS command window and typing **telnet 172.16.30.1** (or **telnet** plus whatever the IP address of the host is).

This example of an Etherpeek network trace shows why Telnet is a great tool for testing all layers of the OSI reference model:

```
Flags:        0x00
  Status:       0x00
  Packet Length:68
  Timestamp:    12:16:05.495000 06/09/1998
Ethernet Header
  Destination:  00:80:c7:a8:f0:3d
  Source:       00:00:0c:8d:5c:9d
  Protocol Type:08-00  IP
IP Header - Internet Protocol Datagram
  Version:              4
  Header Length:        5
  Precedence:           0
  Type of Service:      %000
  Unused:               %00
  Total Length:         50
  Identifier:           23
  Fragmentation Flags:  %000
  Fragment Offset:      0
  Time To Live:         254
  IP Type:              0x06  TCP
  Header Checksum:      0x468a
  Source IP Address:    172.16.20.2
  Dest. IP Address:     172.16.10.2
  No Internet Datagram Options
TCP - Transport Control Protocol
  Source Port:      23  TELNET
  Destination Port: 1032
  Sequence Number:  2665776445
  Ack Number:       17009601
  Offset:           5
  Reserved:         %000000
  Code:             %011000
          Ack is valid
          Push Request
```

```
    Window:              2093
    Checksum:            0xffe7
    Urgent Pointer:      0
    No TCP Options
  TELNET - Network Virtual Terminal
    TELNET Data:
    ..                    0d 0a
    TELNET Data:
    RouterB#              52 6f 75 74 65 72 42 23
  Frame Check Sequence:  0x00000000
```

Not only did Telnet use Ethernet_II frames at the Data Link layer, it also used IP at the Network layer and TCP at the Transport layer. It goes all the way up to the Application layer. Thus, if you can telnet, you know that you have solid TCP/IP communication between two hosts.

`ping` (Packet Internet Groper)

If you can't telnet in to a host, or if you want to test physical network connectivity between two or more hosts, using Packet Internet Groper (`ping`) is a great choice. Try using the `ping` command, making sure to remember the type of output you receive.

```
RouterC#ping 172.16.10.1
Type escape sequence to abort.
Sending 5, 100-byte ICMP Echos to 172.16.10.1, timeout
is 2 seconds:
.!!!!
Success rate is 80 percent (5/5), round-trip min/avg/
max = 64/65/68 ms
RouterC#
```

Table 4.5 explains some of the `ping` responses you might see.

TABLE 4.5: `ping` Responses

ping Response	Meaning
!	Successful receipt of an echo reply
.	Time-out

TABLE 4.5: ping Responses *(cont.)*

ping Response	Meaning
U	Destination unreachable
C	Congested experience packet
I	Ping interrupted
?	Packet type unknown
&	Packet time-to-live exceeded

trace (Trace Route)

The trace command can be used to discover routes to remote destinations. The following examples show how to use the trace command. Practice using this command yourself and remember to look carefully at the output.

```
RouterA#trace ?
  WORD        Trace route to destination address or
hostname
  appletalk  AppleTalk Trace
  clns        ISO CLNS Trace
  ip          IP Trace
  oldvines   Vines Trace (Cisco)
  vines       Vines Trace (Banyan)
  <cr>

RouterA#trace ip ?
  WORD  Trace route to destination address or hostname
  <cr>

RouterA#trace ip 172.16.40.2

Type escape sequence to abort.
Tracing the route to 172.16.40.2
```

```
  1 172.16.20.2 24 msec 24 msec 28 msec
  2 172.16.40.2 44 msec 44 msec *
RouterA#
```

When `trace` reaches the target destination, an asterisk (*) is reported in the display. In response to the probe packet, it's typically reported because of a port-unreachable packet plus the time-out.

Some other responses are given in Table 4.6.

TABLE 4.6: trace Responses

trace Response	Meaning
!H	The router received the probe but didn't forward it because of an access list.
P	The protocol was unreachable.
N	The network was unreachable.
U	The port was unreachable.
*	There was a time-out.

Exam Essentials

For the CCNA exam, you need to remember the tools used to test connectivity and verify IP addresses, as well as the output each one returns.

Remember the tools to test for IP connectivity on your Cisco network. Telnet, `ping`, and `trace` can be used to test for IP connectivity.

Remember the output each command gives you. By practicing on a Cisco router, you can see the output each command displays. It is important to remember the different kinds of output for each.

Key Terms and Concepts

`ping`: An acronym for Packet Internet Groper, `ping` is used to test connectivity between IP hosts.

Telnet: Terminal emulation program used to create a virtual window to a remote device.

`trace`: Also called Trace Route, `trace` is used to find the route a packet travels through an internetwork to a remote node.

Sample Questions

1. Which of the following commands or programs can be used to test IP connectivity?

   A. Telnet

   B. ARP

   C. `ping`

   D. `trace`

   Answer: A, C, D. Telnet, `ping`, and `trace` are used in IP networks to test for connectivity.

2. Which command uses all the layers of the OSI layer to run?

   A. `ping`

   B. ARP

   C. Telnet

   D. `trace`

   Answer: C. If you can telnet to a node on the network, you must have good IP connectivity. Telnet uses the specifications of all layers of the OSI model. Therefore, if you can telnet you should be able to pass data. However, this is not always the case, as Telnet only checks for IP connectivity. For example, if you are using NT, it is possible that you could telnet to a device but still not communicate between applications because of a name-resolution problem.

3. Which of the following commands or programs will show output such as the following?

```
1 172.16.20.2 24 msec 24 msec 28 msec
2 172.16.40.2 44 msec 44 msec *
```

A. `ping`

B. Telnet

C. ARP

D. `trace`

Answer: D. `trace` uses TTL time-outs to find the route to a destination host. Each time the TTL hits a router or hop, it sends back an ICMP message.

List the required IPX address and encapsulation type

Encapsulation, or framing, is the process of taking packets from upper-layer protocols and building frames to transmit across the network. As you probably recall, frames live at the Data Link layer of the OSI model. When you're dealing with IPX, encapsulation is the specific process of taking IPX datagrams (used in the Network layer) and building frames (used in the Data Link layer) for one of the supported media.

Whether you are building a NetWare network with Cisco routers or just studying for the exam, you must pay careful attention to this exam objective and the one that follows. These sections cover the encapsulation methods and keywords used by Cisco routers and NetWare servers. If you do not use the correct keyword when setting your router's interface encapsulation, your routers and servers will not communicate.

Critical Information

NetWare supports multiple, incompatible framing methods, and it does so on the same media. When you use Ethernet, NetWare gives you four different frame types to choose from depending on your needs, and each one of those frame types is incompatible with the other ones. When you configure any IPX device (including a router) on a network, the frame type has to be consistent for things to work.

Before you configure a router, you'll need to know both the frame type and the IPX network address information for each segment that you plan to attach that router to. To find this information, go to one of the NetWare servers and type `config` at the server console. This will show your network numbers and frame types. Table 4.6 shows the different Ethernet frame types and the Cisco keyword for each. It would be a really good idea to memorize these.

TABLE 4.7: Novell IPX Frame Types

Interface Type	Novell Frame Type	Cisco Keyword
Ethernet	Ethernet_802.3	novell-ether (default)
	Ethernet_802.2	sap
	Ethernet_II	arpa
	Ethernet_snap	snap
Token Ring	Token-Ring	sap (default)
	Token-Ring_snap	snap
FDDI	Fddi_snap	snap (default)
	Fddi_802.2	sap
	Fddi_raw	novell-fddi

You'll need the IPX network address and frame type information from the config screen of your NetWare servers when specifying the encapsulation type on the router. Make sure to use the Cisco keyword, *not* the Novell frame type.

NOTE In the next section, "Enable the Novell IPX protocol and configure interfaces," you will learn how to configure the different encapsulation methods on a Cisco router.

Exam Essentials

It is essential that you memorize the Cisco keywords (encapsulations) when studying for the CCNA exam.

Remember the encapsulation methods used on an Ethernet LAN. Studying and practicing on a Cisco router will help you remember the different keywords Cisco uses to set an encapsulation method used on an interface.

Key Terms and Concepts

Encapsulation: A method to encase data in a digital format to be transmitted and understood on a network medium like Token Ring, Ethernet, FDDI, and WAN links.

FDDI: FDDI, or Fiber Distributed Data Interface, is a 100Mbps fiber ring LAN network.

Token Ring: Originally created by IBM, Token Ring defines a token-passing media access method that describes a method for nodes transmitting on a star physical medium.

Sample Questions

1. Which encapsulation method would you use on a Cisco router interface to configure 802.3?

   A. ARPA

   B. Ethernet II

   C. SAP

   D. Novell-ether

   Answer: D. You must remember the Cisco encapsulation methods used on an Ethernet network. 802.3 is the default encapsulation, and Cisco calls it *Novell-ether.*

2. Which encapsulation method would you use on a Cisco router interface to configure 802.2?

   A. ARPA

   B. SNAP

   C. SAP

   D. Novell-ether

   Answer: C. SAP encapsulation used on Cisco routers is referred to as 802.2.

3. Which encapsulation method would you use on a Cisco router interface to configure Ethernet II?

   A. SNAP

   B. ARPA

   C. Ethernet II

   D. SAP

   Answer: B. To encapsulate the Ethernet II frame type on a Cisco router interface, use the ARPA keyword.

Enable the Novell IPX protocol and configure interfaces

This topic brings us right where we left off in the last section. You will now learn how to configure a Cisco router with IPX routing, set IPX network numbers, and use various encapsulation methods on router interfaces.

If you have a network admin job—or if you are reading this book because you want to pass the CCNA test and get such a position—chances are you will need to know IPX. Novell still has a large install base of servers, and they will not be going away anytime soon. To successfully configure Cisco routers and pass the CCNA exam, you need to know how to enable IPX routing and set the network numbers and encapsulation methods on Cisco router interfaces.

Critical Information

This section discusses the commands used to enable IPX on Cisco routers.

Enabling IPX Routing

To enable IPX, use the `ipx routing` command when you are in global configuration mode. As the command name implies, it enables IPX routing on the router. You will not be able to configure IPX on any interface until IPX routing is enabled.

Enabling IPX on Individual Interfaces

Once you have IPX routing enabled on the router, the next step is to enable IPX on individual interfaces. To enable IPX on an interface, first enter the interface configuration mode and then issue a command with the following syntax:

```
ipx network number [encapsulation encapsulation-type]
[secondary]
```

The various parts are defined as follows:

- *Number* is the IPX network address.
- Encapsulation *encapsulation-type* is optional.
- *Secondary* is used to indicate a secondary encapsulation (frame type) and network address on the same interface.

Adding Secondary Addresses

There are two methods for adding additional frame types to an interface. The first is to use the `secondary` option; the second way is to use subinterfaces.

If you wanted to add a second IPX network to your router interface, you can use the `secondary` command at the end of an `ipx network number` command. If you do not use the `secondary` command, the first IPX network number will be overwritten. Here is a sample command:

```
config t
int e0
ipx network abcd1234 encapsulation arpa secondary
```

Subinterfaces allow administrators to create virtual interfaces on a Cisco router and are the new way to run secondary IP, IPX, and other addresses on the same interface. To define subinterfaces, use the `interface` *`[ethernet slot/port number]`* command. For the interface, you can use any number between e0.0 and e0.4292967295—that's a lot of subinterfaces!

Parallel Interface Configuration

If you set up parallel IPX paths between routers, by default the Cisco IOS will not learn about these paths. The router will learn a single path to a destination and discard information about alternative, parallel, equal-cost paths. You need to add a command such as `ipx maximum-paths 2` (with the variable set at any number up to 64), which will allow the router to accept the possibility that there might be more than one path to the same destination.

The Cisco IOS will perform per-packet load-sharing by default over these parallel lines. Packets will be sent on a round-robin basis between all equal-cost lines, without regard to the destination. However, if you want to ensure that all packets sent to a destination or host will always go over the same line, use the `IPX per-host-load-share` command.

Necessary Procedures

Let's start by enabling IPX routing on a router. We will then demonstrate how to verify that IPX is set, using the `show protocol` command.

Enabling IPX Routing

```
RouterA#config t
RouterA(config)#ipx routing
RouterA(config)#^Z
RouterA#sh prot
Global values:
  Internet Protocol routing is enabled
  IPX routing is enabled
Ethernet0 is up, line protocol is up
  Internet address is 172.16.10.1/24
Serial0 is up, line protocol is up
  Internet address is 172.16.20.1/24
Serial1 is administratively down, line protocol is down
RouterA#
```

Once IPX routing is running, you need to add network numbers to the interfaces on which you want to run IPX networking.

Configuring IPX Interfaces

Notice in the above output that IPX routing is enabled, but that the interfaces do not have an IPX address assigned. To configure IPX on the router's interfaces, use the `ipx network` command.

```
RouterA#config t
RouterA(config)#int e0
```

```
RouterA(config-if)#ipx network 2100 encapsulation ?
  arpa          IPX Ethernet_II
  hdlc          HDLC on serial links
  novell-ether IPX Ethernet_802.3
  novell-fddi   IPX FDDI RAW
  sap           IEEE 802.2 on Ethernet, FDDI, Token Ring
  snap          IEEE 802.2 SNAP on Ethernet, Token Ring, FDDI
RouterA(config-if) ipx network 2100 encapsulation arpa
RouterA(config-if)#int s0
RouterA(config-if)#ipx network 2200
RouterA(config-if)#^Z
RouterA#
```

In the example above, we chose ARPA as the encapsulation method for Ethernet 0. This is the Cisco keyword for Ethernet II. The serial 0 interface uses HDLC encapsulation by default. You cannot add LAN encapsulation methods on a serial interface.

Creating Secondary Addressing

To add a second IPX network to the same interface, you can use the `secondary` (`sec`) command at the end of the `ipx network` command line, as demonstrated here:

```
RouterA#config t
RouterA(config)#int s0
RouterA(config-if)#ipx network 3200 encap hdlc sec
RouterA(config-if)#exit
RouterA#sh prot s0
Serial0 is up, line protocol is up
  Internet address is 172.16.20.1/24
  IPX address is 2200.0000.0c8d.5c9d (HDLC)
  IPX address is 3200.0000.0c8d.5c9d (HDLC)
```

The command `show protocol` shows both of the IPX network numbers assigned to serial 0.

The other way to configure a second IPX network in a Cisco router interface is to use the `subinterface` command, as shown in the example below. (Note that this output was cut for brevity.)

```
RouterA(config)#int e0.100
RouterA(config-subif)#ipx network 2300 encap sap
RouterA(config-subif)#^Z
RouterA#sh prot e0
Ethernet0 is up, line protocol is up
  Internet address is 172.16.10.1/24
  IPX address is 2100.0000.0c8d.5c9d
RouterA#sh prot e0.100
Ethernet0.100 is up, line protocol is up
  IPX address is 2300.0000.0c8d.5c9d
RouterA#sh run
Building configuration...

Current configuration:
!
version 11.2
no service password-encryption
service udp-small-servers
service tcp-small-servers
!
hostname RouterA
!
enable secret 5 $1$iEbq$4zS1yXIkb3HxJNQVlWC39/
enable password simple1
!
ipx routing 0000.0c8d.5c9d
!
interface Ethernet0
 ip address 172.16.10.1 255.255.255.0
 ipx network 2100
!
interface Ethernet0.100
 arp timeout 0
 ipx network 2300 encapsulation SAP
!
interface Serial0
 ip address 172.16.20.1 255.255.255.0
 bandwidth 56
```

Notice that this output indicates that there are two Ethernet ports instead of one. You can define a limitless number of subinterfaces on a given physical interface—but keep memory limitations in mind when doing this.

Configuring a Parallel Interface

To configure a router to have more than one IPX link to the same location, use the `ipx maximum-paths` command.

```
RouterA#config t
RouterA(config)#ipx maximum-paths 2
```

Exam Essentials

To pass the CCNA exam, you must understand IPX routing with Cisco.

Know the encapsulation methods used on a Cisco router Ethernet LAN interface. Study the different encapsulation methods used in Cisco routers.

Remember how to configure a Cisco router to route IPX. To configure a Cisco router to route IPX, you must first enable IPX routing with the `ipx routing` command. Then you need to configure each interface used in the IPX network with a network number and encapsulation method.

Key Terms and Concepts

Encapsulation: A method to encase data in a digital format to be transmitted and understood on a network medium like Token Ring, Ethernet, FDDI, and WAN links.

IP (Internet Protocol): A protocol specified at the Internet layer of the Department of Defense (DOD) model. IP is used to route packets through an internetwork and for network addressing.

IPX (Internetworking Packet Exchange): A protocol stack developed by Xerox and originally called XNS. Novell copied the protocol and called it IPX. It is used for routing packets through an internetwork and for network addressing.

Network Number: A number assigned to a router interface or server to describe the network segment the interface or server is associated with.

Routing: The process of sending packets, or datagrams, through an internetwork.

Sample Questions

1. Which two of the following will allow you to add a second IPX network number to a Cisco router interface?

   A. ARPA

   B. Secondary addresses

   C. Subaddresses

   D. Subinterfaces

   Answer: B, D. You can use the `secondary` command or create a subinterface to put more than one network number on the same Cisco router interface. Remember that each number must be a different frame type and that the numbers must match the numbers set on the Novell servers.

2. Which of the following statements is true?

   A. Because subnets are logical entities of a physical interface, any interface-configured parameters that you specify on an individual subinterface are applied to all subnets for a given interface.

   B. You can only apply subinterfaces with IPX network numbers to serial interfaces.

   C. You can configure an IPX network number on any Cisco router interface, as long as all different networks configured on the same physical LAN use the same encapsulation.

D. You can configure an IPX network number on any Cisco router interface, as long as all different networks configured on the same physical LAN use distinct encapsulation.

Answer: D. Remember that each IPX network number set on a Cisco router interface must be of a different frame type and that the IPX network numbers must match the numbers set on the Novell servers.

3. Which of the following statements is true?

A. Subinterfaces are logical entities of a physical interface, and any interface-configured parameters that you specify on an individual subinterface are applied to all subnets for a given interface.

B. Subinterfaces are logical entities of a physical interface, and any interface-configured parameters that you specify on an individual subinterface only apply to that subinterface.

C. You can configure an IPX network on any Cisco router interface, as long as all networks configured on the same physical LAN use the same encapsulation.

D. You can only apply subinterfaces with IPX network numbers to serial interfaces.

Answer: B. The advantage of creating a subinterface, rather than a secondary interface, is that you can create logical interfaces and make configuration changes only to that subinterface instead of the complete interface.

4. If you have more than one link between routers and you want to run a round-robin data flow, what command should you add to your Cisco routers?

A. `ipx round-robin`

B. `ipx maximum-paths`

C. `maximum-ipx paths`

D. `ipx igrp-paths`

Answer: B. The `ipx maximum-paths` command allows up to 64 links to the same location by using IPX routing and round-robin delivery of datagrams.

Identify the functions of the TCP/IP transport-layer protocols

This section covers the protocols found at the Host-to-Host layer of the DOD (Department of Defense) model. Even though the CCNA exam does not test your knowledge of how the OSI model correlates to the DOD model, you still must understand how the protocols in the DOD model work with the specifications of the OSI reference model.

Understanding the IP protocols is important regardless of the type of internetwork you are building or working in. To successfully create and troubleshoot a network or internetwork, you must have a fundamental understanding of how the IP protocol stack works. Cisco really wants you to know the specifications of each protocol, and the CCNA exam reflects the importance they assign to this topic.

Critical Information

The TCP/IP protocol stack refers to the Transport layer (from the OSI model) as the Host-to-Host layer (from the DOD model). This layer's main purpose is to shield the upper-layer applications from the complexities of the network. This layer says to the upper layer, "Just give me your data, with any instructions, and I'll begin the process of getting your information ready for sending." The following sections describe the two main protocols at this layer.

TCP (Transmission Control Protocol)

TCP takes large blocks of information from an application and breaks them down into segments. It numbers and sequences each segment so that the destination's TCP can put the segments back in the order that the sending application intended. After these segments have been sent, TCP waits for acknowledgment for each one from the receiving end's TCP, retransmitting the ones that haven't been acknowledged.

Before it starts to send segments down the model to the Network layer, the sender's TCP contacts the destination's TCP in order to establish a connection. What is created is known as a *virtual circuit.* This type of communication is called *connection-oriented.* During this initial handshake, the two TCP layers also agree on the amount of information that's going to be sent before the recipient's TCP sends back an acknowledgment. With everything agreed upon in advance, the path is paved for reliable Application-layer communication to take place.

TCP is a full-duplex, connection-oriented, reliable, accurate protocol, and establishing all these terms and conditions, in addition to checking for errors, is no small task. It's very complicated and, not surprisingly, very costly in terms of network overhead. Using TCP should be reserved for use only in situations when reliability is of utmost importance. This is because today's networks are much more reliable than those of yore, so the added reliability is often unnecessary.

TIP It would be a good idea to read more about the protocol TCP in the *CCNA Study Guide* published by Sybex.

UDP (User Datagram Protocol)

This protocol can be used in place of TCP. It doesn't offer all the bells and whistles of TCP, but it does do a fabulous job of transporting information that doesn't require reliable delivery—and it does it using far fewer network resources.

There are some situations in which it would definitely be wise to opt for UDP rather than TCP. Remember the watchdog SNMP up there at the Process/Application layer? SNMP monitors the network and sends intermittent messages and a fairly steady flow of status updates and alerts, especially when running on a large network. The overhead needed to establish, maintain, and close a TCP connection for each one of those little messages could reduce what would be an otherwise healthy, efficient network to a dammed-up bog in no time.

UDP receives upper-layer blocks of information (instead of streams of data) and breaks them into segments, as TCP does. Also like TCP, each segment is given a number for reassembly into the intended block at the destination. However, UDP does *not* sequence the segments and does not care in which order the segments arrive at the destination. After numbering the blocks, UDP sends them off and forgets about them. It doesn't follow through, check up on, or even allow for an acknowledgment of safe arrival. Because of this, it's referred to as an *unreliable* protocol. This does not mean that UDP is ineffective, only that it doesn't offer as much reliability as some other protocols.

There are other things TCP does that UDP doesn't do. UDP doesn't create a virtual circuit, and it doesn't contact the destination before delivering information to it. It is therefore considered a connectionless protocol.

Key Concepts of Host-to-Host Protocols

The following list highlights some of the key concepts that you should keep in mind regarding the two protocols just discussed.

TCP	UDP
Reliable	Unreliable
Sequenced	Unsequenced
Connection-oriented	Connectionless
Virtual circuit, acknowledgments	Low overhead

Exam Essentials

The CCNA exam covers the protocols used at each layer of the DOD model.

Remember the specifications of each protocol. You should know that TCP is a connection-oriented protocol and UDP is a connectionless protocol, for example.

Key Terms and Concepts

Connection-Oriented: A term usually used to refer to a connection that uses a virtual circuit

Connectionless: A term typically applied to protocols that do not use a virtual circuit or acknowledgments

TCP (Transmission Control Protocol): A connection-oriented protocol specified at the Host-to-Host layer of the DOD model

UDP (User Datagram Protocol): A connectionless protocol defined at the Host-to-Host layer of the DOD model

Sample Questions

1. Which of these terms match the description given here?

   A. TCP: connectionless

   B. UDP: connection-oriented

   C. TCP: uses windowing

   D. UDP: uses acknowledgments

   Answer: C. TCP is a connection-oriented protocol and UDP is a connectionless protocol. Both reside at the Transport layer. Windowing is used in a connection-oriented session for setting flow-control parameters.

2. Which of these descriptions is correct?

   A. TCP: connection-oriented

   B. UDP: datagram filtering

   C. TCP: datagram acknowledgment

   D. UDP: connection-oriented

   Answer: A. TCP is a connection-oriented protocol and UDP is a connectionless protocol. Both reside at the Transport layer.

3. Which protocol at the Transport layer uses flow control?

A. TCP

B. IP

C. ARP

D. UDP

Answer: A. TCP and UDP both reside at the Transport layer. TCP uses flow control, which helps prevent a receiving device from overflowing its buffers.

Identify the functions of the TCP/IP network-layer protocols

This section covers the protocols defined at the Internet layer of the DOD (Department of Defense) model. As with the last objective, the CCNA exam does not test your knowledge of how the OSI model correlates to the DOD model, but you must understand how the protocols in the DOD model work with the specifications of the OSI reference model.

Understanding the IP protocols is important regardless of the type of internetwork you are building or working in. To successfully create and troubleshoot a network or internetwork, you must have a fundamental understanding of how the IP protocol stack works. Cisco really wants you to know the specifications of each protocol.

Critical Information

There are two main reasons for the Internet layer's existence: routing and network addressing. None of the upper-layer protocols nor the lower-layer protocols perform any functions relating to routing. The complex and important task of routing is the job of the Internet layer.

IP (Internet Protocol) essentially *is* the Internet (Network) layer. The second job of IP is to address network devices with software, using logical addressing called an *IP address*.

Internet Protocol looks at each packet received and checks its IP address. Then, using a routing table, it decides where a packet is to be sent next, choosing the best path.

The following sections describe the protocols at the Internet layer.

IP (Internet Protocol)

Identifying devices on networks requires answering these two questions: Which network is it on, and what is its ID on that network? The first answer is the *software,* or *logical* address (analogous to the correct street in a postal address). The second answer is the *hardware* address (the correct mailbox). All hosts on a network have a logical ID called an IP address. This is the software, or logical, address.

IP receives segments from the Host-to-Host (Transport) layer and fragments them into datagrams (packets). IP can also segment datagrams and reassemble them back into segments on the receiving side. Each datagram is assigned the IP address of the sender and the IP address of the recipient. Each router that receives a datagram makes routing decisions based upon the packet's destination IP address.

ARP (Address Resolution Protocol)

When IP has a datagram to send, it will have already been informed by upper-layer protocols of the destination's IP address. However, IP must also inform a network access protocol, such as Ethernet or Token Ring, of the destination's hardware address. If IP doesn't know the hardware address, it uses ARP (Address Resolution Protocol) to find this information. As IP's detective, ARP interrogates the network by sending out a broadcast asking the machine with the specified IP address to reply with its hardware address. In other words, ARP translates the software (IP) address into a hardware address—for example, the destination machine's Ethernet board address—and from that, it deduces the machine's whereabouts. This hardware address is technically referred to as the media access control (MAC) address, or physical address.

RARP (Reverse Address Resolution Protocol)

When an IP machine happens to be a diskless machine, it has no way of initially knowing its IP address, but it does know its MAC address. The Reverse Address Resolution Protocol (RARP) discovers the identity of these machines by sending out a packet that includes its MAC address and a request to be informed of what IP address is assigned to that MAC address. A designated machine called a *RARP server* responds with the answer, and the identity crisis is over. RARP uses the information it does know about the machine's MAC address to learn its IP address and complete the machine's ID portrait.

BootP

BootP stands for Boot Program. When a diskless workstation is powered on, it broadcasts a BootP request on the network. A BootP server hears the request and looks up the client's MAC address in its BootP file. If it finds an appropriate entry, it responds by telling the machine its IP address and the file—usually via the TFTP protocol—that it should boot from.

BootP is used by a diskless machine to learn the following:

- Its IP address
- The IP address of a server machine
- The name of a file that is to be loaded into memory and executed at boot up

DHCP (Dynamic Host Configuration Protocol) still uses BootP, but administrators no longer have to create a table of MAC-to-IP addresses; DHCP does that for us now.

ICMP

Internet Control Message Protocol (ICMP) is a Network-layer protocol that is used to send messages between routers. ICMP is covered in detail in the next section of this chapter.

Exam Essentials

The CCNA exam covers the protocols used in the DOD stack at the Network layer of the OSI model or at the Internet layer of the DOD model.

Know all the protocols used and their functions. It is important to remember the protocols used at the Network layer and what each one does.

Key Terms and Concepts

ARP (Address Resolution Protocol): ARP is described at the Internet layer of the DOD model and is used to find a hardware address, given the IP address.

BootP: Boot Program, or BootP, is described at the Internet layer of the DOD model and is used for giving diskless workstations an IP address.

IP (Internet Protocol): A connectionless protocol described at the Internet layer of the DOD model.

RARP (Reverse Address Resolution Protocol): Described at the Internet layer of the DOD model, RARP is used to find a IP address, given the hardware address.

Sample Questions

1. Which of the following protocols use a connection-oriented service at the Network layer?

   A. TCP

   B. IP

   C. ARP

   D. BootP

E. None of the above

Answer: E. The Internet Protocol (IP) stack has no protocols that use a connection-oriented service at the Network (Internet) layer.

2. Which protocol at the Network layer is used for addressing of hosts and routing?

   A. TCP

   B. IP

   C. ARP

   D. RARP

   Answer: B. IP is defined at the Network (Internet) layer and is used for routing and addressing of hosts.

3. Which protocol finds an IP address, given a hardware address?

   A. IP

   B. ARP

   C. TCP

   D. RARP

   Answer: D. Reverse Address Resolution Protocol (RARP) is used to find an IP address, given the MAC (or hardware) address.

4. Which protocol uses broadcasts to find the MAC address of a device, knowing its IP address?

   A. IP

   B. ARP

   C. BootP

   D. RARP

   Answer: B. Address Resolution Protocol (ARP) is used to find an IP address, given the MAC (or hardware) address.

Identify the functions performed by ICMP

Internet Control Message Protocol (ICMP) is one of the protocols used at the Internet layer of the DOD model. ICMP is important to Cisco because this protocol is used for many different things, mainly to send updates to routers about problems with network routes or packets that are undeliverable in the internetwork.

When studying for the CCNA exam, be sure to remember what the protocol ICMP does when IP is configured with Cisco routers.

Critical Information

ICMP (Internet Control Message Protocol) is a management protocol and messaging service provider for IP. Its messages are carried as IP datagrams.

Periodically, router advertisements are announced over the network, reporting IP addresses for its network interfaces. Hosts listen for these network broadcasts to acquire route information. A router solicitation is a request for immediate advertisements and may be sent by a host when it starts up. The following are some common events and messages related to ICMP:

Destination Unreachable: If a router can't send an IP datagram any further, it uses ICMP to send a message back to the sender advising it of the situation. For example, if a router receives a packet destined for a network that the router doesn't know about, it will send an ICMP Destination Unreachable message back to the sending station.

Buffer Full: If a router's memory buffer for receiving incoming datagrams is full, it will use ICMP to send out this message.

Hops: Each IP datagram is allotted a certain number of routers that it may go through, called *hops*. If it reaches its limit of hops before arriving at its destination, the last router to receive that datagram deletes it. The executioner router then uses ICMP to send an obituary message, informing the sending machine of the demise of its datagram.

ping: Packet Internet Groper (`ping`) uses ICMP echo messages to check the physical connectivity of machines on an internetwork.

trace: Trace Route (`trace`) uses ICMP and TTL (Time to Live) time-outs to find a packet's destination through an internetwork.

The following output is from a network analyzer catching an ICMP echo request. Notice that even though ICMP works at the Network layer, it still uses IP to do the `ping` request. The type field in the IP header is 0x01h for the ICMP protocol.

```
  Flags:         0x00
  Status:        0x00
  Packet Length:78
  Timestamp:     14:04:25.967000 05/06/1998
Ethernet Header
  Destination:   00:a0:24:6e:0f:a8
  Source:        00:80:c7:a8:f0:3d
  Protocol Type:08-00  IP
IP Header - Internet Protocol Datagram
  Version:               4
  Header Length:         5
  Precedence:            0
  Type of Service:       %000
  Unused:                %00
  Total Length:          60
  Identifier:            56325
  Fragmentation Flags:   %000
  Fragment Offset:       0
  Time To Live:          32
  IP Type:               0x01 ICMP
  Header Checksum:       0x2df0
  Source IP Address:     100.100.100.2
  Dest. IP Address:      100.100.100.1
```

```
    No Internet Datagram Options
  ICMP - Internet Control Messages Protocol
    ICMP Type:               8  Echo Request
    Code:                    0
    Checksum:                0x395c
    Identifier:              0x0300
    Sequence Number:         4352
    ICMP Data Area:
    abcdefghijklmnop    61 62 63 64 65 66 67 68 69 6a 6b
  6c 6d 6e 6f 70
    qrstuvwabcdefghi    71 72 73 74 75 76 77 61 62 63 64
  65 66 67 68 69
  Frame Check Sequence:  0x00000000
```

Exam Essentials

The CCNA test covers all the protocols at the Network (Internet) layer.

Remember what ICMP can do. ICMP sends "destination unreachable" and "buffer full" messages. ICMP can find the number of hops to a destination host.

Remember which programs use ICMP. Packet Internet Groper (`ping`) uses ICMP echo messages to check the physical connectivity of machines on an internetwork. Trace Route (`trace`) uses ICMP and TTL (Time to Live) time-outs to find a packet's destination through an internetwork.

Key Terms and Concepts

ICMP (Internet Control Message Protocol): Described at the Internet layer of the DOD model, ICMP is used for testing, verification, and notification services.

Sample Questions

1. Which protocol is used to send "destination unreachable" messages to other routers?

   A. IP

   B. RARP

   C. BootP

   D. ICMP

   Answer: D. ICMP sends "destination unreachable" messages to neighboring routers if a problem occurs and packets can't be sent to a remote destination.

2. Which of these use ICMP to test network connectivity? (Choose all that apply.)

   A. Telnet

   B. `trace`

   C. `ping`

   D. ARP

   Answer: B, C. Both `ping` and `trace` use ICMP messages.

3. Which of these does ICMP help accomplish? (Choose all that apply.)

   A. "Destination unreachable" messages

   B. "Buffer full" messages

   C. Hops

   D. `ping`

   E. ARP

   F. `trace`

   Answer: A, B, C, D, F. ICMP is an important protocol at the Network (Internet) layer. It is used to send "destination unreachable" messages, to find the distance to a network (`trace`), and to send "buffer full" messages, echo requests, and replies.

Configure IPX access lists and SAP filters to control basic Novell traffic

This section covers the IPX access list commands featured in the CCNA exam. It is important that you pay close attention to the fine details of the output that a command provides.

Be aware that this text focuses on how your IPX access list knowledge is tested on the Cisco CCNA exam. We assume that you have a basic understanding of Cisco routers with access lists and we are only supplying the information needed to pass the exam.

NOTE To get a full understanding of access lists used with Cisco routers, read Chapter 10 of the Sybex *CCNA Study Guide.*

Critical Information

In this section you will learn how IPX access lists are used to control IPX traffic. We will cover standard IPX access lists, extended IPX access lists, and IPX SAP filters.

You should have a basic understanding of how access lists are created and how they are applied to an interface.

Standard IPX Access Lists

Standard IPX access lists allow or deny packets based on source and destination IPX addresses. With standard IP access lists, you can only use a source IP address. The syntax for each line of an IPX standard access list is as follows:

```
access-list [number] [permit or deny] [source] [destination]
```

The second argument is a list number. This tells the router what type of access list is being used. Below is an example of the types of access lists that can be used. Notice that standard IPX access lists use any number from 800 to 899.

```
RouterA(config)#access-list ?
  <1-99>        IP standard access list
  <100-199>     IP extended access list
  <1000-1099>   IPX SAP access list
  <1100-1199>   Extended 48-bit MAC address access list
  <1200-1299>   IPX summary address access list
  <200-299>     Protocol type-code access list
  <300-399>     DECnet access list
  <600-699>     Appletalk access list
  <700-799>     48-bit MAC address access list
  <800-899>     IPX standard access list
  <900-999>     IPX extended access list
```

Extended IPX Access Lists

Standard IPX access lists only filter on source or destination access lists. Extended IPX access lists can filter based on any of the following:

- Source network/node
- Destination network/node
- IPX protocol (SAP, SPX, etc.)
- IPX socket

Extended access lists are in the range 900–999 and are configured just like standard access lists, with the addition of protocol and socket information. Here's a template for building lines in an IPX extended access list:

```
access-list [number] [permit or deny] [protocol]
[source] [socket] [destination] [socket]
```

When you move from standard into extended access lists, you're simply adding the ability to filter based on protocol, socket (or port, for IP), and destination node/network.

NOTE It is important to note that if you create an access list (regardless of protocol), the Cisco router will apply an explicit "deny any" at the end of the list. For example, if you apply a "deny" statement for IP and you do not add any type of "permit" statement, you will effectively shut down the interface to which you applied the list.

IPX SAP Filters

IPX SAP filters are implemented using the same tools discussed above. They have an important place in controlling IPX SAP traffic. Why is this important? Because if you can control the SAPs, you can control the access to IPX devices. Access lists in the 1000–1099 range are used to specify IPX SAP filters. Here's the template for each line of an IPX SAP filter:

```
access-list [number] [permit or deny] [source] [service type]
```

Applying an Access List to an Interface

After you build an access list, it won't do anything until you apply it to an interface. You do this with the `ipx access-group` command. Your only options are to choose whether the access list will filter on incoming or outgoing packets. Here is an example:

```
config t
int s0
ipx access-group 110 out
```

Necessary Procedures

Practice what you learned above by configuring your Cisco routers with the different IPX access lists.

IPX Standard Access List

This sample program sets up an IPX access list allowing IPX network 30 to access IPX network 10, but disallowing IPX network 50 from accessing the same network:

```
RouterA#config t
RouterA(config)#access-list 810 permit 30 10
RouterA(config)#access-list 810 deny 50 10
RouterA(config)#int e0
RouterA(config-if)#ipx access-group 810 out
RouterA(config-if)#^Z
RouterA#
```

Let's map these two lines against a template to see what's happening:

access list	number	permit or deny	source	destination
access-list	810	permit	30	10
access-list	810	deny	50	10

The number 810 corresponds to the range 800–899 that's reserved for IPX standard access lists. The permit/deny parameter is the same as it is with IP packets. Here the specified source and destination are based on IPX network addresses. No wildcard masking is required to specify an entire IPX network—just list the network address and you are done!

Just as with IP access lists, there's an implicit "deny any" at the end of the IPX access list. In this case, any networks other than 30 will be denied access to network 10. If you wanted to allow all IPX networks except 50, you could proceed as follows:

```
RouterA#config t
Enter configuration commands, one per line. End with CNTL/Z.
RouterA(config)#access-list 811 deny 50 10
RouterA(config)#access-list 811 permit -1 -1
RouterA(config)#int e0
RouterA(config-if)#ipx access-group 811 out
 RouterA(config-if)#^Z
RouterA#
```

Once again, let's put these two lines into our template to see what we have:

access list	number	permit or deny	source	destination
access-list	811	deny	50	10
access-list	811	permit	–1	–1

It's important to note here the use of the –1 network address, because in IPX access lists, the –1 network address refers to any IPX network address. It's just like using the *any* keyword when referring to network addresses in IP access lists to specify any IP network.

Extended IPX Access Lists

Use the online help to wade through the syntax of creating an extended IPX access list.

```
RouterA(config)#access-list?
  <1-99>       IP standard access list
  <100-199>    IP extended access list
  <1000-1099>  IPX SAP access list
  <1100-1199>  Extended 48-bit MAC address access list
  <1200-1299>  IPX summary address access list
  <200-299>    Protocol type-code access list
  <300-399>    DECnet access list
  <600-699>    Appletalk access list
  <700-799>    48-bit MAC address access list
  <800-899>    IPX standard access list
  <900-999>    IPX extended access list

RouterA(config)#access-list 910 ?
  deny    Specify packets to reject
  permit  Specify packets to permit

RouterA(config)#access-list 910 permit ?
 –1        Any IPX protocol type
  <0-255>  Protocol type number (DECIMAL)
  <cr>
```

```
RouterA(config)#access-list 910 permit -1 ?
  -1            Any IPX net
  <0-FFFFFFFF>  Source net
  N.H.H.H       Source net.host address
  <cr>

RouterA(config)#access-list 910 permit -1 -1 ?
  <0-FFFFFFFF>  Source Socket (0 for all sockets)
HEXIDECIMAL
  <cr>

RouterA(config)#access-list 910 permit -1 -1 0 ?
-1            Any IPX net
  <0-FFFFFFFF>  Destination net
  N.H.H.H       Destination net.host address
  <cr>
RouterA(config)#access-list 910 permit -1 -1 0 -1 ?
<0-FFFFFFFF>  Destination Socket (0 for all sockets)
HEXIDECIMAL
  <cr>

RouterA(config)#access-list 910 permit -1 -1 0 -1 0 log
```

The `log` command could be used to log any attempts from network 50 to access network 10 and record the following information:

- Source address
- Source socket
- Destination address
- Destination socket
- Protocol type

IPX SAP filters

Now practice creating an IPX SAP filter. Assume that on your Admin LAN network, you have three NetWare servers but you want only the one with internal IPX network address 11.0000.0000.0001 to be seen by the outside world. To accomplish that, you'd configure and apply an access list as follows:

```
RouterA#config t
RouterA(config)#access-list 1010 permit 11.0000.0000.0001 0
RouterA(config)#int e0
RouterA(config-if)#ipx input-sap-filter 1010
RouterA(config-if)#^Z
RouterA#
```

Here's how the one line in the above access list maps to the template:

access list	number	permit or deny	source	service type
access-list	1010	permit	11.0000.0000.0001	0

The number 1010 falls into the range 1000–1099, reserved for IPX SAP filters. The source network is the network/node address of the server. The resulting access list allows packets from 11.0000.0000.0001 to enter the Ethernet interface and be included in SAP updates across the network. As with other access lists, there's an implicit "deny any" that blocks all other SAP updates arriving at the router on the Ethernet interface. Finally, the 0 entered for service type indicates that all services should be allowed:

```
RouterA#config t
RouterA(config)#access-list 1010 permit 11.0000.0000.0001 ?
  <0-FFFF>  Service type-code (0 matches all services)
  N.H.H.H   Source net.host mask
  <cr>
```

Exam Essentials

The CCNA exam will include questions about access lists. Study the different types of IPX access lists.

Know the difference between the different IPX access lists. It is important to understand what each type of list can filter on.

Remember how to apply an IPX list to an interface. By using the `ipx access-group` command, you can apply access lists to an interface.

Key Terms and Concepts

Access List: Used in routers to filter packets either trying to enter an interface or leave an interface.

Extended Access List: A type of access list that can use source and destination logical addresses, port, socket, and protocol to filter a network.

Standard Access List: An access list in routers that can filter only by source or destination logical address. (IP can only filter by source address.)

Sample Questions

1. If you create the following IPX access list, what will happen?

```
access-list 873 permit 30 4d
int e0
  ipx network 4d
  ipx access-group 873 out
int e1
  ipx network 30
int e2
  ipx network 50
```

A. Interface e1 can send packets out e0.

B. Interface e0 can send packets out e1.

C. Interface e1 can send packets out e2

D. Network 50 can send packets out to network 4d.

Answer: A. The access list 873 is a standard IPX access list that can only filter on source and destination network/node. This list permits network 30 out network 4d. This is applied to an interface with the `ipx access-group` command. Remember that an explicit "deny any" is attached to the end of any list so that with this list, only network 30 will be allowed out network 4d; everything else is denied.

2. IPX extended access lists can filter based on which of the following?

   A. Source network

   B. Source node

   C. Destination node

   D. Socket

   E. Default gateway

   F. IP protocol

   G. SAP

   Answer: A, B, C, D, G. Extended lists can filter on more than just a source and destination address. They can use protocols and sockets to make a filtering decision.

3. Which of these commands are valid?

   A. `access-list 810 deny  -1 50 0 10 0`

   B. `access-list 910 deny  -1 50 0 10 0`

   C. `access-list 899 permit  -1 -1 0  -1 0`

   D. `access-list 999 permit  -1  -1 0  -1 0`

   Answer: B, D. The answers A and C are wrong, because they use the access list numbers 800–899, which are reserved for standard IPX access lists. These cannot filter on protocol and port like extended access lists, which use numbers 900–999.

CHAPTER 5

Routing

Cisco CCNA exam objectives covered in this chapter:

- **Add the RIP routing protocol to your configuration.** *(pages 223 – 230)*
- **Add the IGRP routing protocol to your configuration.** *(pages 231 – 238)*
- **Explain the services of separate and integrated multiprotocol routing.** *(pages 239 – 241)*
- **List problems that each routing type encounters when dealing with topology changes and describe techniques to reduce the number of these problems.** *(pages 241 – 247)*
- **Describe the benefits of network segmentation with routers.** *(pages 248 – 250)*

In this chapter you will learn how to run the dynamic routing protocols RIP and IGRP. Routing Information Protocol (RIP) is a distance vector routing algorithm that can send updates of its routing table to its neighbor routers. Interior Gateway Routing Protocol (IGRP) is also a dynamic routing protocol that can send updates of its routing table to its neighbor routers. We will demonstrate how to configure both protocols and explain what the difference is between the two.

This chapter also covers how both routing and routed protocols can run together on the same network as well as what causes routing loops and how to correct them.

Routers are used to create and name internetworks and send data between these internetworks. You will learn the benefits of using routers to segment your network. Since Cisco has designed a way for you to segment your network and create internetworks, they find these objectives important for you to understand. If you are working in a production network, you need to know why to segment your network and with what devices you can do that. This chapter will give you that knowledge.

Add the RIP routing protocol to your configuration.

In this section, you will learn about the RIP routing protocol, its features, and how it works in an internetwork.

It is important to be able to configure RIP on your Cisco routers, and it is also crucial to understand the theory behind RIP and the problems that RIP can cause in your internetwork. The CCNA exam covers only the RIP and IGRP routing protocols. It does not cover static or default routing.

Critical Information

Before we demonstrate how to add RIP to a router, you need a little background on the protocol.

RIP was invented a long time ago, when networks were smaller. RIP uses an algorithm called *distance vector.* This means that the router finds the best route to another network by determining how many hops (routers) it has to go through to get to the remote network. RIP has an upper hop count limit of 15; 16 hops is considered unreachable.

Take a look at Figure 5.1, and you'll see how this hop limit can be a problem when a network starts to grow.

In Figure 5.1, Router 1 is directly connected to Router 2 at 10Mbps, and Router 1 is connected to Router 3 through a 56K link. Router 2 is connected to Router 3 via a T3 (45Mbps). To get from Network 1 to Network 3, RIP would choose the route from Router 1 to Router 3 through Network 2. The better route (with a significantly higher bandwidth) would be to go from Router 1 to Router 2 (through Network 4) and then from Router 2 to Router 3 (through Network 5) to reach Network 3.

FIGURE 5.1: Distance vector networks

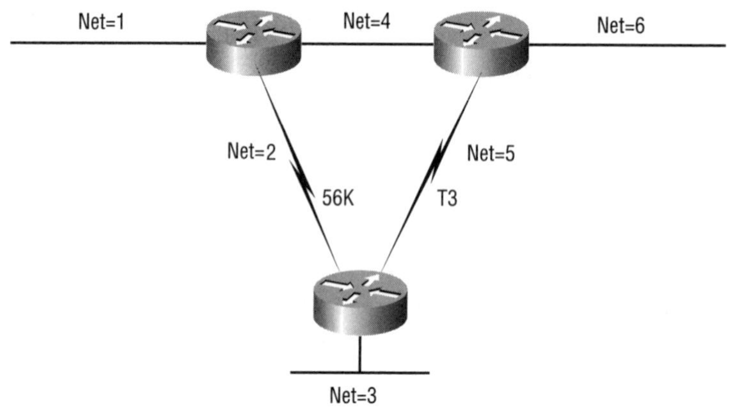

To configure your router to use RIP, use the global configuration command `router rip`. Next you need to tell the router which network numbers you want to advertise. Since you can have more than one network configured on your network, you have to add all networks that you want to participate in the RIP network. Use the `network` command, as shown in this example:

```
RouterA#config t
RouterA(config)#router rip
RouterA(config-router)#network 10.0.0.0
RouterA(config-router)#^Z
```

The global configuration command `router rip` tells your router that it will participate in an RIP network. However, this command does nothing if you don't tell the router which network you want to participate in. In this example, we used 10.0.0.0. This means that the router will broadcast all information it knows about Network 10 out all its interfaces every 30 seconds.

It is important to understand here that RIP only uses classful routing, which means you cannot enter subnets to broadcast, only a full address class. In other words, you can't just broadcast a little part of your network; RIP uses all or nothing. The routers will find their directly connected networks and tell their neighbors about them. The neighbors will put the data in their routing tables and then broadcast that information out to all their neighbors.

Necessary Procedures

Before we work through the steps for adding RIP to a router, let's take a look at a sample internetwork. Figure 5.2 shows an internetwork and the three routers it is using: A, B, and C.

FIGURE 5.2: An internetwork

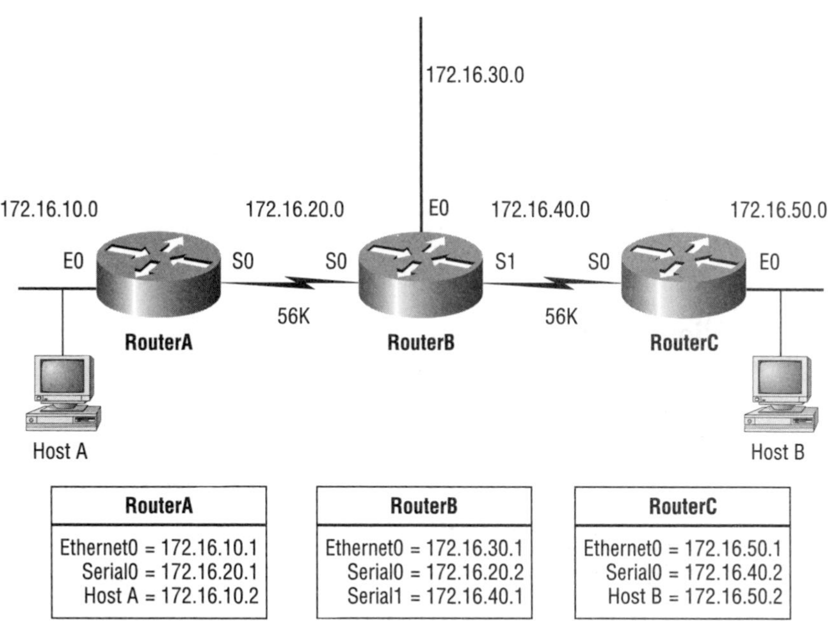

Adding RIP

The first example shows how to add the RIP protocol in RouterA and then tell the router what networks to advertise. Since there is only one network (172.16.0.0) in this example, that's the only entry to be set in the router. A RIP router will accept only major networks. For example, if a specific address such as 172.16.10.10 is entered, the router will accept it and discard the host portion, retaining only the major network information.

RouterA

```
RouterA#config t
RouterA(config)#router rip
RouterA(config-router)#network 172.16.0.0
RouterA(config-router)#^Z
RouterA#copy run star
Building configuration...
[OK]
```

Once the same thing is done for RouterB and RouterC, this little internetwork should be communicating. Remember, if the RIP commands are not added to routers B and C, this will not work.

SEE ALSO This section covered RIP very quickly. We highly recommend that you read Chapter 7 of the Sybex *CCNA Study Guide,* which covers dynamic routing protocols in more detail.

Viewing the Routing Table

After you've configured an internetwork to use RIP, as in the example above, you can test to see if it's working by taking a look at the routing tables. Notice the R in the routing tables below? That stands for RIP entries. This is an example of output you'd see for RouterA:

```
RouterA#sh ip route
Codes: C - connected, S - static, I - IGRP, R - RIP,
   M - mobile, B - BGP, D - EIGRP, EX - EIGRP external,
   O - OSPF, IA - OSPF inter area, E1 - OSPF external
   type 1, E2 - OSPF external type 2, E - EGP, i - IS-
   IS, L1 - IS-IS level-1,  L2 - IS-IS level-2, * -
   candidate default
Gateway of last resort is not set
   172.16.0.0 255.255.255.0 is subnetted, 5 subnets
R  172.16.50.0 [120/2] via 172.16.20.2, 00:00:12, Serial0
R  172.16.40.0 [120/1] via 172.16.20.2, 00:00:12, Serial0
R  172.16.30.0 [120/1] via 172.16.20.2, 00:00:12, Serial0
```

```
C  172.16.20.0 is directly connected, Serial0
C  172.16.10.0 is directly connected, Ethernet0
```

You can restrict the view to RIP networks that have been found by typing **sh ip route rip**. For RouterA, the command output would look like this:

```
RouterA#sh ip route rip
   172.16.0.0 255.255.255.0 is subnetted, 5 subnets
R  172.16.50.0 [120/2] via 172.16.20.2, 00:00:12, Serial0
R  172.16.40.0 [120/1] via 172.16.20.2, 00:00:12, Serial0
R  172.16.30.0 [120/1] via 172.16.20.2, 00:00:12, Serial0
```

Looks like RIP is enabled! This will work great for a small internetwork. Take a look at the Etherpeek trace to see the RIP updates in action, as shown in this example:

```
RIP - Routing Information Protocol
  Command: 2 Response containing network distance pairs
  Version: 1
  Zero:     0x0000
Info on Net # 1
  Network Number:    2
  Zero:              0x0000
  Net Address:       172.16.50.0
  Zero:              0x0000000000000000
  Distance:          3
Info on Net # 2
  Network Number:    2
  Zero:              0x0000
  Net Address:       172.16.40.0
  Zero:              0x0000000000000000
  Distance:          2
Info on Net # 3
  Network Number:    2
  Zero:              0x0000
  Net Address:       172.16.30.0
  Zero:              0x0000000000000000
  Distance:          2
```

```
Info on Net # 4
  Network Number:    2
  Zero:              0x0000
  Net Address:       172.16.20.0
  Zero:              0x0000000000000000
  Distance:          1
Frame Check Sequence:  0x00000000
```

RIP is sending a broadcast of its whole table. Notice that within the RIP packet, the only information about the subnet is the network address and the distance (hop count).

In addition to the command `show ip route`, there is one other command that will tell you if you are receiving routing updates from your neighbors, `debug ip rip`:

```
RouterA#debug ip rip
RIP protocol debugging is on
RouterA#
RIP: received update from 172.16.20.2 on Serial0
     172.16.50.0 in 2 hops
     172.16.40.0 in 1 hops
RIP: sending update to 255.255.255.255 via Ethernet0
(172.16.10.1)
     subnet 172.16.50.0, metric 3
     subnet 172.16.40.0, metric 2
     subnet 172.16.20.0, metric 1
RIP: sending update to 255.255.255.255 via Serial0
(172.16.20.1)
     subnet 172.16.10.0, metric 1
RIP: received update from 172.16.20.2 on Serial0
     172.16.50.0 in 2 hops
     172.16.40.0 in 1 hops
RIP: sending update to 255.255.255.255 via Ethernet0
(172.16.10.1)
     subnet 172.16.50.0, metric 3
     subnet 172.16.40.0, metric 2
     subnet 172.16.20.0, metric 1
RouterA#undebug ip rip
```

```
RIP protocol debugging is off
RouterA#
```

Notice that this output is different from what you'd see by using `show ip route`. The command `debug ip rip` returns real-time updates.

Exam Essentials

You must understand how RIP works and how to add it to your router, as well as what problems can occur when you use RIP networks and how to solve them. These problems and solutions are discussed in more detail later in this chapter.

Understand how RIP works in an internetwork. RIP uses hop counts to determine the best route to a network. It has an upper hop count limit of 15.

Go through the commands to add RIP to your router. To add the RIP routing protocol to your router, go into global configuration mode and type the command router rip. You then need to add the number(s) of the network(s) for which your router will advertise.

Know how to view the routing table. To view routing tables, you can use the commands `show ip route` or `sh ip route rip`.

Understand what the routing table shows. You must know how to read a routing table. Make sure you can find the hop count, destination network, and next hop router address.

Key Terms and Concepts

Distance Vector: A routing algorithm that typically uses hop counts to find the best path to a network. Some of the newer distance vector algorithms use other variables such as bandwidth, delay, and line speed. RIP only uses hop count.

Metric: The distance or weight of a link. This value can be used to find the best path to a remote network.

RIP: An acronym for Routing Information Protocol, RIP is a routing algorithm that uses the distance vector method of finding the best path to a network (hop count).

Sample Questions

1. What is the routing metric used by RIP?

   A. Distance link

   B. MTU

   C. Hop count

   D. BW

   Answer: C. RIP only uses hop count when determining the best route to a destination network.

2. What does a metric of 16 hops represent in an RIP network?

   A. The packet has passed through 16 routers.

   B. It is an RIP broadcast.

   C. The host is unreachable.

   D. The network is unreachable.

   Answer: D. Remember, routers know about networks, not hosts! Sixteen hops in an RIP network is considered unreachable.

3. Which commands can you use to see if your router is receiving RIP updates from other routers? (Choose two.)

   A. `sh ip rip`

   B. `sh ip route`

   C. `debug rip`

   D. `debug ip rip`

   Answer: B, D. The commands `show ip route` and `debug ip rip` will show whether you are receiving updates from neighbor routers.

Add the IGRP routing protocol to your configuration

In this section, we will demonstrate how to configure IGRP routing to your Cisco routers. We will start by talking about the Interior Gateway Routing Protocol and the differences between it and RIP.

IGRP is a Cisco proprietary routing protocol and is basically an upgrade to RIP. Cisco recommends using IGRP over the RIP protocol because of its features. It is important to understand the new features that Cisco has included with IGRP and how they differ from those of RIP.

Critical Information

The main benefit of using Interior IGRP rather than RIP is that it can handle larger networks. As discussed previously, RIP has an upper hop count limit of 15, and 16 hops is considered unreachable. IGRP's hop count limit is 255. Another benefit of IGRP is that it can handle multiple path connections. This means you can connect more than one path to the same network, and IGRP will do a round-robin of data flow between the links.

Configuring IGRP is not unlike configuring RIP. You use the `router igrp` command followed by the network number you want the router to advertise. But there is one major difference: Since you can have multiple networks running between routers, you have to enter the autonomous system number. All the routers that you want to exchange router information must use this same number. This allows you to advertise a small part of your network, not necessarily the whole network, as RIP requires.

For example, Figure 5.3 shows two sites connected with a WAN link. They won't update each other with routing information, because they're in different autonomous systems. (Location A is using AS 10 and Location B is using AS 20.) Location A and Location B would both have to use the same AS number in order to communicate and exchange route information.

FIGURE 5.3: Different AS networks won't communicate with different AS numbers configured.

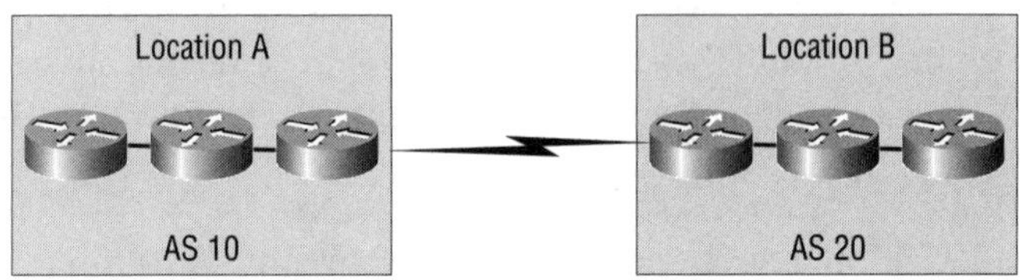

There is another major difference between RIP and IGRP. That difference is the way that IGRP finds routes to a remote network. As you know, RIP only uses hop count to find the best path, but IGRP can use other parameters. If you type in the router command **sh int s0** on an IGRP network, you'll see output that looks like this (this example was cut for brevity):

```
Router#sh int s0
Serial0 is up, line protocol is up
Hardware is HD64570
MTU 1500 bytes, BW 1544 Kbit, DLY 20000 usec, rely 255/
255, load 1/255
Encapsulation HDLC, loopback not set, keepalive set
(10 sec)
```

Notice the third line of output? All of those parameters are being taken into consideration when IGRP tries to find the best route to a destination network. `MTU` stands for Maximum Transmission Unit; `BW` is the bandwidth; `DLY` shows the delay in the link; `rely` represents the level of reliability; and `load` is the load on the link. Notice the bandwidth by default is a T1 line, or 1.544Mbps? If you are using IGRP or any routing algorithm that uses bandwidth as a parameter, you should change this with the `bandwidth` command, as shown here:

```
Router#config t
Enter configuration commands, one per line.  End with
CNTL/Z.
Router(config)#int s0
Router(config-if)#bandwidth ?
  <1-10000000>  Bandwidth in kilobits

Router(config-if)#bandwidth 56
```

This is important, because if you have two links to the same location—one a T1 and the other a 56K line—the router will think both links are a T1 and send equal amounts of packets down each link, unless you change the bandwidth setting on the appropriate link.

Necessary Procedures

The following examples show how we configured the three routers in our internetwork example with IGRP.

RouterA

```
RouterA#config t
 RouterA(config)#router igrp ?
  <1-65535>  Autonomous system number

RouterA(config)#router igrp 10
RouterA(config-router)#network 172.16.0.0
RouterA(config-router)#^Z
RouterA#wr mem
Building configuration...
[OK]
```

In this example, we chose IGRP and typed ?. The router asked for the autonomous system number. We entered **10**. You can choose any number between 1 and 65,655. (That can be a lot of networks!) We'll need to go through the same process at routers B and C or the network won't work.

WARNING It is extremely difficult to pass the CCNA exam without hands-on experience. We recommend running through the labs in Chapters 6 and 7 of the Sybex *CCNA Study Guide* repeatedly.

Viewing the Routing Tables

After configuring your internetwork for IGRP as shown above, you can take a look at the routing table on RouterA:

```
RouterA#sh ip route
Codes: C - connected, S - static, I - IGRP, R - RIP,
   M - mobile, B - BGP, D - EIGRP, EX - EIGRP external,
   O - OSPF, IA - OSPF inter area, E1 - OSPF external
   type 1, E2 - OSPF external type 2, E - EGP, i - IS-
   IS, L1 - IS-IS level-1,  L2 - IS-IS level-2, * -
   candidate default
Gateway of last resort is not set
   172.16.0.0 255.255.255.0 is subnetted, 5 subnets
I  172.16.50.0 [100/182671] via 172.16.20.2, 00:00:22,
Serial0
I  172.16.40.0 [100/182571] via 172.16.20.2, 00:00:22,
Serial0
I  172.16.30.0 [100/182571] via 172.16.20.2, 00:00:22,
Serial0
C  172.16.20.0 is directly connected, Serial0
C  172.16.10.0 is directly connected, Ethernet0
```

Notice the I in this sample output; that means IGRP routing entry. The following example shows some of the IGRP updates on an Etherpeek network analyzer:

```
IGRP - Inter-Gateway Routing Protocol
  Protocol Version:      1
  Op Code:               1  Update
  Edition:               2
  Autonomous Sys:        10
  Local Subnets:         4
  Networks Inside AS:    0
  Networks Outside AS:   0
```

```
  Checksum:                21456
 InteriorRouting Entry #1
    Net Number:                 16.50.0
    Delay (microseconds):       41000
    Bandwidth (Kbit/sec):       178571
    Max. Transmission Unit:     1500
    Reliability:                100%
    Load:                       0%
    Hop Count:                  2
 InteriorRouting Entry #2
    Net Number:                 16.40.0
    Delay (microseconds):       40000
    Bandwidth (Kbit/sec):       178571
    Max. Transmission Unit:     1500
    Reliability:                100%
    Load:                       0%
    Hop Count:                  1
 InteriorRouting Entry #3
    Net Number:                 16.30.0
    Delay (microseconds):       40000
    Bandwidth (Kbit/sec):       178571
    Max. Transmission Unit:     1500
    Reliability:                100%
    Load:                       0%
    Hop Count:                  1
 InteriorRouting Entry #4
    Net Number:                 16.20.0
    Delay (microseconds):       20000
    Bandwidth (Kbit/sec):       178571
    Max. Transmission Unit:     1500
    Reliability:                100%
    Load:                       0%
    Hop Count:                  0
 Frame Check Sequence:    0x00000000
```

There are some big differences between this IGRP packet and the RIP packet shown earlier in this section. Notice that the delay, bandwidth, reliability, and load features are not present in the RIP packets. These factors are all taken into consideration when a router is looking for the best route to a destination or if it's trying to do load balancing.

Also, remember that the IGRP packet is sent out every 90 seconds by default—a much better time period than the 30-second interval RIP uses.

There is one more command that is relevant here: `show ip protocol`.

```
Router#sh ip protocol
Routing Protocol is "rip"
Sending updates every 30 seconds, next due in 12 seconds
Invalid after 180 seconds, hold down 180, flushed after 240
Outgoing update filter list for all interfaces is not set
Incoming update filter list for all interfaces is not set
Redistributing: rip
Default version control: send version 1, receive any
version
  Routing for Networks:
    172.16.0.0
  Routing Information Sources:
    Gateway         Distance      Last Update
  Distance: (default is 120)

Routing Protocol is "igrp 10"
  Sending updates every 90 seconds, next due in 0 seconds
  Invalid after 270 seconds, hold down 280, flushed after 630
  Outgoing update filter list for all interfaces is not set
  Incoming update filter list for all interfaces is not set
  Default networks flagged in outgoing updates
  Default networks accepted from incoming updates
  IGRP metric weight K1=1, K2=0, K3=1, K4=0, K5=0
  IGRP maximum hopcount 100
  IGRP maximum metric variance 1
  Redistributing: igrp 10
  Routing for Networks:
    172.16.0.0
```

```
  Routing Information Sources:
    Gateway         Distance      Last Update
  Distance: (default is 100)

Router#
```

Notice that the `show ip protocol` command displays all the running routing protocols. It also shows the specific parameters for each protocol, their update times, and the AS number, if used.

Exam Essentials

The CCNA exam does not ask any direct questions regarding RIP or IGRP. However, there may be related questions that require your understanding of the subject.

Remember what an AS is. An autonomous system (AS) is a group of routers that share the same routing information.

Understand the difference between RIP and IGRP. RIP only uses hop counts in determining the best route to a destination network. IGRP can look at bandwidth, load, reliability, MTU, and hop count to find the best route to a destination network.

Key Terms and Concepts

Bandwidth: The transmission capacity of a communications channel, measured kilobits per second (Kbps).

IGRP: An acronym for Interior Gateway Routing Protocol, IGRP is a proprietary Cisco distance vector routing algorithm.

MTU: An acronym for Maximum Transmission Unit, MTU is the largest packet size that can be sent out of the interface onto the line. If a packet is larger than the MTU of the link, the router will fragment the packet.

Sample Questions

1. Which of the following parameters does IGRP use in deciding the best route through an internetwork? (Choose all that apply.)

   A. BW

   B. Delay

   C. Reliability

   D. TTL

   E. Hop count

   F. Load

   G. MTU

   Answer: A, B, C, E, F, G. When you use the command `sh interface s0`, the third line of output shows the parameters that IGRP uses to decide the best route to a destination network. These are bandwidth (BW), MTU, reliability, hop count, load, and delay.

2. What command can you use to verify the broadcast frequency of IGRP?

   A. `sh ip route`

   B. `sh ip protocol`

   C. `sh ip broadcast`

   D. `debug ip igrp`

   Answer: B. The only command that will show you the update frequency is `sh ip protocol`.

3. What is the default update frequency for IGRP networks?

   A. 30 seconds

   B. 60 seconds

   C. 90 seconds

   D. 180 seconds

   Answer: C. The default update frequency for RIP is 30 seconds, but for IGRP it is 90 seconds.

Explain the services of separate and integrated multiprotocol routing

In this section, we'll explain how routing and routed protocols can work together. Cisco internetworks can run many different types of protocols simultaneously. This is called "ships in the night" routing. Each protocol is busy doing its basic duties of sending user data or updating routers of known networks, and each is unaware of what the other protocols are doing.

You should be aware of the differences between routed and routing protocols, so we will go over those in this section as well. This section will also cover how to manage your internetwork when running multiple protocol simultaneously. Since most production shops run multiple protocols, this is an important thing to know.

Critical Information

There is sometimes confusion when the similar terms *routed protocols* and *routing protocols* are used. *Routed* protocols are used between routers to direct user traffic such as IP or IPX. Both IP and IPX can provide enough information in the network header of packets to enable a router to direct user traffic. The only job that *routing* protocols do is to maintain the routing tables that are used between routers.

For example, in Figure 5.4, routed protocols IP and IPX are transmitting user data, and RIP and IGRP are sending router information between each router, but none of the protocols is aware the other protocols are running.

Exam Essentials

Although multiprotocol routing is not a major focus of the CCNA test, you should comprehend this subject.

FIGURE 5.4: "Ships in the night" routing

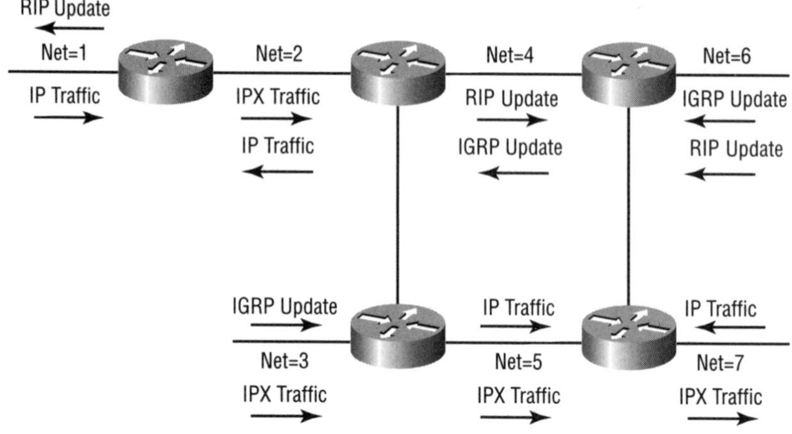

Remember the difference between routing and routed protocols. *Routed* protocols route user data with protocols like IP and IPX. *Routing* protocols send updates between routers and only send information about networks, not data.

Key Terms and Concepts

Routed Protocols: Protocols like IP or IPX, which are used to send packets through an internetwork and deliver user data.

Routing Protocols: Protocols like RIP and IGRP, which are used to send packets between routers to tell each other about networks.

Sample Questions

1. Which of the following protocols are considered routed protocols? (Choose all that apply.)

   A. IP

   B. IPX

C. RIP

D. IGRP

Answer: A, B. IP and IPX are examples of routed protocols.

2. Which of the following protocols are considered routing protocols? (Choose all that apply.)

   A. IP

   B. IPX

   C. RIP

   D. IGRP

   Answer: C, D. RIP and IGRP are examples of routing protocols.

List problems that each routing type encounters when dealing with topology changes and describe techniques to reduce the number of these problems

Routing loops and ways to solve them are key points to study before you take the CCNA exam and before you troubleshoot a router on your network. Cisco considers routing loops a serious problem, but fortunately many solutions have been documented. This section covers routing loops, what causes them, and a variety of solutions for them.

Critical Information

A potential problem with distance vector algorithms is routing loops. These can occur because every router is not updated at approximately the same time. Let's say that the interface to Network 5 in Figure 5.5 fails.

FIGURE 5.5: Routing loops

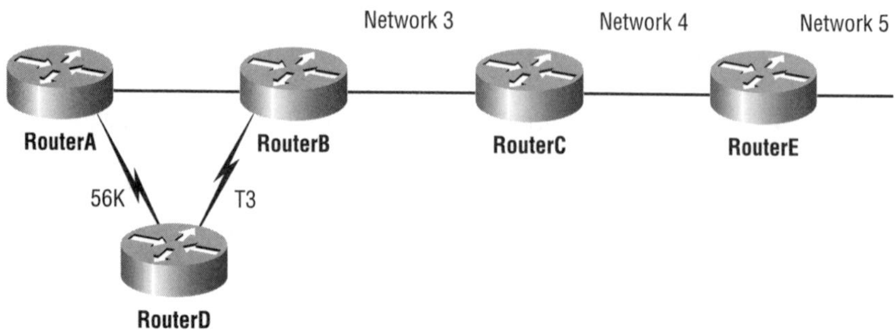

All routers know about Network 5 from RouterE. RouterA, in its tables, has a path to Network 5 through Routers B, C, and E. When Network 5 fails, RouterE tells RouterC. This causes RouterC to stop routing to Network 5 through RouterE. But routers A, B, and D don't know about Network 5 yet, so they keep sending out update information. RouterC will eventually send out its update and cause RouterB to stop routing to Network 5, but RouterA and RouterD are still not updated. To RouterA and RouterD, it appears that Network 5 is still available through RouterB with a metric of three.

So RouterA will send out its regular 30-second "Hello, I'm still here—these are the links I know about" message, which includes reachability for Network 5. Routers B and D then receive the wonderful news that Network 5 can be reached from RouterA. So Routers B and D send the information that Network 5 is available. Any packet destined for Network 5 will go to RouterA, to RouterB, and then back to RouterA. This is known as a *routing loop*.

The routing loop problem just described is called *counting to infinity*, and it's caused by wrong information being communicated and propagated throughout the internetwork. Without some form of intervention, each time a packet passes through a router, the hop count will increase indefinitely in a routing loop.

Hop Count

As discussed previously in the section on RIP, hop counts are used in distance vector networks to find the best path to an internetwork. RIP uses an upper count limit of 15, while IGRP has a hop count limit of 255.

Counting to Infinity

One way of solving long routing loop problems is to define a maximum hop count. Older distance vector routing protocols permit a maximum hop count of up to 15, so anything that requires 16 hops is deemed unreachable. In other words, after a loop of 15 hops, Network 5 in the example above would be considered down. This means that counting to infinity, also known as exceeding TTL (Time To Live), will keep packets from going around the loop forever. Though a good solution, it won't remove the routing loop itself. Packets will still be attracted into the loop, but instead of traveling on it unchecked, they'll just whirl around for 16 bounces and then die.

Split Horizon

Another solution to the routing loop problem is called *split horizon.* It reduces incorrect routing information and routing overhead in a distance vector network by enforcing the rule that information cannot be sent back in the direction from which that information was received. This would have prevented RouterA in the example above from sending the updated information it received from RouterB back to RouterB.

Route Poisoning

Another way to avoid problems caused by inconsistent updates is called *route poisoning*. To use the example above again, when Network 5 goes down, RouterE can initiate route poisoning by entering a table entry for Network 5 as 16 or unreachable (sometime referred to as *infinite*). By poisoning its route to Network 5, RouterE is not susceptible to incorrect updates about the route to Network 5. RouterE will keep this information in its tables until Network 5 comes up again, at which point it will trigger an update to notify its neighbors of the event.

Route poisoning and triggered updates will speed up convergence time, because neighboring routers don't have to wait 30 or 90 seconds (an eternity in the computer world) before advertising the poisoned route.

Hold-Downs

Another way to solve routing loop problems is with hold-downs. These work with route poisoning to prevent regular update messages from reinstating a route that's gone down. Hold-downs help prevent routes from changing too rapidly by allowing time for either the downed route to come back or for the network to stabilize somewhat before changing to the next-best route. These also tell routers to restrict, for a specific time period, any changes that might affect recently removed routes. This prevents inoperative routes from being prematurely restored to other routers' tables.

Hold-downs use triggered updates, which reset the hold-down timer, to let the neighbor routers know of a change in the network. There are three instances in which triggered updates will reset the hold-down timer:

- The hold-down timer expires.
- The router receives a processing task proportional to the number of links in the internetwork.
- The hold-down timer receives another update indicating that the network status has changed.

Static Routes

There is one more method that can be used to solve dynamic routing loop problems: using a static route instead. Remember however, that routing loops can be caused by incorrect network information. If a network administrator puts a bad static route in the router, then it can also cause a loop.

TIP To learn more about configuring static routes, read Chapter 6 in the Sybex *CCNA Study Guide*. As you study for the CCNA test, learning the material presented here is enough.

To configure a static route, use the following arguments and syntax:

```
ip route [destination network] [subnet mask] [next-hop
address] [metric]
```

As an example, here is a real static route command:

```
ip route 172.16.0.0 255.255.255.0 172.16.20.1 3
```

The command starts with `ip route`. The first address is the destination network, and the next is the subnet mask. 172.16.20.1 is the default gateway, or next-hop address, which is followed by the metric, or the weight of the link.

Exam Essentials

To be successful on the CCNA exam, you need to know why routing loops arise and what can be done to resolve them.

Know what causes routing loops and how to correct them. You must understand the reasons a routing loop can occur and know all the ways of correcting them.

Understand the differences between the various routing loop solutions. Be able to distinguish between each of these methods: counting to infinity, split horizon, poison reverse, and hold-downs, which use triggered updates.

Remember the reasons that hold-downs send triggered updates. There are three instances in which triggered updates will reset the hold-down timer:

- The hold-down timer expires.

- The router receives a processing task proportional to the number of links in the internetwork.
- The hold-down timer receives another update indicating that the network status has changed.

Remember what the arguments are in a static route. To create a static route, use the `ip route` command followed by the destination network, subnet mask, next-hop address, and the metric.

Key Terms and Concepts

Convergence: The time it takes for all routers to update their routing tables to have the same information.

Hold-Downs: A method of stopping routing loops by not sending out updates about networks that have gone down.

Metric: The distance or weight of a link. This value can be used to find the best path to a remote network.

Route Poisoning: A method of stopping routing loops by not sending an update over an invalid number of hops (16 in RIP) whenever a link outage occurs.

Split Horizon: A method of stopping routing loops by not sending updates out the same interface through which they were received.

Sample Questions

1. Which of the following statements is true regarding split horizon?
   - **A.** A router sets the metric for a downed link to infinity.
   - **B.** When routing information is received by an interface, it can't be advertised out that same interface.
   - **C.** This prevents regular update messages from reinstating a router that has gone down by not advertising that network.
   - **D.** None of the above.

Answer: B. When an update is received by a router, it will never send that same information out the interface through which it was received.

2. Which statement describes poison reverse?

   A. A router sets the metric for a downed link to infinity.

   B. When routing information is received by an interface, it can't be advertised out that same interface.

   C. This prevents regular update messages from reinstating a router that has gone down by not advertising that network.

   D. None of the above.

   Answer: A. When a link goes down, the router will immediately update the routing table with a metric of 16 to that network.

3. Which of the following describes hold-downs?

   A. A router sets the metric for a downed link to infinity.

   B. When routing information is received by an interface, it can't be advertised out that same interface.

   C. This prevents regular update messages from reinstating a router that has gone down by not advertising that network.

   D. None of the above.

   Answer: C. Hold-downs prevent regular update messages from reinstating a downed link by removing that link from update messages.

4. Which of these methods can be used to reset the hold-down timer?

   A. Triggered updates

   B. Split horizon

   C. Reverse poison

   D. Hold-downs

   Answer: A. Hold-downs use triggered updates to reset the hold-down timer.

Describe the benefits of network segmentation with routers

Cisco wants you to understand how routers work in an internetwork. They also want you to know when you should use a router instead of a switch or bridge. (This information will be covered in more detail in Chapter 7.) Not only does Cisco want you to sound smart in meetings once you hold the CCNA certification, but they want you to be able to make smart business decisions. Being knowledgeable about the benefits of segmentation using routers, which we'll focus on in this section, will help you decide when to use a router.

Critical Information

Routers work at the Network layer and are used to route packets to destination networks. Routers, like bridges, use tables to make routing decisions. However, routers keep information only on how to get to remote networks in their tables, not to hosts; they use this information to route packets through an internetwork. For example, routers use IP addresses instead of hardware addresses when making routing decisions. The router keeps a routing table for each protocol on the network.

These are some of the general benefits of routers:

Manageability: Multiple routing protocols give the network manager who's creating an internetwork a lot of flexibility.

Increased Functionality: Cisco routers provide features that handle the issues of flow, error, and congestion control, plus fragmentation, reassembly, and control over packet lifetime.

Multiple Active Paths: Routers can have more than one active link between devices, which is a definite plus. They can also use a routing algorithm that supports round-robin data delivery (IGRP) or unequal cost load balancing (EIGRP).

To provide these featured advantages, routers must be more complex and more software-intensive than bridges. Routers provide a lower level of performance than bridges in terms of the number of frames or packets that can be processed per unit.

These are benefits of segmenting with routers:

Creates Internetworks: An administrator assigns logical network numbers, for example IP addresses, to each network that connects to a router. The router forwards requests only to the destination network, not to all networks in the internetwork.

Doesn't Forward Broadcasts: By default, routers do not forward broadcasts, which means they can stop broadcast storms from propagating throughout the internetwork. Also, segmenting with routers keeps local broadcast traffic where it belongs: on the local network.

Exam Essentials

On the CCNA exam, you may not see any specific questions on the difference between bridges, switches, and routers, but understanding how each segmentation device works is crucial.

Understand the difference between a router, a bridge, and switch. You need to know how each of these hardware devices works in order to answer related exam questions correctly. (See Chapter 7 for information on each of these devices.)

Key Terms and Concepts

Bridge: A Data Link layer device that segments a network by creating filter tables of MAC addresses. Bridges forward all broadcasts throughout the network.

Router: A Network layer device that adds logical addressing to a network and creates internetworks. Routers do not forward broadcasts.

Switch: A multiport bridge that filters a network by MAC address.

Sample Questions

1. Which of the following statements is true?

   A. Routers filter by hardware address.

   B. Bridges filter by logical address.

   C. Switches filter by port or socket number.

   D. Routers filter by logical address.

   E. Bridges filter by MTU.

   Answer: D. Routers create internetworks by naming the directly attached networks with logical network numbers.

2. Which of the following are benefits of using routers to segment your network? (Choose two.)

   A. Multipath routing

   B. Passes broadcasts

   C. Filters by MAC address

   D. Creates internetworks

   Answer: A, D. Routers create internetworks by naming directly attached networks with logical network numbers. They can have more than one connection to the same network, either load balancing or doing a round-robin data flow, and they do not pass broadcasts through the internetwork by default.

CHAPTER 6

Network Security

Cisco CCNA exam objectives covered in this chapter:

- **Configure standard and extended access lists to filter IP traffic.** *(pages 252 – 261)*
- **Monitor and verify selected access list operations on the router.** *(pages 261 – 266)*

The proper use and configuration of access lists is a vital part of router configuration because access lists are such a vital networking accessory. Contributing mightily to the efficiency and optimization of your network, access lists give network managers a huge amount of control over traffic flow throughout the internetwork. With them, managers can gather basic statistics on packet flow, and security policies can be implemented. Sensitive devices can also be protected from unauthorized access.

Access lists are essentially lists of conditions that control access. They're powerful tools that control access both to and from network segments. They can filter unwanted packets and can be used to implement security policies. With the right combination of access lists, a network manager is armed with the power to enforce nearly any access policy he or she can invent.

To be successful on the CCNA exam, you need a complete understanding of IP and IPX access lists. IPX access lists are covered in Chapter 4.

Configure standard and extended access lists to filter IP traffic

IP and IPX access lists work similarly—they're both packet filters that packets are compared with, categorized by, and acted upon.

Once the lists are built, they can be applied to either inbound or outbound traffic on any interface. Applying an access list makes the router analyze every packet crossing that interface in the specified direction and take action accordingly.

There are a few important rules a packet follows when it's being compared with an access list:

- It's always compared with each line of the access list in sequential order—line 1 and then line 2, line 3, and so on.
- It's compared with lines of the access list only until a match is made. Once the packet matches a line of the access list, it's acted upon, and no further comparisons take place.
- There is an implicit "deny any" at the end of each access list. This means that if a packet doesn't match up to any lines in the access list, it'll be discarded.

Each of these rules has powerful implications when you filter IP and IPX packets with access lists.

Critical Information

There are two steps to configuring standard and extended IP access lists:

1. Configure the access list.
2. Apply the access list to an interface.

Standard Access Lists

Standard IP access lists can analyze the source IP addresses of TCP/IP packets and then take action based upon that analysis. Each line of a standard IP access list uses the following format:

```
access-list [number] [permit or deny] [source address]
```

To define access lists, use the `access-list` command in configuration mode. Each access list is assigned a unique number to distinguish it from the other lists. IP standard access lists are given numbers between 1 and 99, but other access list types require different number ranges. Here is an example command:

```
access-list 10 permit 172.16.30.2
```

The *permit* or *deny* keyword indicates whether to allow or discard matching packets, and the *source address* is used to define which source IP addresses should be acted upon.

Applying the Access List to an Interface

Even though you configure an access list, it won't filter anything until you apply it to an interface. First, enter configuration mode and select the Ethernet 0 interface. Then, we'll use the `ip access-group` command to specify `10 out`. Here is an example:

```
(config-int)ip access-group 10 out
```

NOTE Use the `access-list` keyword to enter the access list, but use the `access-group` keyword to apply that access list to an interface.

The number 10 refers to the access list 10 created in the example above. The variable *out* tells the router to compare outbound packets—not inbound packets—with the list. This can get a bit confusing. It helps to remember that the command is being applied to the router, not the network, so the *out* and *in* designations refer to the router's perspective, not that of the nodes on the network.

To the router, `out` means packets leaving its interface(s) and going out to the network; `in` means packets arriving at the router's interface(s) from the network. In this example, we're seeking to control the outbound packets leaving from the router, so we'll use the `out` command.

Wildcard Masking

Wildcard masking allows you to specify either an entire network or a specific host. You can use wildcard masking in both standard and extended access lists.

In this example, we've used a wildcard mask to specify the source address:

Address:	172.	16.	30.	0
Mask:	0.	0.	0.	255

It consists of a 32-bit binary string of 0s followed by 1s, broken into octets, and written in decimal. 1s are considered *throwaway* bits, meaning that their corresponding positions in the address are irrelevant. By specifying the source address and mask as shown above, we're saying that the 172, 16, and 30 are required to match up, but the last octet of the IP address can be any value (remember that 255 is 1111 1111 in decimal format). Likewise, when you specify a mask as follows:

Address:	172.	16.	50.	2
Mask:	0.	0.	0.	0

you're requiring 172, 16, 50, and 2 all to match up exactly, because you've set all mask values to 0.

Extended Access Lists

The function of extended access lists is pretty much the same as that of standard access lists. The difference centers on what can be filtered. In standard IP access lists, your decisions to permit or deny packets are limited to comparisons with the packets' source address information. But with extended IP access lists, you can act on any of the following:

- Source address
- Destination address
- IP protocol (TCP, UDP, ICMP, etc.)
- Port information (WWW, DNS, FTP, etc.)

So with extended access lists, your abilities are extended. You can make much more detailed lists than you can with the standard type.

The syntax for each line on extended access lists is similar to that of standard access lists. The first three fields—*access-list, number,* and *permit* or *deny*—are exactly the same. But you can additionally specify a protocol before the source and create destination and port fields after the source address. Here's a template for each part of an extended IP access list:

```
access-list [number] [permit or deny] [protocol]
[source] [destination] [port]
```

Necessary Procedures

Following are examples for configuring both a standard access list and an extended access list.

Configuring a Standard Access List

Here is an example of configuring with standard access lists:

```
RouterA#config t
RouterA(config)#access-list ?
  <1-99>         IP standard access list
  <100-199>      IP extended access list
  <1000-1099>    IPX SAP access list
  <1100-1199>    Extended 48-bit MAC address access list
  <1200-1299>    IPX summary address access list
  <200-299>      Protocol type-code access list
  <300-399>      DECnet access list
  <600-699>      Appletalk access list
  <700-799>      48-bit MAC address access list
  <800-899>      IPX standard access list
  <900-999>      IPX extended access list
```

To apply this configuration to an Ethernet interface, you could use this example:

```
RouterA#config t
Enter configuration commands, one per line. nd with CNTL/Z.
RouterA(config)#int e0
RouterA(config-if)#ip access-group 10 out
```

```
RouterA(config-if)#^Z
RouterA#
```

Wildcards can be used in a standard access list as follows:

```
RouterA#config t
RouterA(config)#access-list 11 permit 172.16.50.2 0.0.0.0
RouterA(config)#access-list 11 permit 172.16.30.0 0.0.0.255
RouterA(config)#int e0
RouterA(config-if)#ip access-group 11 out
RouterA(config-if)#^Z
RouterA#
```

Configuring Extended Access Lists

Here is an example program that could be used to configure an extended access list:

```
RouterA#config t
RouterA(config)#access-list 110 permit tcp host 172.16.50.2
host 172.16.10.2 eq 8080
RouterA(config)#access-list 110 permit tcp 172.16.30.0
0.0.0.255 host 172.16.10.2  eq 8080
RouterA(config)#access-list 110 permit tcp any any eq www
RouterA(config)#int e0
RouterA(config-if)#ip access-group 110 out
RouterA(config-if)#^Z
```

Here's how the three lines map to our new template for extended IP access lists:

Protocol	Source	Destination	Port
TCP	host 172.16.50.2	host 172.16.10.2	eq 8080
TCP	172.16.30.0 0.0.0.255	host 172.16.10.2	eq 8080
TCP	any	any	eq www

The new field is for the protocol, and it's specified as TCP. In this case, you chose to allow TCP connections to your proxy on port 8080.

Earlier we presented three different methods of specifying source and destination addresses and an example of wildcard masking, but there are two new methods presented here. In reality, we're just using some keywords to save ourselves the effort of typing in the masks.

- *host 172.16.10.2* is the same as specifying 172.16.10.2 0.0.0.0 with wildcard masking. Setting all the bits in the wildcard mask to 0s basically says there are no wildcards, so you can be referring to only a single machine or host. This means you can use the *host* keyword instead of the mask of 0.0.0.0.
- *any* is equivalent to specifying 0.0.0.0 255.255.255.255 with wildcard masking. When you set all bits in a wildcard mask to 1s, you get 255.255.255.255, so you're saying that none of the bits really matter. You can use this when you don't care about source or destination addresses because you're filtering based on some other parameter. In this example, you're filtering based upon the port.

Finally, you can specify the port to be acted upon. How well do you remember your TCP ports? You can press question mark to get the list of available ports, as shown below. At this point, you could have just ended the command without specifying any port information, and if you did that, all ports would have been allowed. You chose to use the `eq` operator, but there are other numeric comparisons available that you could have selected to specify more than one port. Once you selected `eq`, you again had many options available:

```
RouterA#config t
RouterA(config)#access-list 110 permit tcp host
172.16.50.2 host 172.16.10.2 eq ?
  <0-65535>      Port number
  bgp            Border Gateway Protocol (179)
  chargen        Character generator (19)
  cmd            Remote commands (rcmd, 514)
  daytime        Daytime (13)
  discard        Discard (9)
  domain         Domain Name Service (53)
  echo           Echo (7)
  exec           Exec (rsh, 512)
```

```
finger        Finger (79)
ftp           File Transfer Protocol (21)
ftp-data      FTP data connections
              (used infrequently, 20)
gopher        Gopher (70)
hostname      NIC hostname server (101)
ident         Ident Protocol (113)
irc           Internet Relay Chat (194)
klogin        Kerberos login (543)
kshell        Kerberos shell (544)
login         Login (rlogin, 513)
lpd           Printer service (515)
nntp          Network News Transport Protocol (119)
pim-auto-rp   PIM Auto-RP (496)
pop2          Post Office Protocol v2 (109)
pop3          Post Office Protocol v3 (110)
smtp          Simple Mail Transport Protocol (25)
sunrpc        Sun Remote Procedure Call (111)
syslog        Syslog (514)
tacacs        TAC Access Control System (49)
talk          Talk (517)
telnet        Telnet (23)
time          Time (37)
uucp          Unix-to-Unix Copy Program (540)
whois         Nicname (43)
www           World Wide Web (HTTP, 80)
```

You can either specify the number of the port or use one of the keywords listed above. Notice that in the description, the port that's actually filtered is listed. If you can't remember that SMTP (Simple Mail Transfer Protocol) uses port 25, just enter **smtp**. This can make reading long access lists a whole lot easier.

Exam Essentials

You need to understand the difference between IP standard and extended access lists to pass the CCNA exam.

Know the difference between standard and extended access lists. Standard access lists can only filter by source address. Also, standard access lists cannot filter by protocol or port. Extended access lists can filter by source and destination address, protocol, and port.

Remember how to filter by port. It is important to remember that when filtering by port, you cannot use IP as the protocol, only TCP, UDP, or ICMP. Try this on your router if possible. For example, `access-list 110 permit tcp any any www log` is okay, but you cannot use `access-list 110 permit ip any any www log`.

Key Terms and Concepts

Extended Access Lists: Security used in Cisco routers that can filter by source and destination address as well as by protocol and port.

Standard Access Lists: Security used in Cisco routers that can filter only by source address.

Sample Questions

1. Which of the following commands allow traffic from network 172.16.30.0 to enter interface Ethernet 0?

   A. `access-list 10 permit 0.0.0.255 172.16.30.0 in`

   B. `access-list 10 permit 172.16.30.0 0.0.0.0, access-group 10 out`

   C. `access-list 10 permit 172.16.30.0 0.0.0.255, int e0, access-group 10 in`

   D. `access-list 10 permit 172.16.30.0 0.0.0.255, int e0, ip access-group 10 in`

   Answer: D. To create a standard access list, you must use numbers between 1 and 99. You can only filter by source IP address. You apply that list by going to an interface and using the `ip access-group` command.

2. Which of the following are valid IP extended access lists?

   A. `access-list 99 permit tcp any 172.16.30.0 255.255.255.0 eq ftp`

   B. `access-list 199 permit ip any 172.16.30.0 0.0.0.255 eq ftp`

   C. `access-list 199 permit tcp any 172.16.30.0 0.0.0.255 eq ftp`

   D. `access-list 109 permit ip any host 172.16.30.5 eq ftp`

   Answer: C. You can only filter by port number when using TCP, UDP, or ICMP.

Monitor and verify selected access list operations on the router

Cisco believes that understanding how to build an access list is important, and that being able to monitor and verify these lists once they are applied is just as important.

Access lists can be extremely tricky at times. To pass exam questions on this objective, you need to know how to monitor and verify access lists that are applied to your router and the interfaces. It is important to understand all the commands discussed in this section, not only for the test, but also to work successfully in a production environment.

Critical Information

Here are some specific access-list commands for monitoring and verifying the lists and what functions they provide:

`show access-lists`

This command lists all of the access lists running on the router. It also lists each line of the access list and reports the number of packets that matched each line. This information is priceless when you are troubleshooting access lists. If you configure an access list and then use this command, you should be able to see the counter increments change as packets hit the access list.

`show ip access-list`

This command shows you only the IP access lists, whereas the `show access-list` command displays all the access lists (IP, IPX, etc.).

`sh log`

If you add this log syntax at the end of your extended access list, a log will be generated with the following information:

- Access list number
- Source address
- Source port
- Destination address
- Destination port
- Number of packets

All of this log information could be redirected to the syslog server and stored for security purposes.

`clear access-list counter`

This command clears the counters for the `show access-list` commands.

Necessary Procedures

Using the extended access-list example given above, let's take a look at monitoring. We'll start by using the commands to verify the access lists on the router and then use the commands to verify which interface has an access-list set.

Displaying the Access Lists

The `show access-list` command shows you all access lists, including IP, IPX, etc. In this example, only IP access lists are set:

```
RouterA#show access-list
Extended IP access list 110
permit tcp host 172.16.50.2 host 172.16.10.2 eq 8080
(34 matches)
permit tcp 172.16.30.0 0.0.0.255 host 172.16.10.2 eq 8080
(11 matches)
permit tcp any any eq www (33 matches)
```

The `show ip access-list` command shows only the IP access lists and the number of times each line was hit:

```
RouterA#show ip access-list
Extended IP access list 110
permit tcp host 172.16.50.2 host 172.16.10.2 eq 8080
(15 matches)
permit tcp 172.16.30.0 0.0.0.255 host 172.16.10.2 eq 8080
(4 matches)
    permit tcp any any eq www (8 matches)
    deny ip any any log (4 matches)
```

To clear the counters, you can use the following command:

```
RouterA#clear access-list counters 110
```

Displaying the Interface

When monitoring access lists, it's often important to find out which interfaces have which access lists applied to them. There are two commands that you can use to display this information: `show ip interface` and `show running-config`.

Here's an example of output for the first command:

```
RouterA#show ip interface e0
Ethernet0 is up, line protocol is up
  Internet address is 172.16.10.1/24
  Broadcast address is 255.255.255.255
```

```
  Address determined by non-volatile memory
  MTU is 1500 bytes
  Helper address is not set
  Directed broadcast forwarding is enabled
  Multicast reserved groups joined: 224.0.0.9
  Outgoing access list is 110
  Inbound  access list is not set
  Proxy ARP is enabled
  Security level is default
  Split horizon is enabled
```

The output above was cut for brevity. The output of the next command, `show running-config`, displays the interfaces for which access lists are set:

```
RouterA#show running-config
Building configuration...

Current configuration:
!
version 11.3
no service password-encryption
!
hostname RouterA
!
enable secret 5 $1$YMNO$Pz1r4tEg1E91wcKrNUIOHO
enable password password
!
!
interface Ethernet0
 ip address 172.16.10.1 255.255.255.0
 ip access-group 110 out
 no mop enabled
!
interface Serial0
 ip address 172.16.20.1 255.255.255.0
 no ip mroute-cache
!
```

```
interface Serial1
 no ip address
 shutdown
!
router rip
 redistribute connected
 network 172.16.0.0
!
ip classless
access-list 110 permit tcp host 172.16.50.2 host
172.16.10.2 eq 8080
access-list 110 permit tcp 172.16.30.0 0.0.0.255 host
172.16.10.2 eq 8080
access-list 110 permit tcp any any eq www
access-list 110 deny   ip any any log
!
line con 0
line aux 0
line vty 0 4
 password password2
 login
!
end
RouterA#
```

Exam Essentials

To correctly answer the questions on the CCNA exam regarding IP access lists, you must know how to create access lists and apply them to an interface.

Practice setting IP extended access lists. The only way to select the right answer for access-list questions is to understand the command syntax.

Know the commands to view access lists. You must remember the commands for viewing access lists set on both global configurations and interfaces.

Sample Questions

1. Which of the following commands will show you which interfaces have IP access lists set? (Choose all that apply.)

   A. `sh int`

   B. `sh run`

   C. `sh ip int`

   D. `sh access-list`

   Answer: B, C. The `sh ip int` and `show run` commands show you which interface has an access list set.

2. Which of the following will be logged when IP access-list logging is enabled? (Choose all that apply.)

   A. Protocol

   B. Access-list line number

   C. Access-list number

   D. Destination port

   E. Destination address

   F. Source port

   G. Source address

   Answer: A, C, D, E, F, G. Everything but the access-list line number will be displayed.

3. Which of the following commands will show only extended access list 187?

   A. `sh int`

   B. `sh ip int`

   C. `sh access-list 187`

   D. `sh access-lists`

   Answer: C. Answer D will show access list 187, but only answer C will show you *extended* access list 187.

CHAPTER 7

LAN Switching

Cisco CCNA exam objectives covered in this chapter:

- **Describe the advantages of LAN segmentation.** *(pages 269 – 272)*
- **Describe LAN segmentation using bridges.** *(pages 272 – 275)*
- **Describe LAN segmentation using routers.** *(pages 275 – 278)*
- **Describe LAN segmentation using switches.** *(pages 278 – 281)*
- **Name and describe two switching methods.** *(pages 281 – 285)*
- **Describe full- and half-duplex Ethernet operation.** *(pages 285 – 289)*
- **Describe network congestion problem in Ethernet networks.** *(pages 289 – 291)*
- **Describe the benefits of network segmentation with bridges.** *(pages 291 – 294)*
- **Describe the benefits of network segmentation with switches.** *(pages 294 – 296)*
- **Describe the features and benefits of Fast Ethernet.** *(pages 296 – 299)*
- **Describe the guidelines and distance limitations of Fast Ethernet.** *(pages 299 – 303)*
- **Distinguish between cut-through and store-and-forward LAN switching.** *(pages 303 – 305)*
- **Describe the operation of the Spanning Tree Protocol and its benefits.** *(pages 305 – 307)*
- **Describe the benefits of virtual LANs.** *(pages 308 – 311)*
- **Define and describe the function of a MAC address.** *(pages 312 – 316)*

This chapter covers a lot of test objectives, many of them similar in concept. The focus of this section of the exam is on understanding the major differences between segmenting a network with various devices, including bridges, routers, and switches. The function and benefits of each device will be discussed.

We will discuss the differences between half- and full-duplex devices and what is required to run each one. Fast Ethernet and its specifications, benefits, and distance limitations will also be covered.

Later in this chapter we will review the features and benefits of the Spanning Tree Protocol (STP) and discuss virtual LANs and how they are used in an internetwork.

Finally, we will discuss in detail the final LAN switching exam objective, "Define and describe the functions of a MAC address." This is an extremely important objective. Although you might not see a test question based specifically on this objective, understanding how frames and packets work in an internetwork is crucial for your success on the CCNA exam.

Describe the advantages of LAN segmentation

This section makes a good lead to the chapter, as the next few objectives discussed are how to segment your LAN with various devices and the benefits of each device. It is important to understand why network segmentation is necessary and the various devices that are used for segmentation.

Because the CCNA exam covers only Ethernet networking, we will talk specifically about segmentation of Ethernet networks.

Critical Information

As a network administrator, you'll need to segment your network when it gets too large or when your business requirements demand more bandwidth. The main reason for segmenting a network is to relieve network congestion. Congestion "chokes" bandwidth. More information on congestion problems can be found in the objective "Describe network congestion problem in Ethernet networks," covered later in this chapter.

A way to solve congestion problems and increase the networking performance of your LAN is to divide a single Ethernet segment into multiple network segments. This maximizes available bandwidth, achieving the administrator's goal of providing more bandwidth per user. Here are some of the technologies you can use to segment an Ethernet:

Physical Segmentation: You can segment the network with bridges and routers, thereby breaking up the collision domains. This minimizes packet collisions by decreasing the number of workstations on the same physical segment.

Network Switching Technology (Microsegmenting): Like a bridge or a router, switches can also provide LAN segmentation capabilities. LAN switches (for example, the Cisco Catalyst 5000) provide dedicated, point-to-point, packet-switched connections between their ports. Since this provides simultaneous switching of packets between the ports in the switch, it increases the amount of bandwidth open to each workstation.

Full-Duplex Ethernet Devices: Full-duplex Ethernet can provide almost twice the bandwidth of traditional Ethernet networks. However, for this to work, the network interface cards (NICs) must be able to run in full-duplex mode and must be connected to a full-duplex–capable device such as a switch.

Fast Ethernet: Fast Ethernet switches can provide 10 times the amount of bandwidth available from 10BaseT.

FDDI (Fiber Distributed Data Interface): An older, solid, token-based media access technology that can provide 100Mbps bandwidth. By running dual rings, it has the capability of running at up to 200Mbps. It's typically used between closets or floors or in a campus environment.

It should be no surprise that reducing the number of users per collision domain increases the bandwidth on your network segment. If traffic is kept local to the network segment, users have more available bandwidth and enjoy a noticeably better response time than if there were only one large collision domain in place.

Exam Essentials

Segmenting a network helps eliminate congestion problems. If you can eliminate congestion problems, or reduce them, your network will perform better.

Understand what causes congestion and how segmentation helps. By segmenting your network, you can effectively cut down on the amount of traffic on your network by making smaller networks.

Key Terms and Concepts

Collision Domain: A segment of network in which all nodes attached to that physical segment share the bandwidth.

Congestion: Network traffic in excess of network capacity.

Ethernet: A LAN specification invented by Xerox Corporation. Uses the IEEE 802.3 series of standards.

Segmentation: Creating subsections of a network by using bridges, routers, or switches.

Sample Questions

1. Which of the following is a solution for network congestion?

   A. 802.3

   B. Segmentation

   C. Ethernet

   D. CSMA/CD

   Answer: B. Segmentation is a good solution for networks with congestion problems.

2. Which of the following is an advantage of network segmentation?

   A. Ethernet

   B. Congestion

   C. Less congestion

   D. Video to the desktop

   Answer: C. If you segment your network correctly, you will have less congestion on your network links.

Describe LAN segmentation using bridges

You may have thought bridges weren't used anymore. Not so. Although they were more popular in the eighties, when routers were considered very expensive, bridges are still used today.

In this section, we will talk about bridging and how bridges fit in an internetwork. It is important to remember that switches are really just multiport bridges that have more functionality than regular bridges. To be fully knowledgeable about Ethernet segmentation, it is important to understand the differences between all available devices, including bridges.

Many of Cisco's CCNA exam objectives relate to segmenting Ethernet networks with various devices. Bridges are one of the devices you'll need to study. Other segmentation devices are covered in the following sections.

Critical Information

A bridge can segment or break up your network into smaller, more manageable pieces, but if it's incorrectly placed in your network, it can cause more harm than good!

Bridges do their work at the MAC sublayer of the Data Link layer. They create both physical and logical separate network segments to reduce traffic load.

As Figure 7.1 shows, bridges work by examining the MAC (or hardware) addresses in each frame and forwarding the frame to the other physical segments if necessary. These devices dynamically build a forwarding table of information that includes each MAC address and the segment on which it is located.

FIGURE 7.1: Segmentation with a bridge

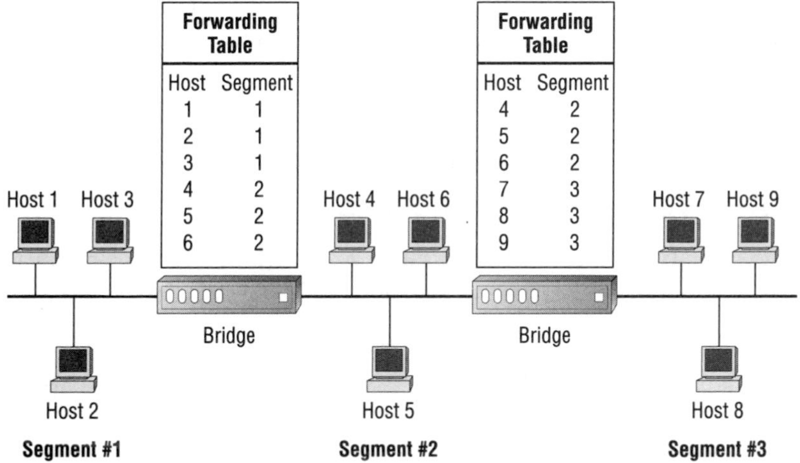

A drawback to using bridges is that if the destination MAC address is unknown to the bridge, the bridge will forward the frame to all segments except the port it received the frame from. Also, a 20 to 30 percent latency period to process frames can occur. *Latency* is the time is takes for a frame to get from the source host to the destination host. This delay can increase significantly if the frame cannot be immediately forwarded due to current activity on the destination segment.

Bridges will forward packets and multicast packets to all other segments that the bridge is attached to. Because the addresses from these broadcasts are never seen by the bridge, and therefore not filtered, broadcast storms can result. This same problem can happen with switches; theoretically, switch ports are bridge ports. A Cisco switch is really a multiport bridge that runs the Cisco IOS and performs the same functions as a bridge (and perhaps additional functions).

Exam Essentials

To answer exam questions on bridges correctly, you'll need to know how bridges segment a network.

Remember how bridges filter a network. Unlike some methods of segmentation, bridges do not break a network into smaller networks; rather, they take a large network and filter it. The size of the network doesn't change. Only routers can break a large network into smaller networks.

Key Terms and Concepts

Bridge: A device that filters a network by MAC, or hardware, address. Bridges are defined at the Data Link layer.

Latency: The delay from the time a device receives a frame to the time it transmits it to another network segment is called the *latency* period.

Router: A device defined at the Network layer that creates internetworks and does network addressing.

Switch: A device that filters a network by MAC, or hardware, address, defined at the Data Link layer.

Sample Questions

1. Which device would you use to segment your network if you were using a non-routable protocol in your network?

   A. Repeater

   B. Bridge

   C. Router

   D. Gateway

   Answer: B. A repeater does not segment a network; it only extends the network's distance. A bridge is protocol-independent and can easily be used to segment a network that uses non-routable protocols.

2. How does a bridge segment a network?

   A. By regenerating the digital signal

   B. By reading the logical address of a packet

   C. By creating a filter table of IP addresses

   D. By creating a filter table of MAC addresses

   Answer: D. A bridge can filter your network by MAC (or hardware) addresses.

Describe LAN segmentation using routers

Routers are a step up from bridges—literally. Bridges work at the Data Link layer and filter a network by MAC, or hardware, address. Routers work at the Network layer and create smaller networks called *internetworks*.

It is imperative that you understand the differences between the way a bridge filters a network and a router segments it. Bridges filter by hardware addresses, which are used in a frame; routers use logical addresses, which are found in a packet.

This section goes into more detail about how a router segments a network. A related topic, MAC addresses and their function, is covered at the end of this chapter.

Critical Information

Routers work at the Network layer and are used to route packets to destination networks. Routers, like bridges, use tables to make routing decisions. However, routers keep in their tables only information on how to get to remote networks, not to hosts; they use this information to route packets through an internetwork. Routers use IP addresses instead of hardware addresses when making routing decisions.

Figure 7.2 shows how a router can break up a network. Notice that a router uses the logical address to name the network and the host. Bridges only keep track of hardware addresses or hosts, not networks.

FIGURE 7.2: Logical addressing

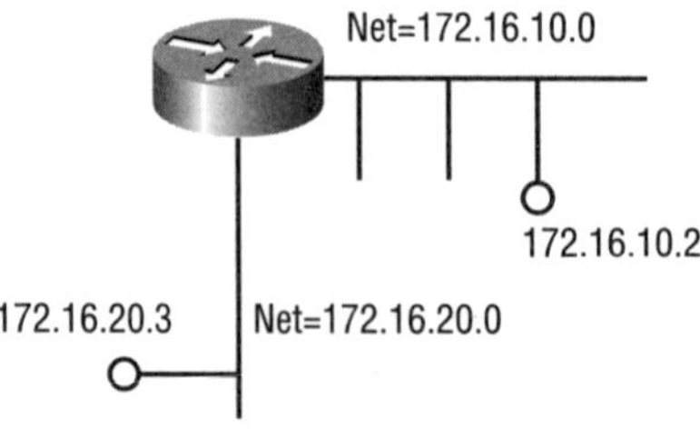

Exam Essentials

To understand how routers are used in LAN segmentation, you must know how frames and packets are used in a network. Review the exam objective "Describe the benefits of network segmentation with routers," found in Chapter 5. Also, the objective "Define and describe the function of a MAC address" at the end of this chapter will tie all of this together.

Remember how routers segment a network. Unlike bridges, routers actually create smaller networks and filter information based on logical address, not MAC address.

Key Terms and Concepts

Bridge: This type of segmentation device filters a network by MAC, or hardware, address. It is defined at the Data Link layer.

Internetwork: A term used to describe LANs and WANs connected by a router.

Latency: The delay from the time a device receives a frame to the time it transmits it to another network segment is called the *latency* period.

MAC address: Also called a hardware address, this is used to address a host on a LAN.

Router: A device defined at the Network layer that creates internetworks and does network addressing.

Switch: A device that filters a network by MAC, or hardware, address, defined at the Data Link layer.

Sample Questions

1. If you want to segment your network and are using the IPX routed protocol, what device should you use?

   A. Repeater

   B. Bridge

   C. Router

   D. Segment

   Answer: C. A router can segment your network by logical address. IPX is an example of a protocol that uses a logical addressing scheme; it was created by Novell.

2. If you want to segment a network by creating smaller networks, not just filtering the large network, what device should you use?

   A. Repeater

   B. Bridge

   C. Router

   D. Gateway

   Answer: C. A router can create smaller internetworks and name the networks.

Describe LAN segmentation using switches

Remember that a LAN switch filters by MAC address, just like a bridge. Of course a switch provides more functionality, but the theory is the same. Unlike bridges, switches allow you to create smaller networks called virtual LANs (VLANs), which will be covered later in this chapter.

For network administration and exam purposes, you need to know the fundamental differences between how bridges, routers, and switches function in an internetwork. This section focuses on switches.

Critical Information

LAN switching is a great strategy for segmentation. LAN switches improve performance by employing packet switching that permits high-speed data exchanges. Like bridges, switches use the destination MAC address to ensure that the packet is forwarded to the right outgoing port.

There are three different types of switching:

- Port configuration switching allows a port to be assigned to a physical network segment under software control. This is the simplest form of switching.
- Frame switching is used to increase available bandwidth on the network. It allows multiple transmissions to occur simultaneously. This is the type of switching performed by all catalyst switches.
- Cell switching—also called ATM, for Asynchronous Transfer Mode—is similar to frame switching. ATM uses small, fixed-length cells (53 bytes) that are switched on the network. It's the switching method used by all Cisco Lightstream switches.

A LAN switch bases the forwarding of a frame on the frame's Data Link layer address (a LAN switch) or on the frame's Network layer address (a multi-layer LAN switch). LAN switches are sometimes referred to as *frame switches* because they generally forward Data Link layer frames, in contrast to an ATM switch, which forwards cells.

As network use increases, more Token Ring and FDDI LAN switches are being used, but Ethernet LAN switches are still the most common type. These are also the type the CCNA exam test objectives are based on.

Exam Essentials

To successfully pass the LAN switching portion of the CCNA exam, you need to understand the differences between a bridge, a router, and a switch.

Remember how a switch works in an internetwork. Switches are really multiport bridges. Unlike routers, they do not by themselves create smaller internetworks. Instead they create a filter table of MAC addresses, just as bridges do.

Key Terms and Concepts

Bridge: A segmentation device that filters a network by MAC, or hardware, address. This is defined at the Data Link layer.

Cell: Fifty-three bytes long, cells are used in ATM networks to encapsulate data and switch it through an internetwork.

Frame: Used to encapsulate a packet to a format understood by the type of media used at the Physical layer.

Latency: The delay from the time a device receives a frame to the time it transmits it to another network segment is called the *latency* period.

MAC Address: Also called a hardware address, this is used to address a host on a LAN.

Port: A number used to describe an upper-layer process or protocol.

Router: A device defined at the Network layer that creates internetworks and does network addressing.

Switch: A device, defined at the Data Link layer, that filters a network by MAC, or hardware, address.

Sample Questions

1. Which of the following statements is true?

   A. Switches receive a frame and forward it to all segments with a server attached.

   B. Routers receive a frame and forward it to all segments.

   C. Switches forward by hardware address.

   D. Switches filter by logical address.

   Answer: C. Switches receive a frame and forward it only to the port where the destination hardware address is located.

2. Which type of switching is used by the Cisco Catalyst 5000 series of switches?

   A. Port

   B. Fast

   C. Packet

   D. Frame

   Answer: D. Cisco Catalyst switches use frame switching.

Name and describe two switching methods

Cisco actually covers three switching methods in their curriculum, and each of these will be described in this section. This topic goes hand in hand with the objective "Distinguish between cut-through and store-and-forward LAN switching," discussed later in this chapter.

Although we will discuss three LAN switch types here, you really only need to understand the difference between two of them: cut-through and store-and-forward.

Critical Information

The latency for packet switching through the switch depends on the chosen switching mode. The three available options are store-and-forward, cut-through, and FragmentFree.

Store-and-Forward

Store-and-forward switching is one of two primary types of LAN switching. With this method, the LAN switch copies the entire frame into its onboard buffers and computes the cyclic redundancy check (CRC). The frame is discarded if it contains a CRC error, if it's a runt (less than 64 bytes, including the CRC), or if it's a giant (more than 1518 bytes, including the CRC). If the frame doesn't contain any errors, the LAN switch looks up the destination address in its forwarding, or switching, table and determines the outgoing interface. It then forwards the frame toward its destination. Because this type of switching copies the entire frame and runs a CRC, latency time can vary depending on frame length. This is the mode used by Cisco Catalyst 5000 series switches.

Cut-Through (Real-Time)

Cut-through switching is the other main type of LAN switching. In this method, the LAN switch copies only the destination address (the first six bytes following the preamble) into its onboard buffers. It then looks up the destination address in its switching table, determines the outgoing interface, and forwards the frame toward its destination. A cut-through switch reduces latency because it begins to forward the frame as soon as it reads the destination address and determines the outgoing interface. Some switches can be configured to perform cut-through switching on a per-port basis until a user-defined error threshold is reached. At that point, they automatically change over to store-and-forward mode. When the error rate falls below the threshold, the port automatically changes back to cut-through mode.

FragmentFree

FragmentFree is a modified form of cut-through switching in which the switch waits for the collision windows, which are 64 bytes long, to pass before forwarding. If a packet has an error, it almost always occurs within the first 64 bytes. FragmentFree mode provides better error checking than the cut-through mode, with almost no increase in latency.

Figure 7.3 shows where the different switching modes take place in the frame.

FIGURE 7.3: Different switching modes within a frame

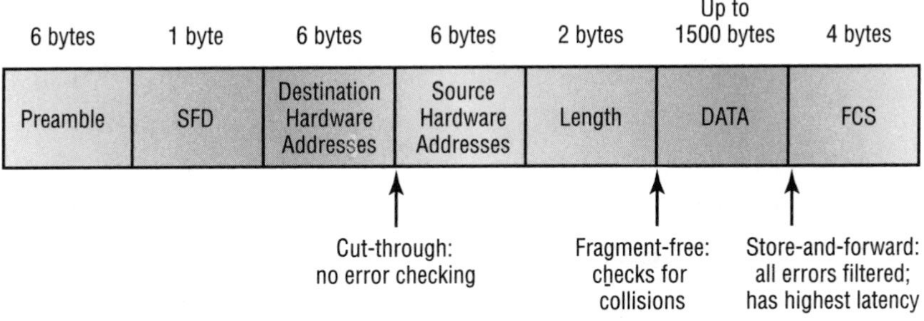

Exam Essentials

You must be able to distinguish between the features of the two primary switching methods, cut-through and store-and-forward.

Remember the difference between cut-through and store-and-forward. The cut-through method of LAN switching has a consistent latency because the switch reads only the first six bytes of the frame after the preamble. Store-and-forward reads the entire frame; therefore, latency varies with frame length.

Key Terms and Concepts

CRC: An acronym for Cyclic Redundancy Check, CRC is a mathematical algorithm used to check for errors when a frame, packet, or segment has been transmitted through a network.

Cut-Through: A LAN switching method that looks only at the destination hardware address in a frame before it makes forwarding decisions.

FragmentFree: A LAN switching method that checks for errors by looking at the first 64 bytes of a frame after it has been received at a switch port.

Latency: The time lapse between when a port receives a frame and when it is forwarded to another port.

Store-and-Forward: This type of LAN switch copies the entire frame to its onboard buffers and runs a CRC before making forwarding decisions.

Sample Questions

1. Which type of LAN switching method only reads the first destination hardware address before forwarding the frame?

   A. Store-and-forward

   B. Port switching

   C. Cut-through

   D. FragmentFree

   Answer: C. Cut-through switching reads only the first six bytes after the preamble in a frame.

2. Which switching method reads the first 64 bytes of a frame before forwarding it?

   A. Port switching

   B. Store-and-forward

   C. Cut-through

   D. FragmentFree

   Answer: D. A FragmentFree switch checks for fragmentation of the frames (collisions) before sending any frames out to any ports.

3. Which type of switching method has the highest latency?

A. Store-and-forward

B. Port switching

C. Cut-through

D. FragmentFree

Answer: A. Store-and-forward has the highest latency of any switching method. In addition, latency varies for each frame depending on its size.

Describe full- and half-duplex Ethernet operation

This section explains the differences between half- and full-duplex Ethernet networks and circuitry. For the CCNA exam, you must be able to differentiate between full- and half-duplex, how each operates, and what it takes to run full-duplex.

When this test objective was written, you could only run full-duplex Ethernet operations with a switch. This is no longer true, but the test has not been changed to reflect this change in technology.

Critical Information

According to Cisco, full-duplex Ethernet can both transmit and receive simultaneously, but it requires a switch port, not a hub, to be able to do so.

Full-duplex Ethernet uses point-to-point connections and is typically referred to as *collision-free* since it doesn't share bandwidth with any other devices. Frames sent by two nodes cannot collide, because there are physically separate transmit and receive circuits between the nodes.

If you have a full-duplex 10Mbps Ethernet operating bidirectionally on the same switch port, you can theoretically have aggregate throughput of 20Mbps. Full-duplex can now be used in 10BaseT, 100BaseT, and 100BaseFL media, but only if all the other network devices (NIC cards, for example) can support full-duplex transmission.

Half-Duplex Ethernet Design

Half-duplex Ethernet has been around a long time. Ethernet II came out in 1984 and is still the most popular of all LAN topologies.

Figure 7.4 shows the circuitry involved in half-duplex Ethernet. When a station is sending to another station, the transmitting circuitry is active at the transmitting station, and the receiving circuitry is active at the receiving station. This circuitry uses a single cable similar to a narrow one-way bridge.

Notice in this figure that loopback detection and collision detect are enabled.

FIGURE 7.4: Half-duplex circuitry

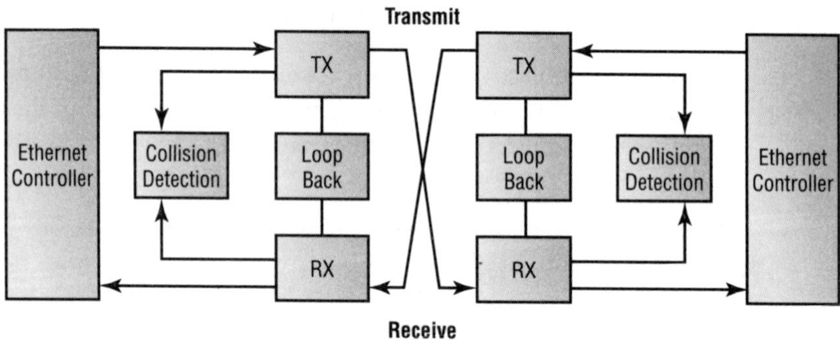

Full-Duplex Ethernet Design

Figure 7.5 shows a diagram of full-duplex circuitry. Full-duplex Ethernet switch technology (FDES) provides a point-to-point connection between the transmitter of the transmitting station and the receiver of the receiving station. With half-duplex circuitry, a standard Ethernet can usually provide only 50 to 60 percent of the bandwidth available. In contrast, full-duplex Ethernets can provide a full 100 percent, because they can transmit and receive simultaneously and because collisions don't occur.

FIGURE 7.5: Full-duplex circuitry

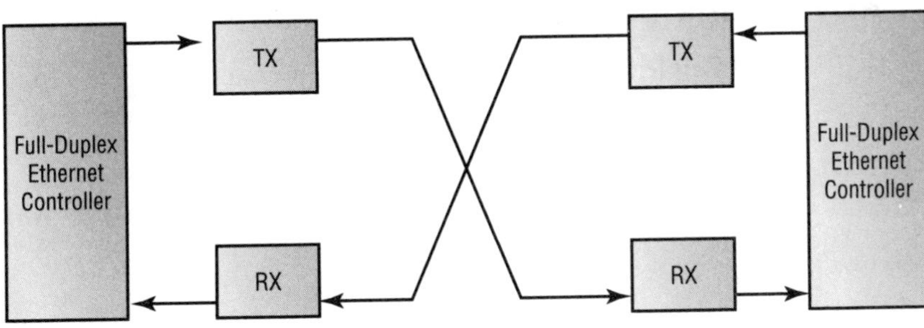

In order to run a full-duplex Ethernet, you must have the following:

- Two 10Mbps or 100Mbps paths
- Full-duplex NIC cards
- Loopback and collision detection disabled
- Software drivers supporting two simultaneous data paths
- Adherence to Ethernet distance standards

Exam Essentials

Remember that the CCNA exam tests you on outdated information regarding full-duplex operations. Your test answers should agree with the information given above.

Remember what is needed to run full-duplex. You do not have to know the distance requirements, but it is important to understand the rest of the requirements for running full-duplex. Do not take for granted that you know what you need. Remember what Cisco says you need.

Understand the definitions of half- and full-duplex. Half-duplex uses a single cable similar to a narrow one-way bridge. Full-duplex provides a point-to-point connection between the transmitter of the transmitting station and the receiver of the receiving station.

Key Terms and Concepts

Full-Duplex: Provides a point-to-point connection between the transmitter of the transmitting station and the receiver of the receiving station

Half-Duplex: Uses a single cable similar to a narrow one-way bridge

Sample Questions

1. Which of the following are needed for running full-duplex? (Choose all that apply.)

   A. Two 10Mbps or 100Mbps paths

   B. SNMP

   C. Full-duplex NIC cards

   D. Loopback and collision detection disabled

   Answer: A, C, D. You need two physical paths, full-duplex NIC cards, and collision detection and loopback detection disabled.

2. Which of the following statements describes half-duplex?

   A. Provides a point-to-point connection between the transmitter of the transmitting station and the receiver of the receiving station

   B. Used in all Cisco switches

   C. Uses a single cable similar to a narrow one-way bridge

   D. No longer supported

   Answer: C.

3. Which of the following statements describes full-duplex?

   A. It provides a point-to-point connection between the transmitter of the transmitting station and the receiver of the receiving station.

   B. It uses a single cable similar to a narrow one-way bridge.

   C. It is used in all Cisco switches.

   D. When you upgrade your servers to full-duplex, all clients must be upgraded at the same time.

   Answer: A.

Describe network congestion problem in Ethernet networks

This requirement is really an offshoot of the exam objective "Describe the advantages of LAN segmentation," which was covered earlier in this chapter.

These are essentially two sides of the same idea: Segmentation is the solution for congestion, which can be a problem in Ethernet networks. We will talk briefly about network congestion in this section. For the exam it is important to understand network congestion and how it happens, but it is even more important to understand how to solve it with segmentation. When working in a production environment, you should know how to segment your network and which devices will meet your business requirements.

Critical Information

With powerful workstations in widespread use, audio and video being delivered to the desktop, and network-intensive applications becoming increasingly common, 10Mbps Ethernet networks no longer offer enough bandwidth to fulfill the business requirements of the typical large business.

As more and more users are connected to the network, an Ethernet network's performance begins to lag. Like too many cars getting onto a freeway at rush hour, this increased utilization creates an increase in network congestion as more users try to access the same network resources.

Congestion typically causes users to scream for more bandwidth. However, simply increasing bandwidth can't always solve the performance issues. Problems like a slow server CPU or insufficient RAM on the workstations and servers also need to be considered.

As discussed earlier in this chapter, Ethernet congestion can be resolved by segmenting the network with bridges, routers, and switches.

Exam Essentials

Along with knowing different ways to relieve network congestion, discussed in several previous sections, you need to grasp what causes this problem.

Understand what causes congestion and how to solve it. Congestion occurs when too many users share the same bandwidth and is exacerbated by the increasing demands put on networks in today's businesses. The solution is to segment the network with bridges, routers, or switches.

Key Terms and Concepts

Bridge: A segmentation device that filters a network by MAC, or hardware, address. It is defined at the Data Link layer.

Latency: The delay from the time a device receives a frame to the time it transmits it to another network segment is called the *latency* period.

Router: A device, defined at the Network layer, that creates internetworks and does network addressing.

Switch: A device that filters a network by MAC, or hardware, address. Switches are defined at the Data Link layer.

Sample Questions

1. Which of the following statements regarding network congestion is true?

   A. It is caused by users printing.

   B. It is caused by Microsoft NT.

   C. It is caused by too many users trying to use the same bandwidth.

   D. It will never happen on a Cisco internetwork.

   Answer: C. Even though a lot of people think *B* would be a great answer, it really isn't. Congestion is caused by too many users trying to get to the same resources.

2. What is Cisco's recommended solution for congestion problems in an internetwork?

   A. Repeaters

   B. Bridges

   C. Gateways

   D. Routers

   Answer: B, D. Bridges, routers, and switches are all possible solutions for network congestion. However, they need to be correctly placed in the network to be effective.

Describe the benefits of network segmentation with bridges

As explained previously in the section "Describe LAN segmentation using bridges," you can use bridges to filter a network by MAC, or hardware, address. In this section we will go over a few benefits of this kind of segmentation.

In production networks, bridges are not typically used anymore. However, it is important when you take the CCNA exam to be able to identify the different types of devices used in segmenting a network and what their benefits are.

Critical Information

There are solid advantages to bridging. If you are segmenting a large network into multiple physical pieces, it ensures:

- Network reliability
- Network availability
- Scalability
- Manageability

These are some of the other benefits of segmentation with bridges:

Few Users per Segment: When filtering with bridges, you can make a large network into smaller collision domains. However, remember that bridges will not stop broadcast storms.

Protocol Independence: Since bridges only work at the Data Link layer, it does not matter what protocols you run at the Network layer.

Exam Essentials

For this exam objective and related ones covered in this chapter, you need to remember the differences between a bridge, a router, and a switch.

Remember what advantages bridging can give you over routing. Bridges are Network layer protocol-independent.

Know the disadvantages of a bridge. Bridges cannot stop broadcast storms.

Key Terms and Concepts

Bridge: A device, defined at the Data Link layer, that filters a network by MAC, or hardware, address.

Sample Questions

1. Bridges filter the network by using what type of addressing?

   A. Logical

   B. Hardware

   C. Port

   D. Socket

   Answer: B. Bridges create a filter table of MAC (hardware) addresses and use this to filter the network.

2. What is a disadvantage to using bridges?

   A. They don't stop broadcast storms from propagating through an internetwork.

   B. They stop broadcast storms from propagating through an internetwork.

   C. They are protocol-independent.

   D. They are easy to install.

   Answer: A. Only routers can stop broadcast storms from propagating throughout a network.

3. What is an advantage to using bridges?

   A. They don't stop broadcast storms from propagating through the internetwork.

   B. They stop broadcast storms from propagating through the internetwork.

C. They are protocol-independent.

D. They have been replaced by switches.

Answer: C. Bridges are not aware of what protocol is running at the Network layer.

Describe the benefits of network segmentation with switches

As described previously in the objective section "Describe LAN segmentation using switches," there are quite a few benefits to using switches. When network traffic affects system performance, as an administrator you need to make more bandwidth available for each user. The best way to accomplish that is generally to segment your network. By understanding the various types of devices available for segmenting a network, you can make good business decisions.

Learning the benefits of network segmentation with switches and how Cisco views segmentation with switches will help you do your job well and succeed on the segmentation portion of the CCNA exam.

Critical Information

LAN switches give you considerably higher port density than standard bridges, and they cost less. Since LAN switches permit fewer users per segment, the average available bandwidth per user increases. This fewer-users-per-segment feature is known as microsegmentation, and it allows you to create dedicated segments. When you have one user per segment, each one enjoys instant access to the full available bandwidth, instead of competing for it with other users. Because of this, collisions—so common with shared medium-sized networks that use hubs—just don't happen.

LAN switches are the only segmentation devices to support some very cool new features, including the following:

- Numerous simultaneous conversations
- High-speed data exchanges
- Low latency and high frame-forwarding rates
- Dedicated communication between devices
- Full-duplex communication
- Media rate adaptation (both 10-and 100Mbps hosts can work on the same network)
- Compatibility with existing 802.3-compliant network interface cards and cabling

Because a LAN switch provides dedicated, collision-free communication between network devices, file-transfer throughput is increased. Many conversations can occur simultaneously because several packets can be forwarded or switched at the same time, which expands the network capacity by the amount of supported conversations.

Full-duplex communication doubles throughput, and media rate adaptation allows the LAN switch to translate between 10 and 100Mbps, to allocate bandwidth on an as-needed basis. Another benefit is that changing over to LAN switches doesn't usually require you to change the existing hubs, network interface cards (NICs), or cabling.

Exam Essentials

As with other objectives covered in this chapter, you should know the advantages and disadvantages of LAN switching and how it differs from other types of segmentation.

Understand the advantages to LAN switching. LAN switching advantages include full-duplex communication, media rate adaption, and easy migration.

Key Terms and Concepts

Switch: A device, defined at the Data Link layer, that filters a network by MAC, or hardware, address.

Sample Questions

1. Which of the following is an advantage to LAN switching?

   A. Makes servers faster

   B. Easier to install than regular hubs

   C. Media rate adaption

   D. Runs only full-duplex communication

   Answer: C. Advantages to LAN switching include full-duplex communication, media rate adaption, and easy migration.

2. Which of the following statements is true regarding switches?

   A. They work the same as routers do.

   B. They work the same as bridges do.

   C. They work the same as a router and a bridge.

   D. Cisco switches can only work with other Cisco switches on the same network.

   Answer: B. Switches are really multiport bridges.

Describe the features and benefits of Fast Ethernet

Having a fundamental understanding of Fast Ethernet is useful for administrators working in a production environment. When you take the CCNA exam, this knowledge will help you answer questions regarding other exam objectives, although there may not be any questions specifically pertaining to Fast Ethernet. It is important not to skip any of the exam objectives as you study for the test, even if you do not expect to see test questions on all the objectives.

This section covers how Cisco views the features and benefits of Fast Ethernet.

Critical Information

In 1995, the IEEE approved the IEEE 802.3u, the 100BaseT Fast Ethernet standard. It defines the Physical and Data Link layers, uses the CSMA/CD (Carrier Sense, Multiple Access with Collision Detect) protocol, and is 10 times faster than 10BaseT. These are some of the new technology stars:

100BaseFX: Ethernet over fiber at 100Mbps using 802.3 specs. It uses a two-strand–, 50/125–, or 62.5/125–micron multimode fiber optic cable.

100BaseT4: Using 802.3 specs, carries 100Mbps over category 3, 4, or 5 UTP cabling with a standard RJ-45 connector.

100BaseTX: Fast Ethernet over category 5 UTP cabling. It's compatible with, and adheres to, 802.3 specifications. It can also use two-pair, 100-ohm shielded twisted pair (STP) cable or type 1 STP cable.

100BaseX: This refers to either the 100BaseTX or 100BaseFX media. This standard was approved to ensure compatibility between the Ethernet CSMA/CD and the ANSI X3T9.5 standard.

100VG AnyLan: IEEE movement into Fast Ethernet and Token Ring that doesn't appear to be taking off, mostly because it's not compatible with the 802.3 standards and Cisco doesn't support it.

Advantages of Fast Ethernet

Migrating or upgrading your network to 100BaseT from 10BaseT can substantially improve throughput and overall performance. Because 100BaseT uses the same signaling techniques as 10BaseT, a gradual migration to 100BaseT doesn't have to be expensive or time-consuming. Partially converting a LAN is a viable alternative to converting all clients simultaneously. These are some of the advantages of 100BaseT over 10BaseT:

- 100BaseT has 10 times the performance of 10BaseT.
- Existing cabling and network equipment can be used.
- It can use 10Mbps and 100Mbps together.
- 100BaseT uses tried-and-true CSMA/CD technology.
- Migration is easy.

Exam Essentials

Work on understanding Fast Ethernet and how it can be implemented in your network.

Remember the advantages of Fast Ethernet. It's much faster than 10BaseT, is easy to migrate, and uses CSMA/CD.

Key Terms and Concepts

100BaseFX: Ethernet over fiber at 100Mbps using 802.3 specs. It uses a two-strand–, 50/125– or 62.5/125–micron multimode fiber optic cable.

100BaseTX: Fast Ethernet over category 5 UTP cabling. It's compatible with, and adheres to, 802.3 specifications. It can also use two-pair, 100-ohm shielded twisted pair (STP) cable or type 1 STP cable.

CSMA/CD: An acronym for Carrier Sense, Multiple Access with Collision Detect, CSMA/CD is a protocol designed to run with Ethernet networks. It helps nodes communicate on a physical medium.

Repeater: Physical device used to extend the distance of a digital signal.

Sample Questions

1. What is an advantage of migrating to Fast Ethernet?

   A. Easier to administrate

   B. Less expensive then 10BaseT

   C. Easy migration from 10Mbps Ethernet

   D. Makes servers faster

   Answer: C. It is easy to migrate to Fast Ethernet because it uses the same signaling techniques as 10Mbps Ethernet.

2. What is the specification for Ethernet over fiber at 100Mbps using 802.3 specs?

   A. 100BaseTX

   B. 100BaseFX

   C. 100BaseT

   D. 100VG AnyLan

   Answer: B. 100BaseFX is the Ethernet over fiber at 100Mbps using 802.3 specs.

Describe the guidelines and distance limitations of Fast Ethernet

Although the CCNA exam does not focus heavily on this test objective, you must be prepared for everything.

Cisco wants you to understand the distance limitations of Fast Ethernet, which are similar to those of 10BaseT. The difference comes in when repeaters are added, but that doesn't happen too often anymore.

Critical Information

100BaseT networks use the same time slots as 10BaseT networks do. What are time slots? They require a station to transmit all its bits before another station can transmit its packet. For 100BaseT networks to transmit in the same time slots, the distance must be reduced. This means that instead of the 5-4-3 rule that the standard Ethernet uses (five network segments, four repeaters, only three segments populated) you can use only two Class II repeaters in a 100BaseT network. The timing in Fast Ethernet is shorter (10% of Ethernet). The maximum frame size, or time slot, is 1518 bytes. The physical distance is reduced because both Fast and regular Ethernet specifications state that the round-trip time must not exceed 512 bit times. Since Fast Ethernet transmits faster, a signal of 512 bits covers a shorter distance.

100BaseT Repeaters

You can still use repeaters in your network to extend the distance of your shared Ethernet network or in switches with dedicated segments. However, repeaters are not used as often anymore because hubs and switches can now do repeating functions. Repeaters may actually reduce 100BaseFX maximum distances, because the repeater delays eat up the timing budget. They will, however, extend 100BaseTX distances. These are the different types of repeaters available:

Class I: A translational repeater that can support both 100BaseX and 100BaseT4 signaling. The allowable delay for a class I repeater is 140 bit times.

Class II: A transparent repeater has shorter propagation delay, but only supports either 100BaseX or 100BaseT4, not both at the same time. The allowable delay for a class II repeater is only 92 bit times.

FastHub 300: A repeater compatible with the IEEE 802.3u standard for Fast Ethernet. The FastHub 300 delivers 10 times the performance of a 10BaseT hub.

Table 7.1 shows the cable type, connector type, and maximum distance between end nodes without repeaters.

TABLE 7.1: Cable Type, Connector Type, and Maximum Distance Between End Nodes

Port Type	Cable	Connector Type	Distance
100BaseTX	Category 5	RJ 45	100 meters
100BaseFX	50/125 or 62.5/125	SC/ST/MIC	412 meters Half-duplex restricted to 412m. No restrictions for full-duplex (distance restrictions due to signal attenuation still applies).

Table 7.2 shows the maximum distance of Fast Ethernet with repeaters.

TABLE 7.2: Maximum Distance with Repeaters

Standard or Repeater Type	Number of Repeaters	UTP Medium	UTP and Fiber Media (TX/FX)
802.3u	one class I repeater	200 meters	261 meters
	one class II repeater	200 meters	308 meters
	two class II repeaters	205 meters	216 meters
FastHub 300	one class II repeater	200 meters	318 meters
	two class II repeaters	223 meters	236 meters
FastHub 300, plus one 3rd party 100BaseT class II repeater	two class II repeaters	214 meters	226 meters

Exam Essentials

You do not have to memorize the tables above, but you should have a general idea of the distance limitations of Fast Ethernet.

Know when a distance problem may occur. You should understand that you might have a distance problem when adding repeaters to your Ethernet 100BaseX network.

Key Terms and Concepts

100BaseFX: Ethernet over fiber at 100Mbps using 802.3 specs. It uses a two-strand–, 50/125–, or 62.5/125–micron multimode fiber optic cable.

100BaseTX: Fast Ethernet over category 5 UTP cabling. It's compatible with, and adheres to, 802.3 specifications. It can also use two-pair, 100-ohm shielded twisted pair (STP) cable or type 1 STP cable.

Repeater: A physical device used to extend the distance of a digital signal.

Sample Questions

1. How many repeaters can you have in a 100BaseT network?

   A. One

   B. Two

   C. Three

   D. Four

   Answer: B. Only two repeaters can be placed in a 100BaseT network and be in spec.

2. What does the *FX* in 100BaseFX represent?

   A. Full-duplex

   B. Fast UTP

   C. Fiber optics

   D. Finally Xerox specifications

   Answer: C. Ethernet over fiber at 100Mbps.

Distinguish between cut-through and store-and-forward LAN switching

This exam objective is closely related to the objective "Name and describe two switching methods," covered earlier in this chapter. In that section we named three types of LAN switching techniques, but Cisco switches only use two of those.

To do well on the exam and to make good decisions as a network administrator, you must understand the different switching methods and how they work. You do not have to know what type of switch is used in each of the different switching methods.

Critical Information

Cisco switches use the cut-through or store-and-forward method of LAN switching. As discussed previously, cut-through switching starts forwarding frames after reading only the destination MAC address. Store-and-forward LAN switching brings the entire frame onto the switch's onboard buffers and runs a CRC to check for errors. Obviously, this technique takes longer than the cut-through method, but it is more dependable. The cut-through method of LAN switching has a constant latency, while store-and-forward latency varies with frame length.

Exam Essentials

Know the fundamental difference between cut-through and store-and-forward switching.

Remember how cut-through switching works. This type of LAN switch only looks at the destination hardware address in a frame before it makes forwarding decisions.

Remember how store-and-forward switching works. With this LAN switching method, the switch copies the entire frame to its onboard buffers and runs a CRC before making forwarding decisions.

Key Terms and Concepts

Latency: The delay from the time a device receives a frame to the time it transmits it to another network segment.

Switch: A device, defined at the Data Link layer, that filters a network by MAC, or hardware, address.

Sample Questions

1. Which of the following switching methods is used in the Catalyst 5000?

   A. Cut-through

   B. FragmentFree

   C. Store-and-forward

   D. Line

   Answer: C. Store-and-forward is a LAN switching method that copies the entire frame to its onboard buffers and runs a CRC before making forwarding decisions. Cisco Catalyst 5000s use this method.

2. Which of the following LAN switching types have a constant latency? (Choose two.)

   A. Cut-through

   B. Store-and-forward

   C. FragmentFree

   D. Distance vector

   Answer: A, C. Both cut-through and FragmentFree have a constant latency.

Describe the operation of the Spanning Tree Protocol and its benefits

Is understanding Spanning Tree Protocol (STP) important? It used to be very important in the old bridged IBM environments. STP is a great, resilient protocol that runs in the background and keeps your network loop-free.

After routing was introduced and administrators began replacing bridges with routers, STP was not used anymore. However, with the invention of the switch, its purpose in life was resurrected! In this section we'll talk about the main purpose of STP, but you don't need to worry about the CCNA test focusing too much on this subject. Don't skip this section, however, because you want to be prepared for anything.

Critical Information

As you've learned previously in this chapter, switches (and bridges) look at the MAC address of a frame and build a forwarding table based on the destination MAC addresses. If the destination MAC address is unknown, the switch floods the frame out all ports, looking for the destination device. The same thing happens with a broadcast frame. This could create a loop problem if more than one link is connected to the same location.

IEEE 802.1d Spanning Tree Protocol (STP) was developed to prevent routing loops in a bridged network. If a router, switch, or hub has more than one path to the same destination, a routing problem could occur. To prevent this, the Spanning Tree Protocol is executed between the devices to detect and logically block redundant paths from the network. The main function of the Spanning Tree Protocol is to allow redundant network paths without suffering the effects of loops in the network.

Cisco Catalyst 5000 switches have STP turned on by default, so you won't get any accidental loops in your network if you start connecting hubs to your switch or multiple connections between switches.

STP uses a calculation called the Spanning Tree Algorithm (STA) to create a loop-free network topology for STP.

These are the benefits of STP:

- Prevents loops in bridged or switched networks
- Allows redundant links
- Prunes topology to a minimal spanning tree
- Resilient to topology changes and device failures

Exam Essentials

You may be tested on the basics of STP—the meaning of the term and the purpose of the protocol.

Remember the difference between STP and STA. Spanning Tree Protocol (STP) uses the Spanning Tree Algorithm (STA) to document a bridged network.

Key Terms and Concepts

802.1D: IEEE specification for STP.

STA: Spanning Tree Algorithm (STA) is used to calculate a loop-free network topology for STP.

STP: An acronym for Spanning Tree Protocol, STP allows data transfer without the existence of a virtual circuit.

Sample Questions

1. Which of the following is a benefit of STP?

   A. Prevents loops in bridged or switched networks

   B. Allows redundant links

   C. Prunes topology to a minimal spanning tree

   D. Resilient to topology changes and device failures

   E. All of the above

   Answer: E. Cisco considers each of these benefits of STP.

2. What does STA stand for and what is it used for?

   A. Spanning Tree Algorithm (STA) is used to calculate a loop-free network topology for STP.

   B. Spanning Tree Always (STA) is used to calculate a loop-free network topology for STP.

   C. Stop-the-Loop Algorithm (STA) is used to calculate a loop-free network topology for STP.

   D. Spanning Topology Algorithm (STA) is used to calculate a loop-free network topology for STP.

   Answer: A. STA is used by STP to map a bridged network and find the links.

Describe the benefits of virtual LANs

Virtual LANs (VLANs) allow you to create LANs virtually within a switched network. This gives you a great tool to use in a production environment. Before VLANs, administrators had to group people into collision domains by physical location. You no longer have to do that. For example, you can group people by the type of workstation they have, by the protocol they use, or by function.

It is good to understand how VLANs work—for exam purposes and for your networking career—and how frame tagging is involved in creating collision domains within a switch.

Critical Information

If you want to allow different ports on a switch to be part of different subnetworks, you need to create virtual LANs within the switch.

Virtual local area networks (VLANs) are a logical grouping of network users and resources connected to defined ports on the switch. A VLAN looks like, and is treated like, its own subnet. By using virtual LANs, you're no longer confined to physical locations. VLANs can be created by location, function, department—even by the application or protocol used—regardless of where the resources or users are located.

VLANs are created using switches, not hubs. The difference between a switch and a hub is that when a hub receives a digital signal, it regenerates the digital signals and then sends it out all connected segments. A switch only sends the signal out the port on the switch the data was destined for.

These are some of the benefits that VLANs offer:

- Simplify moves, adds, and changes
- Reduce administrative costs

- Give you better control of broadcasts
- Tighten network security
- Provide microsegmentation with scalability
- Distribute traffic load
- Relocate server into secured locations

Frame Tagging

Frame identification (frame tagging) uniquely assigns a user-defined ID to each frame. This technique was chosen by the IEEE standards group because of its scalability.

VLAN frame identification is a relatively new approach that was specifically developed for switched communications. In this approach, a unique user-defined identifier is placed in the header of each frame as it's forwarded throughout the switch fabric. The identifier is understood and examined by each switch prior to any broadcasts or transmissions to switch ports of other switches, routers, or end-station devices. When the frame exits the switch fabric, the switch removes the identifier before the frame is transmitted to the target end station. All this means is that the switch tags a frame with a VLAN identifier that is only used within the switch fabric itself. Before that frame leaves the switch, it removes the VLAN ID, because nothing outside the switch would be able to understand the VLAN ID. There is one exception: When you run inter-switch link (ISL), the VLAN ID is preserved as it passes over the ISL link.

The following points summarize frame tagging:

- Used by Catalyst 3000 and 5000 series switches
- Specifically developed for multi-VLAN, inter-switch communication
- Places a unique identifier in the header of each frame
- Identifier is removed before frame exits switch on non-trunk links
- Functions at the Data Link layer
- Requires little processing or administrative overhead

Exam Essentials

Although switching and VLANs are not mentioned in many of the exam objectives, the CCNA test may focus heavily on these topics. It is very important that you know all of the following points.

Understand the difference between a switch and a hub. A hub receives a digital signal and regenerates it, sending it out to each network segment plugged into the hub. Even intelligent hubs cannot send information out through only one hub port. Switches read the digital signal, extract the 1s and 0s, and place the binary data into a logical group called a *frame*. Switches read the hardware address and only send the frame out the destination switch port.

Know the benefits of VLANs. VLANs allow you to create collision domains by groups other than just physical location. You can create networks by function, protocol, hardware type, and so on. Regular LANs only allow collision domains by physical location.

Remember how frame tagging works in a VLAN environment. Frame tagging places a unique identifier in the header of each frame.

Key Terms and Concepts

Frame Tagging: Used in a switched network to tag a frame with VLAN information.

Hub: Different from a switch. When a hub receives a digital signal, it repeats this signal out to all hub ports.

Switch: Different from a hub. When a switch receives a digital signal, it extracts the 1s and 0s and creates a frame. It then reads the hardware destination address and forwards it to only the port or ports it was destined for.

VLAN: An acronym for virtual LANs, VLANs are created within a switched network and used to group users by location, application, protocol, hardware, etc.

Sample Questions

1. Which best describes VLANs?

   A. A physical grouping of network users and resources connected to logical ports on the switch

   B. A logical grouping of network users and resources connected to defined ports on the switch

   C. Proprietary Cisco internetworks only

   D. Used with VIP cards with 7000 series routers

   Answer: B. You can create VLANs by logical grouping rather than physical location.

2. Which of the following statements is true regarding frame tagging?

   A. It's used to build frames in a switched network.

   B. It's used to identify users in a routed network using MAC addresses.

   C. It places a unique identifier in the header of each frame.

   D. It's used to identify users on an active hub network.

   Answer: C. When using VLANs, frame tagging is used to identify the user and also to identify what VLAN the user is a member of when traversing the switched fabric.

3. Which of the following is true?

   A. VLANs must be set up by physical location.

   B. VLANs only work with Cisco switches.

   C. VLANs work with any hub or switch.

   D. VLANs allow you to create collision domains other than by physical location.

   Answer: D. VLANs are gaining in popularity because of how easy they are to configure using other parameters besides physical location.

Define and describe the function of a MAC address

Chapter 1 explained what a Media Access Control (MAC) address is and where it is defined in the OSI reference model. This section covers the functions that a MAC address plays in an internetwork.

It is important to understand where hardware (MAC) addresses are used in an internetwork, because they are a basic part of routing. You will learn how packets and frames work together to deliver user data to remote networks.

This is an important subject. Understanding how frames and packets are used is fundamental to internetworking, and your knowledge of this will be tested on the CCNA exam.

Critical Information

To understand how a MAC address is used, you must know the difference between a packet and a frame. It is also important to understand the basic routing functions that use both a packet and a frame.

Packets

Packets, or datagrams, are defined at the Network layer of the OSI reference model. These are used to carry user data to remote networks. The header contains information about logical networks, not hosts. Its main job is to get user data to the correct network. Once that happens, the frame and MAC address are used.

Frames

Frames are used to send packets to a host or network device on a LAN. The header of a frame contains both the source and destination hardware (MAC) address. Once the router determines that the final destination of the packet is on a local network, it places the packet in a frame with the destination hardware address of the host. If the router doesn't know the hardware address of the destination host, it will send an ARP (Address Resolution Protocol) broadcast requesting the hardware address from a known IP address. The router then places the hardware address of the router interface connected to the local LAN in the header of the frame as the source MAC address.

Basic Routing

To fully understand how a MAC address is used in an internetwork, you must first be clear about how routing works. In this example, we'll use IP routing.

When a datagram's destination is located on a neighboring network, the IP routing process is fairly direct. With this kind of situation, a router follows a simple procedure, as shown in Figure 7.6.

FIGURE 7.6: Simple routing

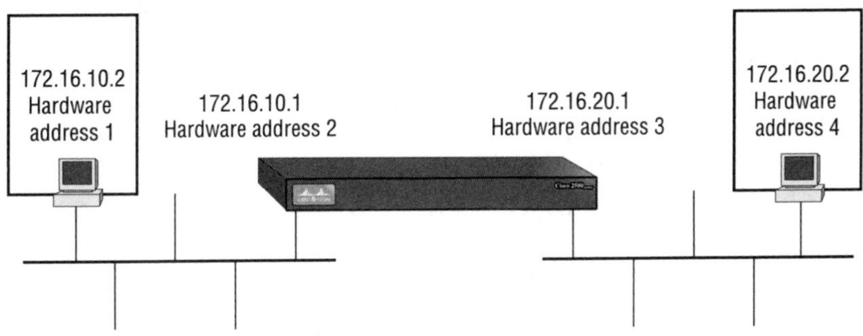

First, when a workstation wants to send a packet to a destination host (in this instance, 172.16.10.2 transmitting to 172.16.20.2), the sending host checks the destination IP address.

If it determines that the address isn't on the local network, then the packet must be routed. Next, 172.16.10.2 calls on ARP to obtain the hardware address of its default gateway. The IP address of the default gateway is configured in machine 172.16.10.2's internal configuration (if all goes well), but 172.16.10.2 still needs to find the hardware address of the default gateway. To do this, it checks the ARP cache, and if the hardware address isn't found, it sends out an ARP request. IP then proceeds to address the packet with the newly obtained destination hardware address of its default router. This is the type of information the router uses to address the packet:

- Source hardware address 1
- Source IP address (172.16.10.2)
- Destination hardware address 2
- Destination IP address (172.16.20.2)

IP, on the receiving router with hardware address 2, establishes that it's not the final, intended recipient by inspecting the packet's destination IP address. That address indicates that the packet must be forwarded to network 172.16.20.0. IP then uses ARP to determine the hardware address for 172.16.20.2. The router puts the newly identified hardware address into its ARP cache for easy reference the next time it's called upon to route a packet to that destination.

This accomplished, the router sends the packet out to network 172.16.20.0 with a header that includes the following:

- Source hardware address 3
- Source IP address (172.16.10.2)
- Destination hardware address 4
- Destination IP address (172.16.20.2)

As the packet travels along network 172.16.20.0, it looks for hardware address 4, with the IP address of 172.16.20.2. When an NIC recognizes its hardware address, it grabs the packet.

It's important to note here that the source IP address is that of the host that created the packet originally (172.16.10.2). The source hardware address is now that of the router's connection interface to network 172.16.20.0. Also significant is that, although the source and destination software IP address remains constant, both hardware addresses change at each hop the packet makes.

Exam Essentials

You need to understand the routing process and the part that MAC addresses play in this process.

Understand the difference between a frame and a packet. A frame is defined at the MAC sublayer of the Data Link layer and contains the hardware address of the source and destination hosts on the local LAN only. The frame destination and source addresses change each time they go through a router. A packet works at the Network layer and holds the logical address of the source and destination network. The packet source and destination logical addresses do not change as they travel through the internetwork.

Know how ARP works. You need to understand how ARP works as well as how IP, TCP, and ICMP work in an internetwork environment and how they relate to the OSI reference model. These protocols and their functions are covered thoroughly in Chapter 4.

Key Terms and Concepts

ARP: An acronym for Address Resolution Protocol, ARP is used to gain a hardware address from an IP address.

Frame: A logical group of 1s and 0s, defined at the Data Link layer, that is used to transmit packets over a LAN.

Packet: A packet, or datagram, is defined at the Network layer of the OSI reference model and is used to route user data to remote networks.

Sample Questions

1. Which of the following statements are true? (Choose two.)

   A. Destination hardware addresses do not change at each hop.

   B. Destination logical addresses do not change at each hop.

   C. Destination hardware addresses change at each hop.

   D. Destination logical addresses change at each hop.

   Answer: B, C. The hardware addresses of both the source and destination hosts change at each hop. Logical addresses stay the same.

2. Which of the following is true? (Choose all that apply.)

   A. Frames are defined at the Network layer.

   B. Frames are defined at the Data Link layer.

   C. Packets are defined at the Network layer.

   D. Packets are defined at the Data Link layer.

   Answer: B, C. Frames use hardware addressing and packets use logical addressing.

3. Which statement is true about a MAC address?

   A. Routers use hardware addresses to find a network device on the remote side of another router.

   B. Routers use hardware addresses to find a network device on a LAN.

   C. MAC addresses are eight bytes long.

   D. MAC addresses are only used in Ethernet networks.

   Answer: B. Any network device, not just a router, uses a hardware address to find a network device on a local network, never a remote network.

Index

Note to the Reader: Throughout this index **boldfaced** page numbers indicate primary discussions of a topic. *Italicized* page numbers indicate illustrations.

A

B

C

D

G

H

I

L

P

Q

R

S

T

U

V

W